Ntombazana

A Story of an African Elephant Family

Michael Garstang

Acknowledgments

The booming call of a baboon greeting the first rays of the sun is never forgotten. Yet, with my life-long partner, our children and their families, a home has been made far from Africa. It was my daughter, Michele, who urged that these memories of origin not be lost. As Ntombazana grew from the early beginnings, all of the family became involved. Elsabe, my wife, and Kathy, our daughter-in-law, produced the text and integrated the drawings. They, together with Michele and nieces, Mary and Jenefer, proofread the text. Tony Eaton took on the mammoth task of editing the entire text. Helpful suggestions flowed from friends, Peter and Jay Tyson, their daughter Anne and her children; Jo and Ann Furber, Virginia and Sandra Fuentes, Mary Morris and many others. This help and support for which I shall be eternally grateful formed a large part of the joy of creating this book.

Copyright 2008 Michael Garstang, Charlottesville, Virginia

All rights reserved. No part of this book may be reproduced in any form or by any means without the permission of Michael Garstang.

Back cover photograph of author by Tony Eaton.
Photograph of elephant skin by Stephen Garstang.

ISBN 978-0-615-18904-8

Ntombazana

Book 1: The Dry Season

Chapter 1 Nkosi's Fight with the Amazulu
Chapter 2 The Place where Ntombi and her Family Live
Chapter 3 Leaving the Balele Highlands
          and the Coming of all the Animals
Chapter 4 Down the Ingagane to the Umzimkulu
Chapter 5 The Baobab Trees and South to the Nyathi Plains
Chapter 6 Ihlosi's Tears
Chapter 7 Lamithi's Long Neck
Chapter 8 Lamithi Saves the Oxpeckers
Chapter 9 Finding Water and Food
Chapter 10 Gathering of the Clans
Ntombi's Family Tree

Book 2: The Wet Season

Chapter 1 Onto the Escarpment
Chapter 2 Ndumeni and the Pass to the Unknown
Chapter 3 Into the Balele Mountains
Chapter 4 The Thlabatini Forest
Chapter 5 The Kranse of the Waterfalls
Chapter 6 The Western Highveld
Chapter 7 Back to the Hidden Valley
Ntombi's Family Tree

Book 3: Loss of our Home Ranges

Chapter 1 A New and Dreadful Danger
Chapter 2 The Arrival of the Bearded Ones
Chapter 3 Indsandlwana and Nkosi
Chapter 4 Coming of Age
Chapter 5 Return of the Amazulu
Chapter 6 Signs in the Forest
Chapter 7 Ndlovu's Toenails
Chapter 8 Sanctuary
Epilogue
Ntombi's Family Tree

Author's Note
A Letter to Zouella and Rodes
Zulu and Afrikaans Names and Words

Book 1

The Dry Season

Chapter 1
Nkosi's Fight for Life

One day long ago, in a wild country of mountains, valleys and plains far away near the southern end of Africa, a great bull elephant called Nkosi was fighting to save his life.

Nkosi had gone into the lands of a tribe of famous hunters and warriors, the Amazulu, and there he had eaten the sweet tall grass called imfi which this tribe grew. An elephant had to be very bold to do this, because whenever one dared to eat their imfi it made the Amazulu furious. The men would join together to form a hunting party, bringing their dogs and the deadly sharp spears called assegaais. Then they would set out to track and kill whoever had eaten their crop of imfi.

Nkosi's ordeal started when he was ambushed and then chased by just such a party of Zulu hunters. During this attack he was speared three times, and he had to turn and charge the hunters because they were trying to surround him. He killed two of the Amazulu that day. Then for five long days the other Zulu hunters tried to catch and kill him, but despite being in pain and losing blood from his three assegaai wounds, he was able to stay ahead of them. He led the hunters into a dry, desolate place called the Dorsland and Gramadoelas.

The Dorsland, or Thirstland, and the Gramadoelas, or Back-of-Beyond, are part of a wide plain that lies between two ranges of mountains, and no one, whether human or animal, goes into this stretch of country if they can possibly avoid it. The veld there is cut up into many deep ravines or dongas. These dongas have steep sides and all animals know that once you get into them, you can't get out again. They run into each other like the branches of a thorn tree. The more you try to get out, the more confused and lost you become. If the day is hot and windy, as days in the Dorsland often are, there can be so much dust in the air that you can't even see where the sun is. There is no food and no water in the Gramadoelas. If you can't find your way out within four days, you are doomed. Nkosi knew all this, but he also knew that with the yelping dogs and the Zulu hunters close on his trail, he had no choice but to go into these badlands and trust that he would remember the signs that his father had told him he must look for if he ever got into the Gramadoelas.

When the Zulu hunters reached the sand dunes on the southern edge of the Gramadoelas and saw that Nkosi's tracks led straight towards the maze of big dongas, they stopped and held an indaba or council meeting. Their leader, the oldest and most experienced hunter, said, "Amadoda – men – we know who this elephant is. He is Nkosi, the largest and wisest bull elephant on the Nyathi Plains."

"Siya vuma – we agree," said all the other hunters.

The leader went on, "We know that to enter the Gramadoelas is to incur almost certain death. With this wind we cannot see the sun and do not know which way is east or west. With this wind, also, our tracks will be obliterated within a very short time. Once our tracks are lost, we will not be able to find our way back out, and to go forward will mean only thirst and hunger. Nkosi is still strong, even though we know he is hurt and we can see his blood on the grasses and on the green tips of the thorn trees. He will go further than we will, and his tracks too will be blown away in the wind. We will lose him in the Gramadoelas, and we will lose ourselves."

"Yebo, Mdala – yes, Old One, you are right," the other hunters agreed.

"Nkosi has tricked us," said the leader of the hunters, "and we will not be able to kill him, but he has also tricked himself. For surely he will die a slow and painful death. His mouth will turn to sand and his throat will dry out until it is like an ox's skin that has lain for days in the burning sun. He will not be able to see, for even his eyes will dry up. He will not be able to breathe, for his trunk will fill with dust. He will try to dig for moisture but he will not find any. In the end, after he has endured day after day of pain and suffering, his spirit will leave the Gramadoelas and his bones and great tusks will bleach white in the sun. Mpisi the Hyena, who finds all dead things, will not find him. Even the vultures will not find him. Nor will his herd, his wives or his children find him. Nkosi has stolen our imfi and trampled our crops many times. Many times we have hunted him. Many times he has outwitted us. This time, Nkosi, you have outwitted yourself."

"Siya vuma – we agree," chorused the hunters, who had been squatting on their heels around their leader during this indaba. They all got up, raised their assegaais and knobkieries in the air and called

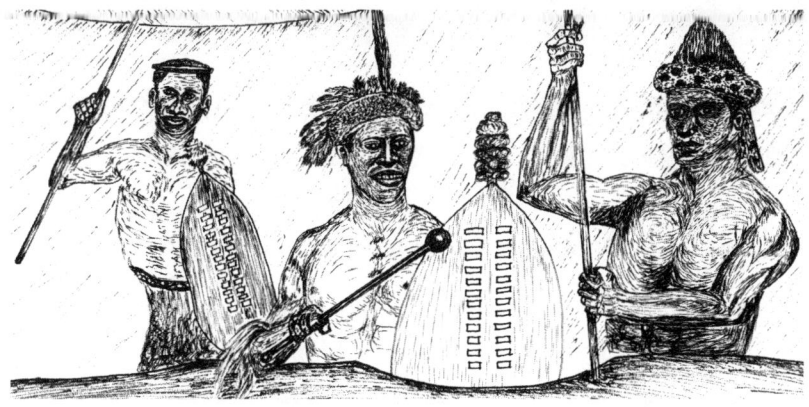

"Bayete!" in a final salute to Nkosi. Then they turned and headed for their kraals far to the south.

Meanwhile Nkosi was beginning to feel the strain of the long chase. The last mile across the soft shifting sands had left him almost completely done in. His lungs were burning and his throat was dry. He had last snatched a quick drink of water just after dawn that morning. The sun was now past its zenith in the sky. His left shoulder was aching and a shaft of pain lanced down his left foreleg each time he took a step. As long as he had been able to hear the faint yelping of the dogs behind him he had ignored the pain and thirst, for he knew that he had to keep going. After he had crossed the last sand dune and entered the mouth of the first large donga, he slowed and then halted to listen. He could hear nothing, but that did not reassure him. The wind was very strong, and in a wind like this, he knew, even his acute sense of hearing was not of much use. But at least the wind was coming from behind him, and not blowing from him towards the hunters, so the dogs would not be able to smell him. Moreover, the wind would quickly cover his tracks on the sand dunes. As long as the hunters did not stumble by luck on this donga that he had entered, he should be able to keep his lead. He felt that he had time now to deal with the assegaais that were still embedded in his left shoulder and in his neck behind his left ear. He knew the danger of bleeding if the spears had cut any large blood vessels. While their blades were still embedded in his flesh, the bleeding was held in check. But once he pulled them out he knew the bleeding could be serious. If only he could find some Euphorbia bushes with their fat leaves and milky sap, for he knew that crushing these leaves on his wounds would stop the bleeding. He searched along the walls of the donga, hoping that some small bushes had survived in the deep crevices, but he could not find a single green thing. Hurting now at every step, he was getting desperate, for of course he had no way of knowing that the hunters had turned back, and he could not take the risk of acting as if they had lost his trail or stopped chasing him. If they found his tracks entering the large donga that he was in, they would quickly catch up with and corner him. The donga was deep, but not wide. He could turn around only with difficulty. He knew that this was the very worst situation he could possibly be in. Not being able to turn quickly and face the hunters with his massive tusks and trunk put him at a great disadvantage. But that was not the most serious threat. He knew that if the hunters came from behind him and he could not turn around, they would slash his Achilles tendons just above the heels of his hind feet. Once they did this, he would be doomed. His back legs would collapse under his huge weight and he would never rise again.

So Nkosi kept going deeper into the donga and deeper into the Gramadoelas, searching without success for plants that would let him pull out the spears and stop the bleeding. At every step he could feel the shafts of the assegaais slapping against his back and shoulders. Each jerk of the assegaais twisted the blades in his shoulder and neck, sending hot stabs of pain through his neck and down his left leg. He could also feel and smell the blood running down his leg. There seemed to be no hope that he would find any living plant in the donga. It was getting drier and drier and he had seen none for a long time. Then suddenly he saw, on the walls of the donga, white powder and crystals clinging to a series of vertical fissures. Dimly he remembered that his mother had used these crystals on a wound that had been suffered by his younger brother Mfanyaan long before, when Mfanyaan had been just one year old and Nkosi himself only about eight. At a river Mfanyaan had carelessly run ahead of his mother and waded into the water, and before she could get there Wenya the Crocodile had grabbed Mfanyaan by the trunk. His mother had saved little Mfanyaan from the crocodile, but his trunk had been very badly cut and lacerated by Wenya's teeth, and she had used fine white crystals to stop the bleeding while young Nkosi looked on. Now, in his exhausted state, he was not sure that the crystals in front of him were the right ones, but he had to take the chance. He had to risk either possibly bleeding to death or leaving the spears in his shoulder and neck and dying anyway. There was no other choice. If the crystals were not the right ones it would be better to have tried and failed than not to have tried at all.

So he reached back with his trunk and, getting a good hold on the shaft of the spear in his shoulder, he closed his eyes against the pain and slowly and carefully pulled the spear out. He could immediately feel the warm blood running like a small stream down his left leg. He moved to the wall of the donga, scraped a mass of the white crystals and powder out of one of the fissures, and holding it in the curl of the end of his trunk, slapped it into the wound. At once it felt as if he had taken a burning brand of ironwood and thrust it into his shoulder. But even as he gasped for air he felt the pain subsiding, and with it the flow of blood. It looked as if he had gambled and won—at least this little battle. He was not safe yet; not by a very long way. But at least he could now pull out the other two spears and walk in reasonable comfort.

By the time he was finished, Nkosi did not know how long it had taken him to pull out the three assegaais and cover his wounds with salt, but he was afraid that it had been much too long. The hunters and dogs could be coming up the donga at that very minute. There was no time to lose. So he set off along the donga again, looking for a fork which could help him to confuse his pursuers. Although he felt that he had to move fast to get ahead of the hunters who he still thought were pursuing him, he was not careless about where he was going. If he was to get through the maze of dongas and out of the Gramadoelas without dying of thirst, he was going to have to be very careful. No one else knew how to find their way through the Gramadoelas, but Nkosi had learnt a way from his father. The strong wind that blows the sand across the Dorsland and forms dunes like those he had crossed earlier in the day comes only from the west. It was the same wind that was still blowing all around him, dry as a bleached bone and hot as the embers left from a bush fire. This wind was so strong that it would move large grains of sand and even small pebbles across the desert floor. When these moving grains and pebbles reached the donga, they spilled over its steep western wall and ended up as a thin pile along the bottom of the wall on that side of the donga.

By keeping careful track at each turn of the donga and at each junction with another ravine, Nkosi could always know where west was. He knew that the Gramadoelas run from west to east across the plains that lie between Mabutu Mountain and the Pumulanga range of mountains. If he always kept the wind-blown pebbles and large sand grains at the base of the wall to his left, he would be heading north across the Gramadoelas. As the dongas continually changed directions, with old channels dying and new channels joining, the piles and thin lines of pebbles were often far from obvious. Many times it took careful feeling with his trunk before Nkosi could tell where the smooth pebbles lay. Although that night he stopped to sleep, the next day and all the next night he kept going. By that time he had not drunk water for three days, and he knew that if he did not get out of the Gramadoelas before the next sunset, he would not make it. Though two days was the most he would usually think about going without water, he could under normal conditions endure four days without drinking. But the past four days had been very far from normal. Since four days back he had been on the run continuously, with only occasional snatches of food and very little water, and for the past many, many hours, he had had nothing to eat or drink at all. He was fairly sure now that the hunters had given up; now his chief enemy, and an even more deadly one, was thirst. So on this last night he kept going, trusting to his trunk to find the way. It was slow going, especially where more than one donga met. There he had to test each wall before deciding which was the western one. He had to be sure that he knew exactly where he had entered the junction for fear that he would make a mistake, unwittingly retrace his tracks, and end up going around in a big circle.

As the eastern sky began to lighten he thought he could see outlines of the Pumulanga Mountains. If this was true, he was nearly through the Gramadoelas. The wind had finally dropped and the sky was clear. Suddenly, as he came around a bend in the donga, he could see the sharp outline of the Pumulanga Mountains with the sun rapidly climbing behind them. He had made it! He knew where there was a spring in a kloof not more than half a mile away. Never had water tasted so good to Nkosi. He had to be careful to drink slowly and only half a trunkful at a time. But he didn't mind.

The cool, damp kloof was as close to heaven as he had ever been. He was hungry, but he spent the whole day in the kloof by the spring. When evening came he left to look for something to eat.

Chapter 2
The Place Where Ntombi and Her Family Live

The story I have just told you is a very important one to me, and one that I know well. How so? Because Nkosi is my father, and if he had died in those badlands, back in the days before he met my mother, I would never have been born.

My name is Ntombazana, although everyone in my elephant family calls me Ntombi, which in Zulu just means "girl". But when my mother and my sisters call me Ntombiyaam they mean I am their special girl. All my family have Zulu names. That is because we live in northern Zululand, where there is a special kloof in the Balele Mountains.

Balele means sleeping or quiet. Our mountains are part of the Inkonto si Quathlaba, the huge Barrier of Spears which we can see far to the west. Because the sun goes down behind them, the northern parts of these mountains are called Ntshonalanga, mountains of the sunset. They are too far away to walk to but we all know they are there when the sun comes up and colors them red in the morning and when they turn purple in the late afternoon. Where the sun comes up the mountains are called IPumulanga, the place of sunrise.

Our favorite place is in a kloof which winds behind Aasvoëlkrans, or vultures' crag. Aasvoëlkrans is a huge cliff much, much higher than even the highest trees. In fact, sometimes it reaches to the sky and clouds sit on top of it. Both the vultures and Mfene the baboons sleep up on the krans because there they are safe from their worst enemy, Ingwe the leopard. Igogo the Klipspringers, with their special hooves that can almost stick to steeply-sloping rocks, live among the boulders, and so do many families of Mbili the Dassie.

On these rocks we also sometimes see Mkulu the Rock Python lying stretched out basking in the sun. This enormous snake, as

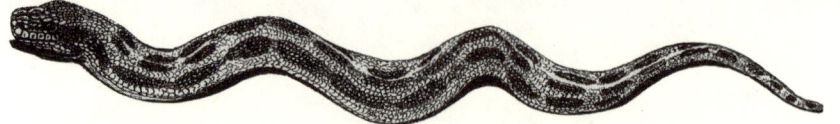

long as my mother, will catch dassies whenever he can, but he will not harm us. Even so, we don't go anywhere near him, just in case, and my mother and aunts keep a wary eye on him whenever he is around.

The hidden valley, where we often sleep, winds behind Aasvoëlkrans. This kloof is the place where I was born, five years ago. It has a clear cool stream in it with pools for swimming, playing and drinking and even a waterfall which splashes and crashes down into an extra-deep pool. That is my very favorite place. Along the banks of the river in the kloof are sweet grasses and reeds and, best of all, fig trees laden with sweet figs. It is quite hard to climb up and down next to the waterfall, but my mother Ndlovu, who knows everything, uses a special path which no one else knows. One of these days I will learn all about it from her.

The Balele Mountains curl around the wide green valley of the Nyathi River. Near the top of the valley is a big vlei with deep clear pools of water called Amanzimtoti, the sweet waters. Here Mvubu the Hippopotamus lives, as well as the one who frightens me more than anything else: Ingwenya the Crocodile.

Further down the Nyathi River is an even bigger vlei called Umzimkulu, meaning "the big waters". We swim there in the dry season. Lots of other animals and bird friends live there. The wisest is Tegwane the Hamerkop, who my mother says can look into the water and see things that haven't yet happened.

The river winds into the grasslands of the Nyathi Plains. We spend the dry season there with lots of other animals. Although it does not rain in that season and everything is hot and parched, there are still sweet grasses and thorn trees to browse on. We can drink from the Nyathi River and eat delicious figs from the big fig trees on its banks.

Now I must tell you about my family.

My father is called Nkosi, or "great chief", because he is the biggest and strongest of all the elephants in the Nyathi Valley. He doesn't stay with our herd, but in the dry season he is always somewhere in the valley.

My mother Ndlovu, my older sisters and my aunts can talk to him even when he is very far away. I can't yet understand what they are saying, nor can I make the sounds they make. These sounds are very low rumbling, grumbling noises. When I am close to my mother and she makes these rumbles, they somehow make my tummy shake and jiggle.

My mother says that when we are little we can't make these low grumbling noises because our heads and trunks are not big enough. To make the noises, she says, you have to start in your throat and then push the air out through the top of your trunk. In the big elephants we can see that the skin covering the top of their trunk where it goes into their forehead start to jiggle when they are rumbling. When we little ones try to make this rumbling sound it just comes out as squeaks. But my mother says not to worry, like all the other things we have to learn, we will eventually find out how to do it.

I have three aunts: Undlebe, who has very big ears; Mabalel, whom I like very much because she often looks after me; and Mathathu, my third aunt. I have three uncles, too, but they don't live with us. They often come to the water when we go to drink in the evenings. Before we go to the water, my mother will make a soft rumbling call which says we are thirsty and want to go and drink. My uncles will answer, especially Umadala, the old one who is nearly as big as my father. My other two uncles are Nsimbi, named for iron because he is very strong and tough, and Mfanyaan or "boy", my father's youngest brother.

We all go together to the water because it is a very dangerous place. Not only does our worst enemy, Wenya the Crocodile, live there, but we frequently come across Ngonyama the Lion, who is very full of himself and likes to think he is the king of the whole place. He and his half-dozen wives, together with a couple of his brothers, often hang out at our best water holes, where they will lie around the drinking place all day. When we and our other friends come to drink and swim they will act as if the water hole belongs to them and they don't want to let us come near and drink.

They like to hide in the long grass around the water hole and then pounce on anyone foolish enough to come to drink without first checking very carefully that it is safe. But while they may catch Idube the Zebra or Nkhonhoni the Wildebeest, who are often quite silly, it won't work for our family. My mother will call to my aunts and uncles and gather all of us together. Then she will lead us to the water with us little ones in the middle and Mdala at the back. If Ngonyama as much as shows his nose, my mother or Mdala will lift their trunks up high, give a terrible shriek, and then charge at Ngonyama with their ears spread out wide. This is terrifying, and "king" Ngonyama at once scuttles away with his tail between his legs. We think it is very funny to see big-headed old Lion cut down to size and chased away like this, but my mother tells us to stay very close to her and remember that we are still small and must not get cheeky towards Ngonyama just because he runs away from a grown-up elephant.

Smelly, ugly Mpisi the Hyena and his gang also hang around our water holes in the hope of finding a free meal. They will try to catch any of us little ones that they can, but unless you are very silly

and don't listen to your mother, they don't
stand a chance. When I was very little I
would stay under my mother's tummy,
and nasty Mpisi could never get at me
there. Now that I am a little bigger I
still stay close to my mother's
side. If she has to shake her ears
at Mpisi to tell him to clear off, I
keep close to Mabalel.

Mvubu the Hippopotamus and his big family are always in one of the deep pools. Mvubu doesn't bother us, and neither does uBhejane the Black Rhinoceros, though my mother says that once upon a time, long, long ago, something happened between uBhejane and us that has affected all black rhinos ever since.

What happened that day was that uBhejane came bumbling along to a water hole where an elephant family was already drinking, swimming and feeding. uBhejane has very bad eyes and can hardly see where he is going. He came blundering out of the long grass and next moment he had almost stuck his great horn into a young elephant calf who was grazing at the side of the water hole. She got a terrible fright and yelled for help as hard as she could. Her mother was under the water having a lovely swim, and couldn't hear her, but her father heard her all right, and he charged out of the water and gave uBhejane a terrible poke with his big tusks. But uBhejane has a very tough skin and is also very bad-tempered, so he didn't run away. Instead he decided to charge the big elephant right there at the edge of the water hole. Unluckily for him, this elephant had been in many fights before. He stepped to one side at the last moment and clouted uBhejane a solid blow with his heavy trunk. This knocked uBhejane clean into the water and he lost his footing on the muddy bottom. As he slipped, the elephant got his tusks under him and threw him into the deep water. uBhejane doesn't really like to swim, and with his side hurting and lots of muddy water going down his throat, he finally came to his senses and decided it would be best to leave. And off he went, grunting grumpily with his tail curled up over his big behind. But the fight had left great gashes in his hide, so he had to borrow a long, sharp quill from Nungu the Porcupine to sew them up. Believe it or not, what that silly rhinoceros did after sewing up his gashes was to go and swallow Nungu's quill. When Nungu wanted his quill back, of course uBhejane couldn't find it. To this day you can still see uBhejane scrabbling around in his dung-heap looking for Nungu's quill. You can also see the mess that he made when he tried to sew up his wounds, for he left all kinds of folds of skin and flabby pieces all over himself.

But now I must come back from crocodiles, lions, hyenas and

rhinos, and finish telling you about my family.

I have two sisters. Mafutha, who is only one year old, is fat, while Ulambile, who is two years older than I am, is just the opposite – she is always hungry and eats all the time, but she is still as skinny as can be, maybe because she is always rushing around playing with the boys, charging bushes and chasing Mpungu the Jackal.

I also have four cousins. The girls are Nyama, the black one, who is the same age as I am, and Umphlophe, the white one, who is Ulambile's age. The boys are Ukhanya, which means "the one who shines" (like the sun) because of his bright eyes and happy ways, and Umvula, "flood", who is called that because he was born during a great storm and nearly died in a flood.

Oh! I have forgotten my brothers, but they are hardly worth mentioning. In fact, they get into so much trouble that we would probably be better off without them — especially Dakiwe. Dakiwe is exactly what his name means: mad. His nickname is Baddy. He really is crazy. Once he sat on Nungu the Porcupine and then had to spend days pulling quills out of his bottom. Another time he got his trunk stuck in Sambane the Aardvark's hole when he tried to pull out a piece of the ants' house and was too silly to let go. My mother had to give him a good whack to make him yell and straighten out his trunk. My other brother is more sensible. He is called Nkosana after my father Nkosi. He is very big and brave and one day I expect he will take the place of my father.

Now I think I really have remembered everyone. Quite a lot! Perhaps I had better go over their names again.

My mother is Ndlovu.

My aunts are Undlebe, Mabalel and Mathatau.

My sisters are Mafutha and Ulambile.

My girl cousins are Nyama and Umphlophe, and my boy cousins are Ukhanya and Umvula.

And my brothers are Dakiwe and Nkosana.

There is also my father Nkosi, and my uncles Umadala, Nsimbi and Umfanyaan; but as I told you, they are not really part of our herd, and they join us only for short spells from time to time.

So there are thirteen of us who are in the herd, counting me. We are always together and if anyone is missing, even for a short time, my mother and my aunts become quite upset. The older ones are always making low rumbling noises which can be heard quite a long way away, even in thick bush or grass. The only trouble is that on very hot and windy days it's hard to hear, and when that happens it is all too easy to get lost. And if you do get lost it won't be long before either Ngonyama the Lion or Mpisi the Hyena will find you. And then you are in big trouble.

This is exactly what happened to Dakiwe once. On a very hot, windy day, instead of staying quietly in the shade of some big trees in a low, sheltered place, Dakiwe got bored and started to follow Logwaja the Hare, who had come wandering into our resting place.

Logwaja is just about as crazy as Dakiwe. He bounced along from one clump of grass to the next, not doing anything except every now and then chasing a grasshopper. It wasn't long before Dakiwe and Logwaja were off around the bend in the river and out of sight of the big trees. Then Dakiwe got bored with following Logwaja and decided he would go back to our resting place. But when he looked around he did not recognize anything. Then he started to cry, and he called and called for Ndlovu. But no one could hear him because of the wind... except nasty old Mpisi, who was resting under a rock up in the kloof, and who did hear him. "Aha!" thought Mpisi, "I can hear a small elephant, and what's more, he is lost. Now if I can only find him, he will make a fine dinner." So Mpisi started down the kloof in his horrible loping way of running. To make matters worse, when Dakiwe started running in fright down the kloof he came to a steep bank that he couldn't get down, so there he had to stop, trapped. And with every moment that passed Mpisi was coming nearer and nearer, down that same kloof. Just as Mpisi was about to come around the last bend in the kloof and come upon poor trapped Dakiwe, what should happen but that Nsele the Badger stepped out into the path. Now nobody hates Mpisi more than Nsele, and Nsele the Badger is not afraid of anyone, especially not of Mpisi the Hyena. Nsele stood up as tall as he could stand on his four short legs and growled a deep growl at Mpisi. Mpisi is such a coward that he stopped dead in his tracks. Then he backed off, turned around, and retreated up the kloof.

By this time Ndlovu had realized that Dakiwe was missing and, raising her trunk, she sniffed and sniffed until she knew which way he had gone. Luckily for Dakiwe, he hadn't gone very far, and as Ndlovu came around the bend of the kloof she could hear and see him up on the bank. She gave a loud low rumble which Mpisi heard, and which made him jump and scuttle off up the kloof even faster. That was the last time Dakiwe ever wandered off by himself.

Ndlovu

Chapter 3
Leaving the Balele Highlands and the Coming of all the Animals

In the rainy season, from about November to March, it is very hot and sticky on the Nyathi Plains. There are also lots of biting insects like Tsetse flies and mosquitoes that can make you very sick. So as soon as my mother Ndlovu knows that it is going to start raining, she leads us up onto the high meadows of the Balele Mountains. She knows the rains are coming because she can hear the rumble of thunder a long, long way off. None of us little ones can hear what she hears. Nor do the other animals hear it. We leave the Nyathi Plains two or three weeks before the other animals like the Idube the Zebra and Nkonhoni the Wildebeest. This is good, because it means that we are the first to find the new shoots of grass and the first green leaves on the thorn trees.

After the rains come to an end in March, the dry season begins. When the nights start getting cold at the end of March my mother leads us down from the Balele Mountains back to the Nyathi Plains. At the end of our stay on the Balele highlands my mother always leads us to the Hidden Valley I have told you about behind Aasvoëlkrans. The clear stream which flows between the steep sides of this beautiful small valley later becomes the Ingagane River, which spills over a waterfall and then eventually flows into the Umzimkulu Lake and from there into the Nyathi River.

By March the days are getting cooler and the nights are cold on the Balele Highlands, but in the Hidden Valley we are sheltered at night, and if we huddle close together we can still keep warm. My mother knows that the nights and even the days will soon be even colder. She says that if you wait too long on the Balele Highlands it can sometimes get so cold that the water becomes as hard as a stone and the rain turns white and sticks to the trees and grasses. When this happens you are in bad trouble because to get down off the Balele Mountains you have to go down a steep, rocky path. When the water goes hard and the rain turns white, this rocky path becomes very slippery. When we travel that path we have to walk all in a line, and a slip by anyone in the family could send everyone in front crashing down. Even if you were not killed in the fall — and you could be, in a place like that — my mother says that breaking a leg is worse than death for a big elephant. My mother and my aunts are so big and heavy that a broken leg could never mend. Soon Mpisi the Hyena would get wind of what had happened and he and his whole gang would come and torment the one who was hurt until they had dragged it down to a horrible death.

So my mother never waits too long in the Hidden Valley before she leads us downstream to the waterfall. The waterfall is very high, as high as five fever trees. The stream tumbles over the edge and crashes into the deep pool below. You can hear the roar of the water long before you get there. Some of the spray rises up just like clouds and sometimes you can see a rainbow in the spray. On a hot day it is lovely and cool near the waterfall. But our big problem is how to get down the sheer kranse that go out like Undlebe's huge ears on either side of the waterfall. We would never be able to get down them if it were not for my mother. She knows the only way down, along a secret path that she learnt from her own mother.

To get to this path you have to wade into the river not far above the edge of the falls. The current is already strong and it is very scary because you feel as if you will be swept away and over the edge of the waterfall. My mother and my aunts form a tight line, with all of us little ones next to them on the side away from the falls. Then, very carefully, my mother and aunts move across the river. But to get to the path you have to go through a narrow cleft in the far rock wall. No one would ever think of going into that cleft with the water rushing through it towards the falls. I don't know how the first elephant found this path. Perhaps it was at the end of a wet season that hadn't been as wet as usual and there was hardly any water in the river. But once this entrance through the rock cleft to the path had been found, we never forgot it.

When we get to the cleft we have to wait, and first my mother goes through, then Mafutha, followed by Mabalel, and then me, so that there is always a big one first and then a little one following. At the other end of the cleft each older elephant waits until she can help the little ones across the last stretch of water.

Once on the other side of the river and through the cleft, we are on the narrow hidden path. Heavy ferns and vines hang down over it, dripping with water from the spray that comes up and over the edge of the falls. The rocks on the path are covered with green moss and very slippery. My mother and aunts show us how to put our feet carefully between the moss-covered rocks so as not to slip on them. This is tricky but vital, because when you step between the moss-covered rocks you can easily get your foot stuck or even twist your ankle. When we get to the edge of the krans on the side of the waterfall, the path disappears over the edge and down towards the deep pool far below. As if this were not frightening enough, the noise of the water crashing into the pool makes you want to run away. But you can't, because there is no room to turn around and everyone is trunk to tail. At the edge where the path disappears downward, ledges of rock run across it. These ledges are just wide enough to put your foot on, one step at a time. The big elephants can feel ahead of them with their trunks, but the little ones' trunks are too short to do this. Our aunts help to keep us safe us by holding onto our tails on the steepest parts. Once over the edge, the path descends along the side of the krans and is not quite so steep and scary, but it is still bad enough, because there is nothing between you and the steep drop to the water below. My mother never stops, but just keeps up a slow, careful pace.

When at last we get down onto the sand around the deep clear pool everyone wants to rush about and shout. The big elephants are just as pleased as we are to be safely down off the krans, but they pretend not to show it. Dakiwe goes rushing off across the sand, shouting and flapping his ears, right into the water, where he makes a big splash. Even though it is the middle of the day the water is freezing, but no one cares. Everyone swims and drinks. The pool is deep and the sand slopes steeply into it. As soon as you are in you have to swim as the water is over your head. Luckily we are all good swimmers.

My mother lets us stay in the water and around the pool all day. There are lots of sweet grasses growing along the banks of the river and a little further downstream there are big fig trees loaded with ripe figs. My mother chooses this place to spend the night, for the next day we will be setting out on the long journey to the Nyathi Plains.

My mother Ndlovu not only knows all the places where there are good things to eat, but she also knows when the grasses and fruits are the sweetest and best-tasting.

All elephants eat many different plants. Most other animals live on only certain grasses or trees or bushes. Then there are others, like vain Ngonyama the Lion, sly Ingwe the Leopard and nasty Mpisi the Hyena, who eat other animals.

My mother says that it was not always so. Once upon a time long, long ago, before there were any animals on the earth, Nkosinkulu, the Great One, and Mantis made a hole in the trunk of a Baobab tree. Out of that hole came, one by one, each of the animals that we know today, such as Idube the Zebra and Nkhonhone the Wildebeest. As each animal came out, Nkosinkulu gave them their names and Mantis told them what part of the mountains, valleys, rivers or plains they must go to and what they must eat.

All this took a very long time. Finally, it was the elephants' turn. When the first elephant came out of the Baobab tree, Nkosinkulu called us Ndlovu, which as you know is my mother's name. But Mantis had by this time given away all the different places and all the different foods. He was in big trouble because Nkosinkulu had especially warned him that there were lots and lots of animals and that he had to be very careful to save some food for each one. Then Mantis had a great idea. Since Ndlovu was so big and so smart, why not let him eat some of all the foods and go to all the places where these foods grew! Nkosinkulu was very pleased and said, "Very well, Mantis, that is a good idea. That is what we will do." So that is how the elephants got to go everywhere and eat all kinds of foods.

My mother also says that when we elephants came out of the Baobab tree, all the animals ate plants and none of them ate each other, which must have been a very nice way to live. But then one more animal came out of the Baobab tree. This animal, whom Nkosinkulu called Abantu, was man.

The first man was a funny-looking animal. He stood up on his hind legs and walked on only two legs, not using his hands to walk on at all — which was really strange because Nkonsinkulu had given all the other animals four legs. It is true that birds walk on only two legs, but most birds fly, apart from the ostrich, of course. Abantu was all skinny, with only tufts of hair that stuck out here and there like those of Ngulube the Warthog, and he was almost as ugly as Ngulube, my mother says.

Now Mantis was in trouble again. What was the Abantu going to eat and where was he going to live? Ndlovu had already been told that he could live everywhere and eat any kind of food. Now the Abantu had come, and Mantis did not know what to do. He was afraid that Nkosinkulu would realize that Mantis was the only one left to eat and that the Abantu would eat him. So he ran away and hid in a green bush, holding up his front feet and praying to Nkosinkulu to spare him. In the meantime the Abantu were getting very hungry and cross waiting for Mantis to tell them what food to eat. Finally the chief of the Abantu said, "There is no food left! We are going to starve!"

Then he saw some fat, shiny Mpala running past. "Why not

eat them?" he said. "Yes!" all the Abantu shouted. "We will eat the Mpala and all the other antelope, which we will call Nyamazane, meat."

When Ngonyama the Lion, Ingwe the Leopard and Mpisi the Hyena heard that, they said, "Yes, we too shall eat Nyama". And so, instead of everyone living happily together, animals started to kill each other for food — all because Mantis hadn't planned everything correctly. And to this day Mantis can still be seen sitting swaying on the bushes with his front feet held up in front of him, asking Nkosinkulu for forgiveness.

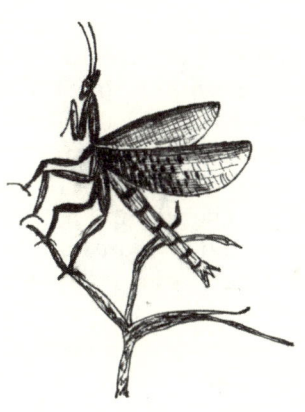

Chapter 4
Down the Ingagane to the Umzimkulu

After leaving the waterfall pool, my mother stays on paths that run through and along the thick bush bordering the Ingagane River. The fig trees there have lots of roots that hang down from the spreading branches and spread the tree outwards from its original large trunk. In this way over time one tree becomes many trees, all joined together. Each fig tree that spreads like this can cover a huge area. The ground under the fig trees is clear of bushes and even grass because so many animals come to feed there. Ngulube the Warthog is especially fond of figs and he and his big family can often be found grubbing and grunting around these trees.

Nkawu the Vervet Monkeys are often up in the fig trees chattering away. The Nkawu teenagers and young ones are particularly mischievous, rushing up and down the roots and branches and chasing each other around the trunks. Sometimes in these games they scamper right between your legs and give you a big fright. Every now and again one of the naughty teenagers will catch a baby monkey by its tail and give the tail a nip. Then the little one will give a loud scream and set all its aunts and its mother chattering. They are a noisy bunch. But they need to be careful, because Ingwe the Leopard, even though he lives mostly in the kranse, sometimes also sleeps in the big trees along the river. And if he can, Ingwe will grab any careless Nkawu and have him for a snack.

Ingwe's other favourite meal, Mfene the Baboon, also loves to feed on the figs. Both baboons and vervet monkeys are messy eaters and drop a lot of half-eaten figs on the ground under the trees. Nungu the Porcupine, Iphiti the Duiker, Imbabala the Bushbuck, and his cousin the Inyala—all these are very happy to feed on the fallen figs. But my mother is careful not to eat the figs on the ground because of the big yellow wasps that also like them. We pick things up with our trunks, of course, and if you picked up a fig, and there was a wasp on it, and the wasp stung the inside of your trunk, it would be terribly sore.

The big fever trees that also grow along the river are the fish eagles' and kingfishers' favorite perches. The weaverbirds build their hanging nests from the branches of the fever trees that spread out over the water. Hanging the nests from the ends of branches stops Nyoga the Spitting Cobra from reaching them and stealing the eggs or, even worse, eating the baby weaverbirds. Mostly we elephants and the snakes don't bother about each other. Our skins are too tough for snakes' fangs, and elephants are much too big for snakes to think about as prey to eat, so there is no reason for a snake to try to bite us. But my mother says that we must always watch out for Nyoga the Spitting Cobra. Nyoga has tiny holes in his fangs which can spray venom into your eye. This can blind you, and you would have a really hard time dealing with all the daily obstacles and dangers with only one eye. So we are very careful not to stumble onto Nyoga, especially along the river banks.

Egrets stand along the edge of the water waiting for Ixoxo the Frog to make a mistake, which would be his last. Another bird we often see along the river is Tegwane the Hamerkop. He builds his huge nest in the fork of a big tree, or on a rocky krans ledge, and keeps on adding to it for many, many years. My mother says she knows of Tegwane nests that my grandmother knew back in her lifetime, and they are still being used. My mother also says that inside a Tegwane's nest you will find all kinds of strange things: pieces of the backbone of Emfene the Baboon, quills from Nungu the Porcupine, and even fangs of Nyoga the Cobra. Tegwane also gathers shiny pebbles and the shells of snails. My mother says she doesn't know what Tegwane does with all these things in his house, but he is clearly up to no good, since the only other place she has heard of such things being kept is in the kraal of Mutwa the Magician. Another strange thing about Tegwane is that you often see him at the edge of a very still and deep pool of water doing nothing but just staring for minutes on end down at his reflection in the water. My mother says that he is trying to look into the future to see what is going to happen, and this also makes her suspect that he is up to no good.

Fish Eagle flies along the river all the time and sits on the highest branches of the fever trees. Whenever we are near the river we can hear his clear fluted whistle. He has terribly long and sharp claws and can swoop down and pluck a fish from the water without any trouble at all. My mother says he can see a fish even when he is flying high above the river.

A strange creature we sometimes see on the branches of the acacia trees along the river is the chameleon. The chameleon is very hard to spot, and when we eat the new green leaves on the acacia trees it is easy to grab a branch with your trunk before you see the chameleon sitting there. The reason it is so easy not to see him is that the chameleon can change the color and patterns of his skin. He can turn green like the acacia leaves with black and white stripes like the branches and thorns. He is unusual in other ways too. He also has eyes that swivel and look in different directions. And he has a tongue which he can shoot out a long way, maybe almost as far as my trunk could reach when I was small. There is sticky stuff on the tip of his tongue so that he can snatch flies and insects off branches around him. Chameleon walks very slowly, carefully lifting each foot (which can grip like a little hand) and moving it forwards and backwards in search of a safe foothold before he finally takes the step. He does this to creep up on flies. My mother says she has heard that once upon a time long, long ago, Chameleon's slow pace got him into big trouble with the Abantu. When the Abantu had just emerged from the Baobab tree, death had not come to the land, and in order to live forever all you needed to do was to drink from a special stream. Nkonsinkulu showed the Chameleon where this stream was and told him to go and tell the Abantu and all the other animals about it. Chameleon set off at his painfully slow pace, slowly lifting each foot and then hesitating before putting it down, so in the end he took just about forever to find the Abantu. When he did, and delivered his message, the Abantu rushed down to where Chameleon said the magic river was. But when they got there all the water was gone. Frantically they tried to find some water, turning over stones and digging holes in the sandy riverbed. They even tried sucking the shiny round pebbles they found under the banks of the river. But they could not find any trace of the magic water. It had all dried up during the long, long time that Chameleon had taken to carry his message from Inkonsinkulu to them. So the Abantu and all the other animals lost the chance to live forever. My mother says she thinks this is just a story, but it is true that the chameleon is the slowest walker I have ever seen.

The paths that we walk on through the thick bush on each side of the river are deep and clear. My mother says that these paths have been there as long as elephants have been in the Balele Mountains and on the Nyathi Plains, and that is a very, very long time. Ndlovu knows all of these paths, the places they lead to and what kind of food is near to each path. She also knows what other animals use these paths and are likely to be nearby. She never gets lost and when we wander down the wrong path she just gives a low rumble to tell us, "You are going the wrong way".

Lots of other animals use these paths, including uBhejane the Black Rhinoceros and Nyathi the Buffalo. You have to watch out for them because they are both near-sighted and bad-tempered. uBhejane is the worse of the two because he will charge you without even thinking. My mother is very careful when she knows from smelling the air and the bushes that uBhejane is somewhere nearby.

Nyathi the Buffalo is not quite as bad as uBhejane. He and all of his herd (and often there are lots and lots of them in one place) come to the river to drink. After they have wallowed in the mud holes they make and have covered themselves from head to foot with black mud, they go and doze under the big fever trees. It's not so bad when there are a whole herd of them because they are always grunting and snorting and you can easily hear and smell them. But we have to watch out for the grumpy old bulls that often stand or lie all by themselves in the thickest thorn bushes. If you wander off the path to browse on some nice green acacia leaves, some ugly old Nyathi bull may be lying under that very tree – and then he will suddenly come charging out at you, which is enough to scare the wits out of anyone.

After we have spent about seven nights and days grazing down the Ngagane River, the thick bush and big trees along the river start to thin out. There are still trees along the banks of the river, but not nearly as many as those around the waterfall pool and farther up the river. When the trees become sparse and the tall grasses take over along the river, we know that we are nearing the great vlei called Umzimkulu, "the big waters." Now we see lots of waterbirds: herons, egrets, and Egyptian and Spurwing geese.

We also have to watch out again for Wenya the Crocodile and Mvubu the Hippopotamus. There are lots of crocodiles and hippo in the Umzimkulu Vlei. Wenya the Crocodile often comes up the Ngagane River a little way, so even before we get to the vlei we have to be careful when we drink.

My mother says that once upon a time, long, long ago, Wenya tried to leave the rivers and the vleis to go and live on the plains. Wenya saw how we came and went and how freely Idube the Zebra could roam across the open veld. So one day Wenya asked a herd of zebra whether he could go with them onto the plains. The Idube stallion told Wenya that that would not be a good idea.

"Wenya, the plains are hot and dry and there is no shade or water," Idube said.

"I know," said Wenya, "but I am tired of living in this same old vlei, and I want to see the world."

"Well, Wenya," Idube said, "I don't think you will be able to keep up with us, but you can try if you like."

So Wenya heaved himself out of the water and rose up on his four big legs. "See how tall I am, Idube."

Idube was impressed that Wenya was nearly as tall as he was. "Yes, I guess you are. You're taller than you look when you are in the water."

This made Wenya feel confident that he would be able to keep up with Idube. So off they went. Soon the veld got stony and the hot stones began burning and hurting Wenya's feet. The zebra kept on going and Wenya lagged further and further behind. Finally Wenya saw a lone acacia and he dragged himself into the little bit of shade under it. He scraped out a shallow hollow and tried to cover himself with tufts of grass. He was so exhausted that he soon fell fast asleep. Idube, who had seen Wenya go towards the thorn tree, came back and looked at him. Wenya was so fast asleep that the zebra thought he was dead. "Well," they said, "we are sorry for Wenya, but we did warn him that he probably would not make it out on the hot plains. There's nothing we can do for him now." So they left Wenya for dead and went on their way towards the hills.

As the sun began to set over the Shonalanga Mountains, Wenya started to cool off and feel better.

When he opened his eyes he saw Logwaja the Hare looking at him. "Greetings, Logwaja, are you well?" said Wenya to the Hare.

"Greetings, Wenya, how are you?" replied Logwaja.

"I am very tired and hungry," said Wenya, "and I think Idube the Zebra was right: I don't belong on the plains. But now I am too weak to get back to the water."

"Don't worry," said Logwaja. "I'll get someone to help and we will get you back to the vlei." Just then, who should turn up but Mpisi the Hyena, always looking for a free meal.

"Well, Wenya, you don't look so good. What are you doing way out here on the veld?" Mpisi said, licking his chops and looking at Wenya's nice fat long tail.

"I don't feel so good," said Wenya. "Will you and Logwaja help me back to the vlei?"

"Sure, sure," smirked the crafty hyena, figuring that as soon as they got poor old Wenya back to the water he would call the rest of his mangy crew and they would have a great feast. So the hare and the hyena helped the crocodile struggle back to the vlei. By the time they got there Wenya was just about done in. He lay in the water with only his nostrils and eyes showing above it. Mpisi could see that the crocodile was not going to move, so he hurried off to gather all his friends to come and feast on poor helpless Wenya. But by the time Mpisi and his gang came back Wenya had recovered. He did not show that he was feeling better. He still lay in the water with only his nose and eyes showing. Mpisi waded into the water, licking his chops and already tasting the first big bite he was going to take out of Wenya's tail. Wenya watched Mpisi with half-closed eyes, still looking as if he was dying. Just as Mpisi was about to bite into Wenya's tail, Wenya lashed out with his powerful tail and knocked Mpisi head over heels into the deeper water. There Wenya grabbed him in his huge jaws and, spinning his whole body around like a whirlwind, he tore Mpisi apart. Ever since that day, my mother says, you can see Wenya the Crocodile lying in the water with only his eyes and nostrils showing and Mpisi the Hyena skulking in big circles well away from the water's edge, while Logwaja the Hare comes to drink without even looking around.

As we near the Umzimkulu, the trees finally disappear completely and the grasses and reedbeds get thicker and thicker. Soon the Tambuti grass is as tall as my mother and we little ones cannot see over it at all. In tall grass like that you have to stay very close to your mother or aunts for fear of getting lost. The grown-ups make a lot of low rumbling noises so that we know where they are. Even so, if it were not for the paths that Mvubu the Hippopotamus makes as he goes from the deep pools to the grasslands around the vlei, we would never be able to get through the thick tall grass. Hippos come out of the water at night to graze on the sweet grasses around the vlei. My mother has told me why this is. She says that once upon a time, long, long ago, Mvubu had a very fine shiny coat of soft brown fur, and also a fine bushy tail. Because of his fine coat, Hippopotamus could spend the whole day grazing in the sun and not get sunburnt. Mvubu was very proud of his fine coat and bushy tail and would often stand on the bank of a deep pool and admire his reflection in the water. One day when he was admiring himself in the pool, Logwaja the Hare came along and sat down beside Mvubu. "Greetings, Mvubu, what are you doing?"

"Greetings, Logwaja. I am admiring myself. Look what a handsome fellow I am. You, on the other hand, look pretty scruffy with your long ears and your moth-eaten tail."

Now Logwaja actually thought that he was very good-looking, and he was furious with Mvubu for insulting him like that. "You are a very vain character, Mvubu," thought Logwaja, "and you need to be taught a lesson." So he hopped away and gathered together a huge pile of dry grass.

"The nights are cold," he said to the hippo. "Here is a pile of grass that will keep you snug and warm."

Mvubu was charmed and said, "Thank you, Logwaja, that is very nice. I'll have a lovely warm sleep tonight." Then he snuggled into the pile of grass and fell fast asleep. As soon as Logwaja heard Mvubu snoring away under the tree, he rushed to the Abantu village on the nearby ridge. There he stole a red-hot coal from the Abantu's fire and, carrying it in a tiny clay bowl that he had also taken from the Abantu, he ran back to the sleeping hippo. He put the glowing coal in the dry grass of the hippo's bed and blew on it as hard as he could. Soon a flame flickered up, then another, and soon the whole pile of dry grass burst into flame.

Poor Mvubu jumped up to find his fine coat and tail on fire. He rushed into the pool and sank to the bottom. When he came out in the morning and looked at his reflection, he was horrified. Instead of being covered with the sleek brown coat that he had been so proud of, he was red and bare-skinned all over with just a few spiky hairs sticking up. He was so ashamed of how he now looked that he took to spending all day in the water with only his nostrils, eyes and little round ears showing. And to this day Mvubu comes out to feed only during the hours of darkness, when no one else can see him.

My mother also says that after Mvubu began to spend all day in the water hiding his red skin and shabby looks, Nkosinkulu became worried, for he did not think that two large animals such as Wenya the Crocodile and Mvubu the Hippopotamus could both live in the same pools of water. He was afraid that with their large mouths and large appetites they would eat all the fish in the pools and in the rivers. But Mvubu begged Nkosinkulu to let him stay in the water.

"Nkosinkulu," Mvubu begged, "please, my skin is tender and sore. If I stay in the sun, I'll burn and die. Please let me spend my days in the water. I promise that I will not eat any of the fish."

Nkosinkulu thought for a long time and then said, "All right, Mvubu, but on one condition. You have to demonstrate to me each day that you have kept your promise and not eaten any fish."

"I promise, Nkosi. Thank you, Nkosi," said Mvubu. And to this day, as my mother says, you can see Mvubu carefully spreading his dung, to show Nkonsinkulu that there are no fish bones in it and that he has not eaten any fish.

Mvubu is a very strange animal. Once my mother saw Wenya the Crocodile rise out of the water, grab a poor careless impala antelope by the nose and face, and drag him under the roiling water. No sooner had Wenya dragged the impala towards a certain watery grave than Mvubu, who had been watching the whole thing, rushed over. He somehow grabbed the impala away from Wenya. Then he gently cradled the terrified impala in his huge mouth and carried him up onto the riverbank. There Mvubu carefully laid the impala on the grass and returned to the river. The impala had some bad cuts about his face and head and one of his ears was torn and bleeding from Wenya's sharp teeth, but otherwise he was not hurt, and soon he shook himself and ran off into the bush. My mother says he recovered and after that was always very cautious when coming to drink at the river. But no one ever knew why Mvubu had so bravely saved the impala's life.

Chapter 5
The Baobab Trees and South to the Nyathi Plains

Instead of going down to the Nyathi River from the Umzimkulu Vlei, my mother leads us westwards towards the Shonalanga Mountains. There where the Nyathi River begins from a spring on the side of Amajuba Mountain, the Hill of Doves, are great trees called Baobab trees. This is the tree out of which all the animals came in the beginning, as I told you, when Nkosinkulu named them and Mantis told them what they could eat and where they would live. At the start of the dry season the Baobab trees have lovely juicy flesh that my mother and my aunts can get to with their tusks.

My mother says that once upon a time long, long ago, when trees could still wander around the earth, the Baobab tree got into trouble with Nkosinkulu. The Baobab tree was not satisfied that it could only creep along like Shongololo the Millipede, for it wanted to be able to run like an impala. Nkosinkulu told the Baobab tree that this was impossible. "Baobab, you are much too big to go running like an impala," said Nkosinkulu. But still the Baobab tree kept on complaining and whining. Finally Nkosinkulu lost all patience. He pulled all the Baobab trees up by their roots, turned them upside down and stuck them into the ground like that. And so to this day all Baobab trees seem to have their roots in the air and their branches in the ground.

When we get to the Baobab trees my mother and aunts go to special trees and push their tusks into the tree trunks. Then they break out big pieces of the tree, which we all love to eat. Even though we ask for more, my mother lets us have only a certain amount. I think this is because if we ate too much we would all get bad tummy-aches. But I think it may also be because she does not want to hurt the Baobab tree too much. In this way we can keep coming back and eating from it every year.

After we have fed on the Baobab trees my mother gives the "Let's go" rumble, turns around and heads down the Nyathi River to the Nyathi Plains. By now it has been nearly one whole cycle of the moon since we left the Hidden Valley and the waterfall pool. The Nyathi River and Plains are named after Nyathi the Buffalo, who live along the river and graze on the plains. I have already told you how mean they are and how they hide in the long grass and bushes near the river and often scare us when we go to the river to drink and look for figs. The Nyathi Plains stretch from the Balele Mountains as far as the eye can see to the south. The Nyathi River runs through the middle of the Nyathi Plains and there are always big trees to find shade under and pools to swim in and drink from.

When you hear the "Let's go" rumble you had better stop playing or fooling around and get in line behind your mother, otherwise you will quickly be left behind. My mother Ndlovu is always in front, and my fat little sister Mafutha comes next behind her. Mafutha is nearly always late and still trips over her trunk when she tries with her funny little waddling run to catch up. Mabalel, my favorite aunt, comes next and I follow her with Undlebe, my oldest aunt, behind me. We always try to stay in place and keep in line — not like my brothers behind us, especially Dakiwe, who is always running after butterflies, or chasing birds, or doing something naughty to remind us why his nickname is Baddy. One day, for example, when we were walking very fast and I was having a hard time keeping up with Mabalel, Dakiwe decided to rush off after Sakabula the Long-tailed Widowbird.

Now Sakabula has such a long, thick and beautiful blue-black tail that he has a hard time flying fast. So Dakiwe nearly caught him, but Sakabulu knows how to trick animals that chase him and he didn't have much difficulty outwitting Dakiwe. He flew straight over the steep bank of one of the streams that run into the Nyathi River. This bank consisted of black clay, which is very slippery when it is wet, and there had been rain the night before. Dakiwe couldn't stop in time and he slid all the way down the bank on his bottom, yelling with fright. Then we all had to stop, because he couldn't get back up the slippery slope. Ndlovu and Mabalel had to stretch their trunks out as far as they could to try to reach Dakiwe. At first they couldn't reach him. Ndlovu had to rumble loudly at Dakiwe to move up the stream to a place where the bank was not as high. Only there were Ndlovu and Mabalel able to hook their trunks around Dakiwe's trunk and pull him out. Ndlovu was very cross and gave him a hard whack on his bottom with her trunk. But we were all very happy that he had been saved, even if it was his own fault that he had needed saving in the first place.

When all thirteen of us are walking in a long line we don't stop to eat or drink but just keep moving on. It is hard to keep up with the grown-ups because they take such big steps and don't trip over the rocks and roots.

Another group of elephants which lives further over near the big mountains often comes to the Nyathi Plains at the same time as we do. My mother knows these elephants and she and they talk to each other at long range in the loud low rumbles that I told you about. My mother tells them that we are moving to the plains and that we may see them at one of the drinking holes in the evening. They tell us what they are doing and in this way we stay in touch even though we are too far away to see each other.

The last mountain that we pass before entering the Nyathi Plains is called Mabutu Mountain. It is not a very big mountain, but it has a cave that goes all the way through it, and in this cave live small people called Bushmen My mother says that they paint pictures of animals on the walls of caves and dance around their fires imitating animals. So far in my life I haven't seen any Bushmen. My mother says that they don't bother us, but that we must still be very careful when we are anywhere near them. As we go past Mabutu we can smell their fires. My mother keeps her trunk up high to smell better and make sure that we are not going anywhere near any Bushman women who may be out gathering roots and berries.

The first animals we usually see after we have passed Mabutu are zebras with their vivid stripes. A strange thing about these stripes is that in some ways they actually make the zebra harder to see. This helps Idube to fool Ngonyama the Lion, because when Idube runs fast the stripes make him all blurry and Ngonyama gets confused and may miss his spring. Idube's stripes also fool the bad fly I mentioned before, the Tsetse fly. Because of Idube's stripes, the Tsetse fly can't see him properly and so doesn't bite him. Sometimes early in the dry season the Tsetse flies bother us on really hot days when we try to cool off under some big shady trees, but my mother knows other kinds of tree which Tsetse flies don't like. So she leads us there. Later on in the dry season the nights become too cold and all the flies leave the Nyathi Plains.

There are other flies that also bother us on the Nyathi Plains, but they would be much worse if it were not for Miskruier, the Dung beetle, whom we call Missy for short. What this little beetle does is to roll up the dung of lots of animals into a perfectly round ball rather bigger than herself. Then she sets to work rolling and pushing the ball along the ground. To do this she goes backwards, pushing the ground with her front legs and controlling and steering the ball of dung with her back legs. She does this until she finds a nice sandy spot where she can bury the ball in the ground. Before she covers it up she lays her eggs in it. Now the flies like to lay their eggs in animal dung too. So both Missy's eggs and the flies' eggs end up in the same place. Missy's eggs hatch out first and the larvae that come out of them immediately gobble up all the flies' eggs. In this way there are far fewer flies to bother us than there would have been if Missy the Dung beetle had not been around.

There are lots of other beetles on the veld, and even one which looks like uBhejane the Rhinoceros. The spiders, scorpions and lizards are all enemies of the beetles. Some of the spiders are very clever. The Trapdoor Spider, for example, builds his nest underground with a tunnel to the surface. He then builds a tight-fitting trapdoor which he camouflages with sand and bits of leaves until it is quite invisible. Then he hides in the tunnel, lifting the trap door just a tiny bit so that he can see whoever is unlucky enough to come walking by. As soon as an insect like an ant or grasshopper comes close enough to his lair, he flings open the trapdoor, pounces on the poor insect and hauls it into his lair. When the trapdoor is closed the spider is safe from enemies such as the scorpion. And when it rains the trapdoor seals the spider's lair off from the water, keeping him snug and dry.

But all the insects have to watch out for Mantis. Mantis is very fierce, for such a small creature, and will attack and kill even insects that are very much bigger than herself.

By the way, when I told you about Idube the Zebra's stripes just now, I forgot to mention that Idube's calves also know who their own mother is by the pattern of the stripes on her bottom. This makes it easier for them to stay behind their own mother if the whole group has to gallop away in a mad dash to escape from Ngonyama's attack. Ngonyama does not always have it all his own way when hunting zebras. If he gets too close to the hooves of a big zebra stallion, those hooves can deliver a terrible kick which can easily break Ngonyama's jaw, and once a lion's jaw is broken he will not live many more days.

Both Idube the Zebra and Nkhonhoni the Wildebeest are our good friends and we often find them together. But Nkhonhoni is not nearly as smart or as brave as Idube. Nkhonhoni calves often fool around, dancing, prancing, jumping and generally showing off for everyone to see. And if Ihlosi the Cheetah should happen to see this, the Nkhonhoni calves had better watch out. Ihlosi is the fastest animal on earth. An Ihlosi can run as fast as seventy miles per hour.

So unless Nkhonhoni calves are warned by their mothers and get a good start, they may find themselves in deep trouble. The only thing that may help them is that although Ihlosi can run like the wind, she can't keep it up for very long.

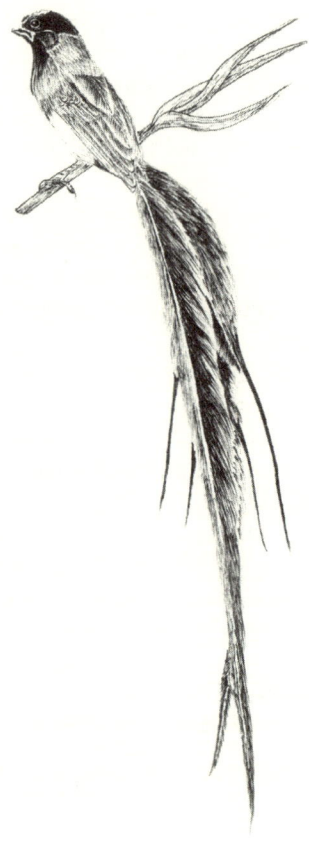

Chapter 6
Ihlosi's Tears

You can always tell Ihlosi the Cheetah from Ingwe the Leopard. First, Ingwe is almost never around in the daytime, whereas you will often see Ihlosi sitting on a big termite mound looking for her dinner. Ihlosi also has single black spots, while Ingwe has groups of black spots each with an orange spot in the middle, like petals on a flower. Ihlosi is leaner in build, with long legs, a long slender body, a very long tail and a small head. But the biggest difference is that Ihlosi has a dark tear-stain leading from the inner corners of her eyes all down her cheeks. My mother says that Ihlosi got this tear-stain from crying and crying because once upon a time long ago a wicked Abantu hunter stole her cubs. It happened like this.

Ihlosi was out hunting for food for her three cubs and caught an Mpala just as an Abantu hunter came along. He was really impressed by how easily she had run down the impala and caught it. The three cubs were very hungry, and soon they had eaten up the whole impala and were begging for more. So their mother Ihlosi went out and quickly ran down another impala.

The Abantu hunter carefully watched Ihlosi's hunting from a ridge where he was hiding. When he saw the second kill he thought, "My word, that Ihlosi is a much better hunter than I am! If only I had an Ihlosi to hunt for me, I would never go hungry." Then he remembered the cubs and thought, "What if I catch one of Ihlosi's cubs? Then it can hunt for me." With this idea in mind he hurried home to fetch a net with which to catch the cub. By the time he got back, the cubs had finished the second impala and were as stuffed full of food as they could be.

"Aha!" he thought. "They will never be able to run away with those big tummies." So he crept up on them very, very slowly, making sure that he was downwind from them, for he was afraid of their mother. But just then she decided that, being really thirsty after the hard work of the two hunts, she needed to go down to the Nyathi River to drink. "What luck," chuckled the hunter to himself. "Now I have got them." He found a small donga that ran right up to where the cubs were now lying with their feet in the air and the warm sun shining nicely on their fat little bellies. He crept up ever so slowly, not making any noise or treading on any dry twigs or leaves. Just then a Kwêvoël, who is also called the Go-'Way Bird, came and sat right on an aloe above the Ihlosi cubs.

The Kwêvoël is a good friend to those who are being hunted because as soon as it sees a hunter it yells, "Go 'way! Go 'way!" to warn the prey and save it from the hunter. The Abantu hunter knew this, so he flattened himself into the grass in the donga and didn't move a muscle. After a while the Kwêvoël got bored and flew away. "Finally!" said the hunter. "Now I'll get them," and he threw his net over all three Ihlosi cubs.

"Help! Help!" they cried out, fighting to get free of the net. But the more they struggled the more they entangled themselves. And soon, panting and very scared, they could only lie still, putting their ears back and hissing and spitting at the hunter.

The hunter was very pleased with himself and thought, "Ha, if I keep all three cubs and make all three hunt for me, I will never be hungry." Now this was being really greedy, because he did not need all three cheetah cubs to hunt for him. And even worse than that, it goes against tribal law not to hunt for yourself. But this hunter was much too greedy to care about that, and he marched home very pleased with himself, carrying all three Ihlosi cubs tied up in the net.

When the mother came back to her den from the river she couldn't find her cubs anywhere. But she knew from the smells that an Abantu hunter had been there, and the flattened grass and broken bushes told her that there had been a struggle. With an awful sinking feeling inside her she realized that something terrible had happened to her cubs. Desperately she called and called with the sharp "Mew mew" sound which her cubs knew well. But there was no answer. She had to find them, so she set off to follow the track of the hunter.

Soon she came to a ridge which looked down on his kraal. And there Ihlosi saw the greedy hunter boasting to his wives and friends about his great feat and how he was now going to live better than anyone else. At his feet, in wicker chicken-cages, were her three cubs.

"But," she heard the hunter's eldest wife say, "you know it is against tribal law to have someone else hunt for you when you can hunt for yourself." And she heard his reply: "I don't care about tribal law, that's for old women and children. I am going to keep these cubs and train them to hunt for me."

That was all the mother cheetah could stand. There was no way she could get into the kraal, for it had a high thorn fence all around it. Even if she did somehow manage to get in, there were too many men and dogs there. All the men had spears, and if a spear didn't get her, she would be torn apart by the dogs. So she turned around and walked slowly and sadly back to the den where she had brought up her three little ones. All that night she cried, and cried, and never slept. Great tears rolled down her cheeks one after the other. She couldn't stop them even as the dawn started to break and the dark bush below the den started to glow in the first rays of light. By then there were dark stains down each of Ihlosi's cheeks.

She had no desire to eat or even go for a drink. All she could think of was that her three cubs were shut up in cages. Nor could she sleep, even though she was dead-tired from her long night of grieving. Just as the sun caught the tops of the trees on the ridge where her den was, she heard the approach of a group of men. She had not been keeping her usual lookout, and when she became aware of them they were right above the den. Then she heard the voice of the Chief of the Abantu. He was praising the sun and the gifts of Nkosinkulu and thanking Nkosinkulu for all the animals. The mother cheetah thought, "How can he say that when one of his hunters has stolen my children?" Though she was deathly afraid of men, she knew the Chief of the Abantu was a good man, so she stepped from her den and showed herself to the Chief. "Greetings, Ihlosi," he said.

"Greetings, O Great One," she replied. "Are you well?"

"I am well, Ihlosi," he answered. "Are you also well, Ihlosi?"

"No, O Great One, I cannot be well. My heart is broken; my children are gone."

"I see that you have much grief, O Ihlosi, for your cheeks are stained with tears."

"Yes, Inkosi, I weep for my children."

"How did you lose your children, Ihlosi?"

"Inkosi, I ask your pardon, for I do not wish to speak badly of one of Inkosi's best hunters."

"Speak, O Ihlosi, speak and let me hear."

"Inkosi," said the mother cheetah, "yesterday one of your hunters came and stole all three of my children. He has them at this moment down in his kraal, caged inside his chicken cages."

"What does my hunter want with your children?"

"Inkosi, he wishes to train them as his hunters to hunt game for himself."

"That, Ihlosi, is against tribal law."

"I know, Sire."

The Chief of the Abantu became very angry and sent his general Ikonto to fetch the hunter. "Bring him back here at once together with Ihlosi's three children. And death to you as well as him if any one of Ihlosi's children suffers as much as a scratch."

Ikonto ran almost as fast as Ihlosi and brought back the hunter and Ihlosi's three children.

"What is your name, you who call yourself a hunter?" asked the Chief, barely able to keep his voice from thundering across the valley.

"O Great One, I am your humble servant, Mposa."

"You are no servant of mine, Mposa. Do you not know the law of the land? If you are able to hunt, you hunt for yourself. Others do not hunt for you."

"I know the law, O Inkosi."

"Then why have you stolen Ihlosi's children?"

"I was greedy and lazy, O Great One."

"You will return them now, and for as long as Ihlosi wishes, you will give her a fat young goat each time the moon is new to make up for the wrong you have caused her. See the stains of grief on her cheeks. See, her cubs too have the same stains. All Ihlosi will carry these marks for all time to ensure that your greed and lazy ways are never forgotten. I have spoken." And before Ihlosi could thank the Chief of the Abantu, he had turned and walked off into the rising sun.

And to this very day, as my mother says, all Ihlosi carry the marks of that mother cheetah's tears down their cheeks.

My mother also says that the cheetah was not always the fastest runner of all the animals. Once upon a time, long, long ago, there were quite a few animals that lived on the plains who thought they could run faster than Ihlosi. After lots of competitions between Mpala, Kudu, Gemsbok, Idube the Zebra, Nkonhoni the Wildebeest and Nondo the Tsessebe, Nondo was chosen as the fastest among this group. Nkosinkulu then arranged a race between Nondo the Tsessebe and Ihlosi the Cheetah to see who was in fact the fastest of all the animals. The race had to be run from a big thorn tree near the Nyathi River to a rock on the slopes of Mabutu.

Skilpad the Tortoise was chosen to start the race because nobody could ever accuse him of having any kind of claim to being the fastest animal. Tortoise was so slow that even the Abantu children could catch him. As soon as Skilpad shouted "Hamba – go!" to start the race, Nondo shot off like the wind. Even though Ihlosi ran as fast as he could, he could not catch Nondo. Igogo the Klipspringer could see Nondo racing up the hill towards the finish at the big rock. He thought, "Poor old Ihlosi is going to be so sad that he lost the race. All the animals will say, You aren't the fastest, Ihlosi, Nondo is the fastest." But just then Nondo stepped in an old anteater hole. In a cloud of dust he tumbled over and over and then lay groaning on the ground. Ihlosi came up like a flash and Igogo, watching, thought: "Oh-oh, Ihlosi is going to win after all". But Ihlosi didn't run past the fallen Nondo. Instead he stopped and gently lifted Nondo's head, asking him if he was all right.

"Yes," said Nondo very shakily, "I think so. My leg hurts but I don't think it's broken."

Ihlosi felt Nondo's front legs and said, "Yes, I think you've just got a bad sprain. The right one is going to hurt for a day or so, but you will be all right."

Nkosinkulu, who of course had also had been watching the race, was very pleased with the way in which Ihlosi stopped to help Nondo instead of just running on to win.

"Ihlosi the Cheetah," said Nkosinkulu, "you did a very good thing to help Nondo when you could easily have won the race. Because of your noble act, I will make you the fastest animal in the whole world."

And from that day to this, Ihlosi has been the fastest of all the animals.

Chapter 7
Lamithi's Long Neck

One of the good friends whom we are sure to see as soon as we get to the Nyathi Plains is Ndhlulamithi the Giraffe. His name is rather a long one (maybe to match his neck) so we just call him Lamithi for short.

Lamithi didn't always have such a long neck. My mother says that once upon a time, long, long ago, Lamithi had a short neck like that of Idube the Zebra. One day, during a terrible year when no rain came in the wet season and all the grass was gone, Lamithi and her friend uBhejane the Black Rhinoceros were searching for food. The sun was blazing down and both Lamithi and uBhejane were boiling hot, hungry and thirsty. But there was no food and no water. They were so hot that they had to find shade under a big spreading camelthorn tree. Lamithi looked up to the top of this tree and said to uBhejane, "Look, uBhejane, how green and sweet the leaves look up at the top of this tree."

uBhejane, with his little black eyes and short neck, could hardly see the leafy crown of the tree, but he grunted, "So what, Lamithi? We can't reach them."

"What if we could?" said Lamithi. "Let's go and ask Mutwa the Sangoma if he can make some medicine so that we can reach the green leaves."

"Very well," said uBhejane. "How far is it to Mutwa's kraal?"

"Quite a long way up the valley towards the Balele Mountains," answered Lamithi.

"Well, there's nothing to eat here," said uBhejane. "We may as well go and look up the valley." So they set off and walked all day, until finally, just as the sun was starting to set behind the Shonalanga Mountains, they came to the kraal of Mutwa, the most powerful magician in the whole country.

Now, you don't just stroll up to a Sangoma's kraal and say casually, "Hi, how's your brew, man?" If you did that you would probably find yourself three inches high, covered in warts and croaking next to a muddy pool. No, what you have to do is wait patiently and respectfully until Mutwa's messenger comes to you and asks what has brought you there. Mutwa's messenger is a Tokolosh, and he is enough to send a chill down anyone's spine. Itokolosh are little wizened dwarfs that are all hairy and wrinkly, with big pointed ears and long crooked teeth. They ride on the backs of baboons, facing backward and holding on to the baboon's tail. Mutwa only sends them out at night and they ride through the bush, not making a sound, to deliver the great magician's muti and messages. So Lamithi and uBhejane had to wait in the bush below Mutwa's kraal for one of the Tokoloshes to come riding by.

As soon as it got dark uBhejane, as big as he was, started to shiver with fright at every sound in the black darkness of the bush all around them. Lamithi, too, was scared because of all the weird sounds. "Ooh! Ooh! Weeja!" came the howling of Mpungu the Jackal; "Whoop! Whoop! Woowa!" rang out the horrible laughter of Mpisi the Hyena; and "Wewa-wewa" went the weird cry of Mhimbi the Bush baby. But with these sounds all mixed up and echoing up and down the kloof, neither Lamithi nor uBhejane knew what they were — all they knew was that it was very, very scary, and that in fact they were too frightened to stay there any longer.

"Let's get out of here!" uBhejane said.

"Yes, let's go!" agreed Lamithi. So they both turned to run down the kloof away from Mutwa's spooky kraal. But just as they started down the narrow kloof, who should be coming up it, blocking their way, but a big baboon with a Tokolosh on its back.

"Yikes!" they both yelled, and froze on the spot. The Tokolosh, who had been facing backwards, swung round to see who had cried out.

"Aha, my fine friends," said he, "what are you doing here? Mutwa will turn you both into toads."

"No, no, please, Mr Tokolosh," cried Lamithi. "Don't let that happen. We only came to ask the Great Mutwa for help to reach the green leaves on top of the big thorn trees."

"Indeed," growled the Tokolosh, "and why should the Great Mutwa help two miserable bags of bones like you two? What presents have you brought him?"

Of course, neither the giraffe nor the rhino had thought about that. They had to do some very quick thinking, so Lamithi reached behind him and pulled off his tail.

"I have brought the Great Mutwa the most wonderful fly-whisk, O Mr Tokolosh," he said.

"And I the most wonderful horn," said uBhejane, pulling off his sharp second horn.

Tokolosh peered closer and saw that, yes indeed, these were two fine presents, better than any he had brought his master in the past. "Well," said the Tokolosh, "they may do. Wait here and I will tell my master what you want."

uBhejane and Lamithi, still shivering with fright and hurting behind and before from having pulled off a tail and a horn, were only too thankful to see the Tokolosh depart up the kloof to Mutwa the Magician's kraal. But no sooner had they begun to breathe a little more easily than there was a great flash of light which lit up the whole kloof and a deafening clap of thunder which echoed up and down the mountains. At this both Lamithi and uBhejane immediately fell to the ground and pleaded to be spared.

"Oh miserable creatures — what do you want?" thundered Mutwa the Magician.

"Oh please, Sir," Lamithi managed to whisper, "we only want longer necks and legs to reach the green leaves on top of the thorn trees."

"You miserable creatures, go! Come back tomorrow as the sun lights the top of the kranse — not a minute before, not a minute after!" thundered Mutwa the Magician.

"Yessir," Lamithi and uBhejane blurted together and turned and ran as fast as they could down the kloof. uBhejane was so scared that he just kept running, but Lamithi soon stopped.

Lamithi thought, "I have lost my tail and I've got nothing in return. I am going to go back at sunrise tomorrow." So he lay down to wait for first light. As soon as he could see the outline of the trees and the rocky wall of the krans, Lamithi started back up the kloof. He came around the corner below Mutwa the Magician's kraal just as the rays of the rising sun caught the topmost rocks of the kloof. "Boohaa-boohaa", the call of Mfene the Baboon, echoed up and down the kloof. And as the sound died away, out of the shadows came the Tokolosh riding on his baboon. "Where is your near-sighted friend, O Painted One?" asked the Tokolosh.

"I don't know," whispered Lamithi.

"Well, no matter. Here is the magic potion my master has prepared for you. One dose for each of you. Take it before the sun strikes the rocks on that side of the kloof." And leaving the muti, the Tokolosh was gone. Lamithi knew that he could not get uBhejane's muti to him in time.

All he could think of to do was to drink both potions himself. So he downed the muti from both gourds. No sooner had the bitter liquid slid down his throat than Lamithi felt pins and needles in his legs and neck. The prickling feeling got worse and worse until his legs and neck were burning. Then he realized that he was looking over the top of a big thorn tree. When he looked down the ground was far below him. His head was fifteen feet in the air.

And that is how Lamithi got his long legs and neck, and why uBhejane is still bumbling around on his short fat legs. Luckily for Lamithi, the medicine was so strong that he even grew a handsome tail again. But from that day to this, poor old uBhejane has had only one horn, with just a stump in the spot where he broke off his second horn to give to Mutwa the Magician.

Chapter 8
Lamithi Saves The Oxpeckers

When we meet Lamithi we almost always see special birds called Oxpeckers running up and down his long neck, cleaning his ears and riding on his back. My mother Ndlovu says that the Oxpeckers became special friends of Lamithi's after a great fire, as I will now tell you.

One day long, long ago, when hot winds were blowing down from the Shonalanga and Balele Mountains over the Nyathi Plains, some klipspringers were playing on the big boulders of Mabutu Mountain. The winds were so hot and dry that all the bush and grass was brown and crackly. One of the klipspringers, bounding up a big rock, happened to kick some small stones loose, and they went tumbling down over the krans. As these stones struck the boulders at the foot of the krans sparks flew in all directions. Some fell into the dry brittle grass, and in another moment flames had sprung up from the sparks and were being fanned by the hot wind. Before you could say FIRE!, a roaring blaze started to sweep down the slopes of Mabutu and into the Nyathi Plains. The flames leapt up into the air and jumped from tree to tree with a terrible roaring noise. All the birds and animals of the Nyathi Plains could see the great pall of smoke rising from the foot of the Mabutu Mountain and hear the distant growl of the flames.

"Run, run! Fire, fire!" the Kwêvoël screamed to Idube the Zebra, Nkhonhoni the Wildebeest, Mpala, Nondo the Tsessebe, Lamithi, uBhejane and all the other animals of the plains. And they all ran from the fire and the flames towards the Nyathi River, for they knew that if they could jump into the water they would be safe from the blazing inferno. Lots of the smaller animals, like Ngulube the Warthog, Mvuzi the Meerkat, Mbili the Dassie and Ngundwaan the Field mouse, rushed for their burrows and hid deep underground where the fire and the smoke could not reach them. The birds all flew away — all, that is, except the Oxpeckers' three children, who were in their nest high up in a yellow fever tree, and who were too young to fly.

The father and mother Oxpecker were frantic with fear. They called and cried out desperately to the animals rushing past the fever tree: "Oh please, please, somebody, save our children from the flames!" But everyone was so frightened that they just kept on running.

All except Lamithi the Giraffe. Lamithi heard the Oxpeckers' cries, and even though smoke and sparks were already filling the air around the Oxpeckers' fever tree, she stopped in her headlong gallop and turned back to the tree. Lamithi was tall enough to reach the Oxpeckers' nest, and carefully she nudged the three baby birds out of the nest and onto her head. "Hold on with your little feet to the hair on my head," Lamithi cried to them. "Hold on as tight as you can!" And when she felt all three Oxpecker chicks gripping the hair between her horns as tightly as they could, she started to lope swiftly towards the Nyathi River. Lamithi does not run or walk as other animals do. Giraffes move both legs on the same side forward and backward together, whereas other animals work their diagonal legs together. Because both legs on each side are moving the same in this unusual way, Lamithi runs with a rolling motion, but with her long legs she can cover the ground almost as rapidly as my father Nkosi can. And now, running as fast as she could, Lamithi got to the Nyathi River and saved the Oxpeckers' three children. The mother and father Oxpecker were so grateful that they promised that from then onwards they would always take care of Lamithi, keeping her ears and neck clean and pecking off any nasty ticks or other insects that tried to hitch a ride on her long neck. And they have kept their promise, for to this day you will see the Oxpeckers riding on Lamithi and keeping her clean.

After a fire like this, lots and lots of birds, from Aasvoël the Vulture to the proud eagles, fly in to the burnt area to find insects and even small animals that have not escaped the flames. Secretary Birds stride through the burnt grass looking for dead or injured snakes, and soon their long legs and large feet are the same pitch-black color as the grass. Even owls come out before sunset to quarter the burnt veld. Bateleur Eagles, who dip their wings like a tightrope-walker balancing on a cable, soar through the air together with the great white-chested Martial Eagle. Flocks of white egrets fly all the way from the Umzimkulu Vlei to see what they can find in the burnt area. Hoopoe, Kiewiet the Crowned Plover, Herons and even the great Crowned Cranes join in. Lots of guineafowl and Hadeda Ibis come too. No matter how bad a fire has been, it soon seems to be doing a lot of animals good. Not many days after the fire, green shoots can be seen in the blackened grass and on bushes that seemed dead. By the first rains, at the end of the dry season, the whole area that the fire burnt is a carpet of green.

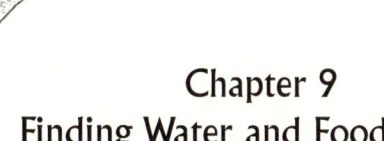

Chapter 9
Finding Water and Food

Lamithi's long neck and long legs make it hard for her to drink. The only way she can reach the water is to spread her front legs wide apart and lower her head right down to the water level. When she does this all her blood wants to rush to her head, because that head was fourteen or fifteen feet above the water a few moments before and now it is lower than almost any other part of her body. But her neck is specially designed to stop this rush of blood from happening, so she can lift and lower her head without blacking out. It is good that she can do this quickly, because when she drinks she is in great danger from Wenya the Crocodile and also from Ngonyama the Lion. With her front legs spread wide and her head so far down, she can't get back to her feet quickly and run away.

So if you watch Lamithi going to the water hole to drink, you will see that she is very careful. She will walk only a few steps towards the water before she stops and, from her great height, looks and listens. When she finally gets to the water she drops her head down and then jumps up and quickly backs away without even touching the water. Only when she is sure that neither Wenya nor Ngonyama are nearby will she finally drink.

Ostrich, with her long neck, has a slightly different problem drinking: she can't suck the water through her beak and up her long throat. So she has to scoop up a beakfull at a time and then lift her head to let the water run down her throat. She has such a long skinny throat that you can see the water going down. It isn't only birds with long necks that can't suck up water: doves and pigeons also have to let the water run down their throats just as Ostrich does,

45

and their necks are short. The Swallow really has the answer: she scoops up water with her lower beak as she skims across the surface of a river or vlei. It looks like fun to me.

But we elephants are much better at drinking than all other animals, because we can fill our trunks with water and then pump it into our mouths. This is not as easy as you may think. We all have a difficult time learning to do it, and have to be taught how by our mothers. When I first tried to drink water, I thought you just sucked it up through your trunk. But that is a very bad idea, because the water goes down the wrong way and gives you a terrible fit of choking, coughing and sneezing. What you have to learn, instead, is to hold the water in your trunk, hold your breath and then lift your trunk and pour the water into your mouth. My mother Ndlovu taught me how to do this by first sucking up some water herself and then letting it run into my mouth from her trunk.

When I caught on to the idea, she wrapped her trunk around mine and let the water run into my trunk. This was much harder to learn, because I kept breathing in and getting the water up my nose. But finally I was able to stop doing that. The secret was to breathe in only a little and then hold my breath and lift my trunk to my mouth. After lots of tries with my mother helping me, I was finally able to do it by myself.

Lamithi the Giraffe has a way of keeping cool which is also different from ours. We keep cool by waving our ears. You can see lots of blood vessels running through the ears of big elephants. When we grow up we really need this, because on the Nyathi Plains in the middle of the day in the dry season there are no clouds and it is blazing hot. It is so hot that even with our thick feet we can feel the hot stones and sand burning through the soles of our feet. When it gets this hot the only way to cool off is either to get into the water and have a nice swim and mud bath, or to find shade under a big spreading thorn tree. Even standing in the shade and waving our ears as much as we can, we still feel very hot.

Lamithi keeps cool in another way. She is actually able to send her blood through the white patterns of her skin when it is hot and through the dark patterns when it isn't. Sunlight makes dark surfaces hotter than light-coloured ones, so in this way she can cool herself down or warm up, which is a pretty neat trick. Sometimes I wonder how Idube the Zebra feels when the sun beats down, heating his black stripes so much more than his white ones. I'm sure he could use Lamithi's cooling system—if he only had it.

We can use our trunks to do lots of things, but you have to learn how to do them. Sometimes you can just copy what your mother and aunts are doing, like picking ripe figs from the branches of the fig trees. You can also pick up the figs that have fallen on the ground, but as I told you earlier, this is risky because lots of the figs on the ground have big yellow wasps on them, and you do not want to have a wasp sting you inside your trunk. So it is better to pick the figs off the branches, and a trunk is perfect for this.

We also have to learn to use our trunks to detect smells in the air. My mother can do this very well. She can tell if Ngonyama the Lion or any of his wives are anywhere nearby. She can tell which of our uncles are around, or whether my father Nkosi has been at the water hole before us, and even how long before us. She can smell the faintest trace of smoke and warn us of a veld- or bush-fire long before we can see it. To do this she lifts her trunk high in the air. She uses the scents she picks up in the air, together with what she can hear. We little ones still can't hear the sounds she hears or the smell the scents she catches. She can tell whether a fire is a bad one or not by listening to its far-off noises. We small ones can't hear the low fire rumbles. These sounds, as well as the faint smell of smoke, are some of the things we must learn to detect as we grow older.

We will also need to learn how to smell water when we can't even see any sign of it. My mother not only knows how to do this: she also knows where to look for this hidden water.

This is vitally important because in very dry years, when the rains don't come at all in the wet season, even the Nyathi River dries up. When we come back to the Balele Highlands at the end of the dry season, we have to cross a long dry stretch where there is no water. My mother goes into the dry riverbeds and in certain places she can smell the water under the sand. There is no sign of this water in the sand or even in the little bits of dry grass on the banks. Everything is brown and bone-dry. But my mother can pick out a spot on the sandy river-bottom where she will start digging. The dry sand is loose and she scoops it out with her front feet. When the hole is as deep as her front knees you can see that the sand is becoming wet. Pretty soon you can see and smell the water in the hole.

Even though everyone is very thirsty, we have to be patient and wait until water seeps into the bottom of the hole that my mother has dug. The big elephants can reach this little pool of water with their trunks. But the little ones, who don't yet know how to suck up the water and hold it in their trunks, can't get to the water in the bottom of the hole. So each one's mother has to suck up water in her trunk and then let it out into her calf's mouth or trunk. All this takes a long time because only one mother and calf can drink at a time. And after each drink we must all wait for the water to seep back into the bottom of the hole before the next one can have a drink. After everyone has had a turn and we leave the dry riverbed, a lot of other animals like Mpala and Idube the Zebra come rushing over to the hole that my mother has dug. But they are not patient and careful like us elephants. They all rush to the hole, trampling its sides into it and filling it with sand before anyone gets even one sip of water. Then they all complain and blame each other for ruining the water hole, but it's really their own fault. In any case, since they don't have trunks they would still wreck the water hole even if they were more careful, because they would trample down its sides trying to get their heads low enough to reach the water. So once again you can see how lucky we are to have trunks.

By now four moons have grown full and waned since we left the waterfall pool. My mother has led us steadily down the Nyathi River with the great wall of the Inkonto si Quathlaba, the Barrier of Spears, on our right. We sometimes graze for two days towards the mountain barrier but always come back to the river. My mother knows where the sweetest water is in springs that rise from the foothills of the Inkonto si Quathlaba. Every afternoon as the sun begins to dip behind the mountains and the deep shadows of the kloofs start to creep towards the Nyathi Plain, my mother gives the assembly rumble. If any of our family, like Dakiwe for example, has wandered away, they hurry back and join the line headed for the water. Often my uncles Amadala and Nsimbi hear the call and join us. My father Nkosi sometimes comes silently through the bush and joins us at the water hole. When this happens we all rumble and squeal with joy because we are so pleased to see him. Even though we are very excited, we are careful to be respectful to Nkosi. Even Dakiwe rushes towards him and then stops and sits down with his forelegs straight out in front of him. This is a respectful greeting to Nkosi, who recognizes it with just a brief wave of his big ears and a sideways step past Dakiwe. My mother and some of my aunts greet Nkosi, twining their trunks around his huge trunk and tusks. They even touch his eyes gently with the tips of their trunks and put their trunks in his mouth. Nkosi towers over everybody and walks very slowly and with great dignity towards the water. Everyone gives way and leaves a path for him and a space at the water's edge. While Nkosi is proud to be treated with such respect, you can also see that he is very pleased to be greeted in this way.

Often the water holes my mother finds in the foothills are only small pools. At such pools everyone is very careful to take their turn and then give way for the next one to drink. You quench your initial thirst and then move away to give the one behind you a turn. If you are still thirsty, you have to wait until everyone else has had their first chance to drink before you go back for more. When everyone has quenched their thirst we move downstream a little way before taking a bath. Mostly these pools are too small to swim in, but it is fun to roll in the mud and slide down the banks. Nkosi or my mother will go into the water where we take our baths and stir up the mud. They go in about knee-deep and then use a front leg to create a tremendous splashing and agitation. Water and mud from the bottom of the pool flies everywhere. Soon you can't see any clear water. The whole pool is mixed up into a black soup of mud and water. Nkosi and my mother take great trunkfuls of this muddy water and spray themselves from head to foot. By the time they have finished they are black all over from the mud. By covering ourselves in mud this way we can stop the big flies from biting us and get rid of the nasty ticks that climb onto us in the long grass. When the mud dries we find an old stump or even an old anthill and rub and scrape ourselves against it. This feels very good and rubs many of the ticks off us. In parts that are hard to reach, like behind our ears, Lamithi's friends the Oxpeckers come and help us get rid of them.

As I have told you, not all the other animals are as careful at water holes as we are, and Nyathi the Buffalo are the worst. They come in a big mob and wade right into the drinking pool. Pretty soon the whole pool is trampled into a mud hole. Ngulube the Warthog is just as bad but at least he is not as big as Nyathi. Fortunately neither Nyathi nor Ngulube likes to come up into the foothills. They mostly stay down in the plain and near the river. As long as the rains have come in the wet season, there is plenty of water in the Nyathi River. When a river is flowing, even a mob of buffalo can't mess it up. But in bad years, especially towards the end of the dry season, even the Nyathi River will stop running. Only a few deep pools will remain, and these are taken over by Mvubu the Hippo, because he has nowhere else to go. Things can get pretty bad when all the animals are forced to use just a few drinking places. All the grass and bushes around the water holes are quickly stripped bare and there is nothing to eat for miles around. Unless the water hole is very deep, it is soon trampled into a mud hole. This can be very dangerous because you can get stuck in the deep mud and be unable to get out. Usually my mother is too watchful to let this happen to us, but every now and then one of us little ones gets into trouble in a muddy water hole. When this happens our mother or one of our aunts reaches in with her trunk and pulls us out. None of the other animals know how to help each other like this, so when they get stuck in the mud they cannot get out of it.

Sometimes when we are in the hills my mother will lead us up a special gully to a soft rock-face. Here she and the other grown-ups break out chunks of a strange soft white rock with their tusks. It seemed weird the first time I was given a piece of this rock to eat, but I soon found that when you chew these chunks they taste quite good and make a fizzy feeling in your mouth and throat. We don't eat very much of this soft rock, but my mother says we must eat some each year to help keep our teeth and tusks strong.

After spending one or two days in the hills, we head back down to the plain and the Nyathi River. By now it has been dry for nearly four moons without a single cloud in the sky. Although the nights are still cold, the days are getting steadily hotter, and every now and then a hot dry wind blows down from the Shonalanga Mountains. This wind blows all day and all night. It usually stops only briefly near sunset. Before the middle of the night, strong gusts come rushing down the valley from the mountains and everyone gets very nervous. Because of the strong wind you can't hear or smell properly. The air is full of dust which gets in your eyes, ears and mouth. Sometimes we can't even see each other when we're trying to walk in a line to the water hole. Because all the grass and most of the bush has by now been eaten for some distance around the water hole, it is especially bad there. Great clouds of dust come sweeping across the open space and you can lose sight of where the water hole is. When you get there you can't even see the water as it is covered by a thick film of dust. When these winds blow, my mother leads us to a deep kloof which comes down to the Nyathi River. Where the kloof meets the river there is a deep pool of water in a rocky hole. It is very difficult to get down to reach the water and only one elephant at a time can go down. My mother knows this and stands at the top rumbling to everyone and keeping us all in order. She lets us go down one at a time, so each of us must wait until the previous one has gone down and come back up. We can stay in this kloof for two or three days until the winds die down. There is not much left to eat in the kloof, but we don't mind. You can hear the wind roaring in the trees up above on the edges of the kloof and it feels nice to be out of it. Dust still swirls down into the kloof but it is much better down there than out in the open. When at last the wind stops and we emerge from the kloof, birds are singing and calling again and everyone is very relieved.

As everywhere gets drier and drier, there are only a few water holes left. Mostly these are deep pools in the Nyathi River. By now the river has stopped running and there are long stretches of dry riverbed with only sand and gravel and no water. The reedbeds and tambuti grass in the river channels and along the banks look dry, but there are still green places hidden down narrow paths. My mother finds these and we get a good meal. Even so, we are now often hungry and have to keep looking for grass and green leaves. My mother and aunts show us how to recognize grasses with sweet roots. They grab these with their trunks and then, pulling the grass, they kick the roots loose from the soil and bang them against a tree trunk or rock to shake off all the soil. After they have done all this the grass tastes quite good. We try to do it but it doesn't work too well for us little ones. The dry grass breaks off and we can't kick the roots loose as the grown-ups can. My mother and Mabalel also push over quite big thorn trees to get to the green leaves up in the high branches. When they do this we can all gather around and eat the green leaves and the sweet bark. We have to use our small tusks to poke under the bark and lift it up. Once you have lifted up a piece of bark, you can pull it off the trunk or branch in long strips.

    My father Nkosi and my uncles can push over quite large trees and we often come across places where they have knocked down trees and broken off big branches. This may look bad but my mother says it helps the veld and the bush. The fallen trees often continue to grow and send up new shoots which soon become the trunks of other small trees in their own right. Food is added to the soil and grasses grow in and around the fallen trees. Lots of small animals like Nsele the Badger, Nungu the Porcupine, and Iphiti the Duiker all find new homes under the fallen trees. Even Mpungu the Jackal may make a den and raise a new litter of cubs under a big acacia tree that my father has pushed over. By pushing trees over, breaking off branches and browsing on the thorn trees, elephants keep the bush open and allow grass to grow. This helps the Mpala and Idube the Zebra, because if the bush were not kept back it would grow together into a dense cover of thick foliage. This would block out all the sunlight and the grass would die. My mother says that a lot of the animals work together to keep the plains healthy. Each kind of animal grazes, browses or feeds on one part. Idube the Zebra grazes the short grass, Nkonhoni the Wildebeest crops the longer grass, Kudu browses the bushes and Lamithi the Giraffe feeds on the taller trees. We elephants eat food in all of these places. And these are just a few of the animals that keep the veld and the bush healthy.

    As the dry season goes into its fifth moon we have to look for dry grass that still has some water in its stems. This grass is very tough and we have to learn how to use a tusk to pull it out. You grab a bunch of the grass with your trunk, then stick your tusk under the tuft and holding tight with your trunk, lift up with your tusk. When you get it right, the grass breaks off and you get a nice mouthful. All the older elephants have worn notches in one of their tusks from doing this. Most use the right tusk, though some use the left one.

Fortunately for us, it is just at this time, when food is becoming scarce, that the Marula seeds ripen. The Marula tree has big pods with large juicy seeds in each one. When they are ripe they are as sweet and almost as good as the figs earlier in the dry season. My mother knows where the biggest and best Marula trees are and when each one of them has ripe pods. Not every Marula tree is ready at the same time, because it depends on whether the tree is on a slope that faces north or south. Marula trees on north-facing slopes ripen first, the ones on south-facing slopes later. Once the Marula seed-pods start to ripen we know that we will have lots of tasty food for the next two weeks. Many of the other animals know this too, so they all gather under the Marula trees. Mfene the Baboon is the worst. When a whole tribe of twenty or thirty baboons finds a Marula tree, they don't leave much for us. Luckily the big old baboon leaders are more concerned with how they look and giving out punishment to anyone in their tribe who they think is misbehaving, than with remembering where the best Marula trees are. But my mother never forgets, and she carefully leads us in a way which confuses the baboons so that they can't follow us. In this way we can keep the best Marula trees a secret from Mfene and his busy fingers. Ngulube the Warthog and most of the antelopes also like Marula seeds, but they only pick up the ones that have dropped to the ground. My mother and my aunts often shake the branches of the Marula trees with their trunks and even their tusks, and this brings down a lot of fruit for everyone.

By the time we have found all of the Marula trees with fruit on them, we have gone far down the Nyathi River and we can see hills and even mountains to the south. My mother knows that this is the end of the Nyathi Plains, and that beyond those hills the Abantu live. The Abantu tribe who live there are called the Amazulu. They can be fierce, as I told you at the beginning of my story, and I have been taught to fear them. Both my father Nkosi and my uncle Nsimbi have been in the country of the Amazulu, and they both carry the scars of assegaai wounds. They were lucky that they were hit in parts of their body which they could reach with their trunks, so that they could pull the spears out and clean the wounds. An assegaai wound that you can't reach is very dangerous because it can go bad, and then get worse and worse. In the end just one wound like this can kill even the biggest and most powerful elephant.

Chapter 10
Gathering of the Clans

When the hills to the north of the land of the Kwazulu come into sight, my mother turns away from the Shonalanga Mountains to go to a drift to cross the Nyathi River. Near the end of the dry season the river may be low, with the flat rocks and sand of the drift showing beneath the shallow water. We youngsters are pleased to see this, although the older ones know it may mean trouble when we cross the plains to the Pumulanga Mountains. But all we are thinking about is that we can now cross the Nyathi River easily and safely. In some years the river is full or even in flood. Then the crossing is very dangerous. When the river is in flood it is too deep even at the drift, and it flows fast. Not many years back Undlebe's calf Mhimbi, who was only one year old, was swept away and drowned. It was a very sad day that none of the herd have ever forgotten, especially when we get to the crossing. Each year Undlebe goes down the river to the big bend where Mhimbi's body was swept ashore. When she found his remains, she carried his skull up and away from the river. The skull is still there, where she placed it, and each year we go back to this sad place. We all circle around Mhimbi's skull and Undlebe tenderly touches it and gently picks it up. She rumbles quietly, talking to Mhimbi's spirit. Now that she has Nyama she is not quite so sad. This year we did not stay as long as usual with Mhimbi's skull, and it seems as though Undlebe is finally getting over the loss of her calf.

There are other places that my mother visits where the bones of our family and friends lie. There are no such things as elephant graveyards. My mother says that story is not true. There are simply places of bones where elephants have died, mostly from old age. Elephants have six sets of teeth, with each set growing out in turn as we get older. When the last set wears out we can no longer chew food properly and this means the end of our life. In the old days, my mother says, most elephants died of old age. Now things are changing, with elephants sometimes being killed by the Abantu people. Of course, elephants die in accidents, as Mhimbi did, and also from sickness. Fortunately, if you have a leader as wise as my mother, most accidents can be avoided. When we visit a place of bones, my mother will identify each skeleton and although we can't understand all of her low rumbles, we can sometimes hear that she is repeating the name of the one who died there.

Soon after crossing the Nyathi River we turn north to avoid the Gramadoelas to the east. We have to go between the Nyathi River and Mabutu Mountain, which we can just see in the haze over the thorn trees to our right.

In a dry year food is scarce and so is water. Then my mother will lead us away from the river towards Mabutu Mountain, because she knows that even in a dry year we will find Bobbejaan-berries there. These red berries are named after Mfene the Baboon, who also loves to eat them. They grow in a very dry area too far from the river to allow us to drink there. There are only a few water holes that may have water in them at the western base of Mabutu Mountain.

All of the other animals, and especially Ngonyama the Lion and Mpisi the Hyena, know about these water holes and gather there at this time of the year. Vultures come down to these water holes even from as far away as Aasvoëlkrans. They know that they will find meals from Ngonyama's kills and from animals that have not made it through the dry season.

The vultures from Aasvoëlkrans have to fly all the way across the Nyathi Plains to reach this spot, but making this long journey is not as tiring for them as you may think, because they have some good tricks under their wings. By the end of the dry season the days are getting very hot as the sun beats down from cloudless skies. As the ground heats up, wind swirling across the baking land gets wound up into dust devils which you can see whirling across the plains. The Aasvoëls can hear these whirlwinds as they are forming, and they take off and head towards them. The dust devil forms a whirling wind which sweeps up dust and leaves from the ground and carries them high into the sky. The vultures get into the same rising air currents and are lifted by them as high as Aasvoëlkrans itself and higher. They reach this height by riding the winds of the dust devil, which they do without moving their wings at all. When they have ridden the rising currents of the dust devil to the very top, far up in the sky, they turn and glide off in long sweeping curves, looking out for food across the vast reaches of the Nyathi Plain. They have excellent eyesight, and if they see any food like a dead Mpala or Nyathi calf, they spiral down to feast on it. If they find no meal they return to their starting point, often one of the water holes at the foot of the western slopes of the Mabutu Mountain.

And to do all this flying, the Aasvoëls use only the little energy that it takes to fly to a dust devil. They are a strange mixture—ugly when you see them on the ground, and yet beautiful once they are on the wing. My mother says that they may not be very handsome birds to look at close up, but they are a lot smarter than people think.

With the days getting hotter and longer, my mother decides that the time has come to leave the Nyathi River and cross the plains to the Pumulanga Mountains. This is a long and dry crossing, for there are no water holes between the Nyathi River and the slopes of the Pumulanga Mountains. My mother leads us first to the Nyathi River, where we spend a lovely lazy day swimming and eating the grass that is still green along the banks of the river and in the riverbed. In the late afternoon, before the sun starts to sink below the Shonalanga Mountains, my mother gives a very firm "Let's go" signal. Then she sets off towards the Pumulanga Mountains on one of the well-used trails at a fast pace. We keep up this pace all night long, with only one short rest around midnight. My mother never varies the pace but just keeps up a fast steady walk. It is not terribly fast for the grown-ups, but we little ones really have to hurry all the time. We get very tired, but each of us has a mother or an aunt behind us who will nudge anyone who slows down or lags and doesn't get on with it. By the time the tops of the Pumulanga Mountains are lit by the rising sun, the slopes leading to the first kranse are already there in front of us. We are all tired and thirsty, and there is no water that we can see or smell. My mother doesn't slow down but keeps up the steady pace, swinging onto one of the game paths that head northwards parallel to the kranse of the Pumulanga Mountains. Our hearts sink because we can't see anything but dry veld and rolling hills in front of us, and it looks as if we are going to go on like this all day. But not long after the sun is clear of the Pumulanga Mountains, the path swings to the right and we enter a narrow kloof that runs into the mountain. No sooner have we entered the kloof than we smell and then hear water. A small stream of crystal-clear water runs out of the kloof. Green bushes and grass grow along it and around the eye of the spring where the water gurgles up between two huge boulders. I think this is the same spring that saved Nkosi's life. We are able to feed and rest there all the remainder of the day and that

night too.

Now my mother relaxes and slows down to our more leisurely feeding pace. Over the next few days we move slowly northwards parallel to the kranse of the Pumulanga Mountain towards the big vlei called Amanzimtoti, the Sweet Waters. We also become aware of low calls from lots of other elephants. We can see that my mother and my aunts recognize many of these calls as those of relatives and friends. Even we little ones recognize Nkosi's calls and those of our uncles Mdala and Mfanyaan. By the next day some of the other elephants, including my father and uncles, have joined us. We can hear and see other herds in the bush, all heading towards the Amanzimtoti. Pretty soon our herd has doubled in size and there are at least four or five other herds as big as ours, or even bigger, moving towards the Sweet Waters. It is very exciting, almost like a huge birthday party. Even the grown-ups are excited, and the sides of their faces become streaked with the black liquid from their temples. Everyone rushes around, squealing with joy at seeing relatives and friends they haven't seen for a long time. We little ones are kept busy learning who they all are and how we can recognize them. The ones we know best are the herd that lives between the Nyathi River and the Shonalanga Mountains. We usually first hear them when we are heading to the Baobab trees after we have left the Umzimkulu vlei early in the dry season. After that we often see them at water holes and along the Nyathi River. We have learnt the names of three of the younger ones who are the same ages as Mafutha, Dakiwe and Nkosana. Mafutha is now nearly two years old, Dakiwe is ten and Nkosana is fourteen. Our new friends are Inyoni, who is two, Tembo, who is nearly ten, and Mpanda, who is nearly grown-up at fifteen and will soon be leaving the herd. Their father is my uncle Umadala.

Once we get to the Amanzimtoti we have great games in the water and in the mud holes. The mud holes are the best because we can slide down a steep bank of black clay which is very slippery. We all end up in a big pile in the mud at the bottom. We little ones have to watch out for Mpanda and Nkosana because they are pretty big and rough. When things get too rough, Mafutha, Inyoni and I get off to the side and let the others pile into the mud. We also like to swim in the deeper pools where the water is often over our heads. If we stick our trunks up out of the water, we can walk along the bottom with our whole body underwater. We play tag like this, and that's great fun because everyone's eyes are underwater and you have to smell and feel with your trunk. After swimming we go to our mothers and aunts to have a dust bath. This is also hilarious, because we have to learn how to pick up the dust with our trunks and throw it over our backs. There are always dust fights, too, with Dakiwe and Tembo throwing great clouds at each other.

Then we play a game we call "Bok-bok", in which everyone piles on top of whoever is "it". We don't do this to Mafutha and Inyoni because they are too small. When you are at the bottom you have to make a secret sound before you can get up. There is so much squealing and shrieking that often some of our aunts join in too. We also play "Charge the Nyathi", where we pretend that some bush is a big old buffalo bull. We raise up our trunks and put out our ears to make ourselves look as big and fearsome as possible. Then we scream and charge the bush. Dakiwe is the best at this game because he can make the most terrible noise. We get so excited playing this game that my mother sometimes has to come over and tell us, and especially Baddy, to calm down.

Now, for the first time since leaving the waterfall pool more than five moons back, we see clouds over the Balele and Pumulanga Mountains. They are only small puffs of white that appear in the late afternoon as the sun sinks over the Shonalanga Mountains. At sunset now you can see my mother standing very still facing the clouds on the horizon. She holds her head very high and her ears out wide. We know that she is listening for the sounds of rain. She soon hears them, much too soon for all of us little ones who still have lots of games to play. But my mother doesn't wait. She gives the "Let's go" rumble and we know we must get into line quickly because she will move off fast. Almost every time Baddy fails to listen and goes on playing with Tembo. At last he suddenly realizes that all the families are getting organized and some, including his own, have already left. Then there is a great screaming and trumpeting and flapping of ears as he runs round in circles calling for his mother. My aunts Undlebe and Mabalel at the back of the line are waiting for this to occur. It happens every time we leave Amanzimtoti nowadays. But by next year Dakiwe will have been forced out of the herd. He is already too old to stay. We will miss him, but I'm sure we will meet him again at the Amanzimtoti. Next year we won't have to wait for him when we leave. He will be with the other young bulls in a bachelor herd and they will leave the Amanzimtoti together. But this time, like last time, and for the last time, Ndlovu turns back and rumbles to Dakiwe, who finally hears her and comes running as fast as he can.

My mother then leads us to the place where the Balele and Pumulanga Mountains meet. Not the exact place where they join, because that is the kloof where Mutwa the Magician has his kraal, and we don't want to go there. Instead it is just south of Mutwa's kloof. Quite a few families are headed this way. The kranse gradually get smaller as they meet and form the kloof. Unlike the Hidden Valley where I was born, this kloof has no waterfall. The stream that goes into the Amanzimtoti just rushes down over rocks. The path winds up the kloof next to the stream, and often crosses it. Because the stream is fairly small these crossings are no problem, but you have to be careful on the slippery rocks or you may hurt your ankles.

We spend the first night in the kloof before starting the final climb out of the Nyathi Plains and back onto the Balele Highlands. It takes us all day to reach the top and by then we are tired and hungry, because during that day we don't spend much time eating. My mother allows us only a few stops and then hurries us along again. This is because the final stretch is through a very narrow gorge, a little like the secret passage that led us down the waterfall krans.

This gorge is just wide enough for the big elephants to fit through and even then they scrape their sides on the rock walls. These walls are polished black where elephants over many years have passed through. My grandmother, my great-grandmother and many earlier generations have passed through this narrow opening that leads from the Nyathi Plains to the Balele Highlands. This is why my mother is always so careful to listen for sounds of the storms on the Highlands. Once it starts raining at the beginning of the wet season in the far north of the Balele Mountains, this tiny stream becomes a raging torrent of brown water. Once that happens there is no way up out of the Nyathi Plains. Even if we went back all the way to the waterfall pool we would not be able to get up that dangerous path or through the cleft in the cliff. We would be trapped on the plains in the heat and humidity of the wet season. The Nyathi Plains are too unhealthy in the wet season for us to stay there, so we rely on my mother to lead us out in time.

In the evening, as we come through the final narrow gorge and up to the rim of the escarpment, we can see the flickering lightning in the far distance over the northern peaks of the Balele Mountains. Once again my mother has led us out – just in time, but in perfect safety.

The air is crisp and clear on the escarpment and we all recognize the sweet fresh smells of spring in the highlands. This is the start of a whole new phase of our year, and it won't be until five more moons have come and gone that we find ourselves once again in the Hidden Valley behind Aasvoëlkrans, where our journey began.

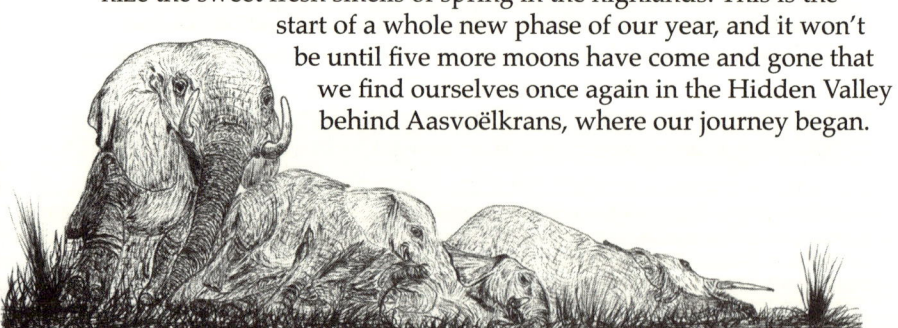

Mpanda *Ntombi* *Nkosana* *Dakiwe*

Ntombi's Family Tree

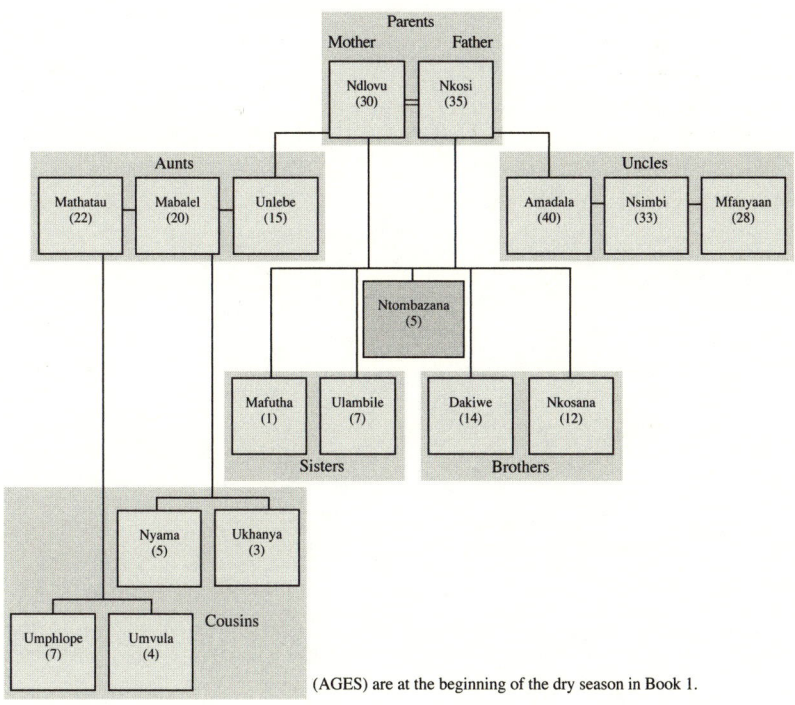

(AGES) are at the beginning of the dry season in Book 1.

Book 2

The Wet Season

Chapter 1
Onto the Escarpment

  I have told you how my mother Ndlovu leads our herd, every dry season, all the way from the Hidden Valley where I was born to the rim of the escarpment where we must be when the wet season comes along. Now I am going to tell you how she leads and guides our journeyings during that season too, to bring us safely back to the Hidden Valley once more when the cycle of the year is complete. Some of the things I am going to tell you about are those that we experience every year; others are things that happened to us on the particular journey we made this year, when I was already five years old and heading towards my sixth year. So let me begin.

  As my mother Ndlovu leads us up onto the Balele Highlands, we can see in the clear mountain air the rolling grasslands of the plateau stretching far away up to the purple-blue hills of the northern horizon. There is still a wall of kranse to our right, as the Pumulanga Mountains continue northwards to meet the last peaks of the Balele Mountains. To our left run the kranse of the Three Waterfalls, and towards where the sun sets we can see the dark mass of the Thlabatini Forest.

  Although the stream that we have followed through the kloof to get here is already running strongly, the rains feeding it are far to the north and east, and the grass of the highlands is still golden brown in the bright sunlight. So my mother leads us north towards Ndumeni, the Place of Thunder and the Pass to the Unknown. This is where the rains of the wet season begin and where we saw lightning on the northern horizon during our last two nights on the plains. We will not go through the Pass of the Unknown, for Ndlovu does not know the land beyond that pass. All she knows is that Nkosi and Amadala have been through that pass and have returned to the Balele Highlands. We will turn westwards at the pass and head into the Balele Mountains themselves. Ndlovu will stay in the valleys between the steep mountains, following the paths that her mother and her mother's mother before her used to follow. By this time the rains will have reached the Balele Mountains and spread across the highlands, spilling onto the Nyathi Plains. New tender sweet grass and leaves will have sprouted almost overnight.

On many days the mountaintops will be shrouded in cloud and mist will hang in the valleys. As the rains come down the mountains we will turn south and out of the Baleles, back onto the highlands, and my mother will lead us into the Thlabatini Forest.

Long before we enter the Balele Mountains we see animals that live in the highlands all the year round or, like us, come to the highlands in the wet season. Like us, some of these spend the dry season on the Nyathi Plains.

The first we see, high in the clear blue sky, is Lammergeyer the great mountain vulture. Lammergeyers seldom leave the rising currents of air which carry them soaring for hours over mountain ridges and peaks. Unlike the vultures of Aasvoëlkrans, they do not live in colonies but in pairs which mate for life. They hunt Mbile the Dassie, Logwaja the Hare, and the young of Nxala the Reedbuck. They also seek out dead animals, carry their bones to great heights and drop them onto the rocks. This splits the bones open so that the Lammergeyers can eat the marrow. We hear their high ringing whistle all along the kranse of the northern Pumulanga Mountains. Another animal on the Balele Highlands that has a shrill whistle is Nxala the Reedbuck. Two kinds of reedbuck live here, the Mountain Reedbuck and the ordinary Reedbuck, though both go by the name of Nxala. One lives close to the mountain streams, the other favors the slopes and rocky places.

Mpofu the Eland, the biggest of all antelopes, lives on the mountain slopes too. The name Mpofu can mean "the golden-skinned one" but it can also mean "the humble one". My mother says that Mpofu got his name because once upon a time, long, long ago, he rescued the Earth Mother, Mbulwane, from the depths of the earth. She had been imprisoned there for being unable to stop the animals and the Abantu from killing each other. While Mother Earth was imprisoned in the bowels of the earth, eternal winter descended on the land. The waters of the rivers and lakes turned to stone. Rain fell like the white round pebbles of the streams and the whole earth shivered in the grip of terrible cold. The only way the animals could survive was to go into a huge cave in the mountain. There they huddled around a fire that they somehow managed to build. Ngonyama the Lion knew that they would not be able to survive long like that, so he called for volunteers to come forward to try and rescue Mbulwane from her prison deep in the earth. No one stepped forward at first, but finally Mpofu the Eland spoke: "Ngonyama, I, Mpofu the Eland, largest of all the antelopes, will go and try to rescue Mbulwane."

"You, Mpofu?" said Ngonyama in surprise. "But you have no fangs or claws with which to fight. Why, you are known as the 'poor one,' the 'humble one'."

"I know, O Lion, but I am also one of the fastest and strongest of all the animals. Is it not possible that in this rescue, speed and strength will be more important than being able to fight?"

"Yes, Mpofu," said Ngonyama. "Strength and speed may be what is needed. If you are willing to go, then go, and may the gods be with you."

Ndlovu the Elephant and uBhejane the Rhinoceros pushed aside a huge boulder which opened a passageway to the nether world.

Mpofu galloped down into the depths of the earth, jumping over yawning chasms and rivers of fire. After running all day and all night, he could see the dark caverns ahead. Calling Mother Earth by her name, he heard her faint response. "Mbulwane, is that you?" called Mpofu.

"Yes, I am here. Who is this?" came the faint reply.

"I am Mpofu the Eland, Mother of the Earth. I have come to rescue you. Are you alone?"

"Yes, O Mpofu, I am alone, but bound hand and foot." Mpofu untied Mbulwane and quickly got her onto his back. Then he ran like the wind, crying to Mbulwane to give him strength. Crossing the rivers of fire and leaping the smoke-filled chasms, he finally came within sight of the tunnel he had come down, the route by which he and Mbulwane would escape back to the light of the surface. Just as Mpofu thought he had made it, Mother Earth screamed. Sondokati, the monster of the depths, was coming after them, riding a flying serpent. "Stop, Mpofu, or I shall destroy you both!" roared Sondokati.

Mpofu could now see the light of the animals' chamber ahead of him and he drew upon the last of his strength. Just as he reached the chamber entrance he felt the searing pain of an arrow fired from Sondokati's bow. It had only grazed his rump, but it was a poisonous arrow, and he felt his strength failing. Mpofu collapsed inside the chamber among all the animals. Mother Earth, her power restored, turned and with a bolt of lightning destroyed Sondokati as Mpofu at her feet drew his last breath.

Crystal tears ran down Mother Earth's cheeks and splashed onto Mpofu's body. As each tear touched his body it rose into the heavens and became one of the stars that form the Mpofu Constellation. Known by others as the Lupus Constellation, it can be seen at the bottom of the Southern Cross. And my mother says that to this day, Mpofu leaps up to his stars, jumping higher than any other antelope.

We also see drawings made by the San Bushmen on the walls of sandstone caves and rock overhangs. There are more of these far to the north in the Balele Mountains, where we pass mountains with bands of sandstone like rivers frozen into the mountainsides. The San people hunt Mpofu but they also revere him. When they do kill an eland with their poison-tipped arrows they speak to Mpofu's Constellation, asking forgiveness for the killing. They praise Mpofu and thank the Constellation for providing so much food for their families. They are especially thankful for the thick layers of fat in Mpofu's hump and dewlap. This they use for many things in addition to cooking. They make ointments from the fat to heal wounds and burns, and they use it also to tan the skins and hides of animals that they use for clothes and sleeping karosses.

Soon after reaching the highlands we see two other large kinds of antelope: Nyala and Mgankla the Kudu. Nyala we have met along the Nyathi River, but he also frequents the highlands. He and his golden-brown wives can be seen along the rivers and on the edges of the Thlabatini Forest. The Nyala bulls with their dark coats, long manes and long hair covering their necks and bellies are beautiful animals. A brilliant white blaze or chevron lies between their eyes and they have sweeping black horns with ivory tips.

Mgankla the Kudu is a close cousin to Nyala and also to Imbabala the Bushbuck. Mgankla gets his name from the clashing of the Kudu's huge spiral horns when two males fight. Female Kudu have no horns. Kudu bulls fight each other for territory and mates in the early wet season. Soon after we reach the highlands we are almost certain to hear the clashing of Mgankla horns echoing loudly through the forest and down the valleys. It can happen that the great spiral horns of two bulls lock together and they are unable to free themselves. We have sometimes come upon the grim sight of the horns of a pair of Mgankla still locked together in a fatal embrace, with nothing else left of the dead fighters, for Mpisi the Hyena has removed all of their remains but the skulls and horns. What a sad, pointless way to die! It is a good thing that when bull elephants fight their tusks cannot get locked together.

Kudu are mainly browsers and particularly like the fresh green leaves and new flowers of the acacia in the early wet season. They browse quickly through the acacia bush, taking only one or two bites from each tree. This is because, believe it or not, the acacias actually know that they are being fed upon and quickly start emitting pungent-smelling gases called tannins through their leaves. These tannins give the leaves a bitter taste which the Kudu do not like. Even more amazingly, the acacia trees downwind from those that the Kudu are browsing on begin releasing tannins as well.

Soon after my mother has led us out of the kloof onto the highlands along the southern end of the Pumulanga Mountains we are likely to see Ndabushe the Caracal, who lives along the river that flows out of the kloof. Although the Caracal looks like one of Ngonyama's young wives, he and Ngonyama the Lion are bitter enemies. My mother says this is because once upon a time, long, long ago, Ndabushe and his wife tricked Lion out of a buffalo that he had killed. Ngonyama was very thirsty after his chase and fight with Nyathi the Buffalo, so he asked Ndabushe to look after the kill while he went for a drink. He warned Ndabushe not to eat any of the kill.

"Very well, Father. My wife and I will guard your meal," promised Caracal. But as soon as Ngonyama had disappeared down the bank of the river, Ndabushe and his wife started to gobble down Ngonyama's dinner. When Lion came back to get stuck into his tasty kill, which was on top of the steep bank above the river, he called up to Ndabushe, "O Ndabushe, help me up this steep bank."

"Just be seated, Father, while I get a rope," called back Ndabushe. He ran off and brought back a piece of old rotten riem made from strips of Nyathi's skin.

"Catch, Father," Ndabushe called as he threw the riem over the bank. Lion caught the rope and climbed up the bank, but just as he got to the top the rope broke and he tumbled down.

"Oh my goodness! We failed, O Father! Catch it again," called Ndabushe. And while he was tricking Ngonyama like this, the wily Caracal's wife was eating all the best parts of Lion's dinner. After three more tries and three more tumbles down the bank, Ndabushe and his wife thought it best to get away as quickly as they could. So off they ran, full of glee at what they had done, leaving Ngonyama to climb back up as best as he could and then discover what had happened to the meal he had been looking forward to eating. My mother says that to this day Ngonyama the Lion keeps an eye out for Ndabushe the Caracal to repay him for tricking him out of his dinner.

Another, even smaller cat that we see on the Balele highlands is Insimba the Genet with her beautiful colouring. My mother says that once upon a time, long, long ago, Insimba used to have a very plain tawny coat like Ngonyama's. She is much smaller than Ngonyama—only as big as a baby lion cub—and Lion's cubs used to make fun of her, calling her "our ugly little cousin". This Insimba did not like at all. She wished that she could find some way to get a beautiful coat like that of Ingwe the Leopard or Ihlosi the Cheetah.

One day when she was out hunting fieldmice in the long grass along the river, Insimba nearly trod on a puff adder. She leapt into the air in fright, since Ibululu the Puff adder usually lived in the caves and rocks on the slopes of the mountains. When she had recovered from her scare, Insimba said to Ibululu, "What are you doing here, Ibululu? Your home is far up that mountain slope in a rocky cave."

"Shss," hissed Ibululu, "I don't know, Insimba. Last night I was following the scent of a plump fieldmouse, but each time I thought I had him, he got away. The next thing I knew, the sun was coming up over the Pumulanga Mountains and I found myself right down here. Now I am very tired and I don't feel at all well. Insimba, please help me to get back to my home."

Insimba could not figure out how she could get the short but heavy puff adder all that way up the slope, so she said, "Ibululu, why don't you come just a little bit further in this long grass to my house? There you can rest until you are strong enough to return to your home in the cave."

"I agree, Insimba. I will come with you to your house." Now Ibululu the Puff adder was much sicker than either she or Insimba the Genet had at first realized, and Insimba had to look after Ibululu for many weeks. Fortunately she ate all the things that Insimba liked, such as insects, scorpions, frogs, mice, moles and small birds. At first Insimba did not have to work very hard at finding food for them both, for Ibululu was too sick to eat much. But things changed quickly as Ibululu got better, and poor Insimba was run ragged keeping up with Ibululu's appetite.

Finally one day, much to Insimba's relief, Ibululu said "I must go, Insimba. Thank you very much."

Then Ibululu surprised Insimba by saying, "You have saved my life, Insimba. Had you not taken me in and cared for me these many weeks, I would most surely have become food for my worst enemy, the Secretary Bird. I will give you anything that is in my power to give."

Insimba did not really think that the puff adder could give her anything that she wanted, but just in case, she said, "Ibululu, I have always wanted a coat as beautiful as Ingwe the Leopard's or Ihlosi the Cheetah's. Could you give me such a coat?"

"It is within the power of my fangs to give you such a coat," Ibululu said. "But I must bite you very carefully, so that just the right amount of poison goes through my fangs into your veins". This sounded rather alarming to Insimba, but she wanted a fine coat so much that she said, "Very well. Bite me carefully, Ibululu".

Ibululu told the Genet to hold out her right front paw and then very gently closed her mouth over it. Insimba felt the sharp prick of the fangs and the burning of the puff adder's venom as it entered her leg. She began to feel dizzy and suddenly feared that Ibululu had tricked her, but almost in the same moment she saw her plain tawny coat beginning to turn a beautiful golden color. As she watched her coat turning gold, black splashes started to appear on it, just like those of Ihlosi the Cheetah. Insimba leaped for joy. She was now one of the most beautiful animals in the bush. And to this day, my mother says, the puff adder and the genet have remained friends and do not bother each other.

Each day as my mother leads us northwards towards Ndumeni, more clouds form over the Balele Mountains ahead of us and over the Pumulanga Mountains to our right. Soon there come days when the air feels heavy and we can smell the rain. Towering white clouds build up ahead of us and as the morning moves to midday my mother leads us into the shade of some big acacia trees. She knows that lightning is a real danger on the exposed highlands. Soon we can feel what she has already sensed: a tingling in the air almost as if someone is pulling the string of a San Bushman's bow tighter and tighter.

As the bowstring is about to break we realize that the calls of the plovers and the whistles of the Lammergeyer have ceased. No lammergeyers are soaring in the darkening sky now, and the emerald-spotted wood doves and rock pigeons fly low and fast towards their roosting places. Our aunts make nervous rumbles but seem unsure what to do, so my mother takes charge and acts quickly. With a loud "Let's go" rumble she swings out from under the acacia trees straight towards a kloof that runs into the Pumulanga Mountains. The entrance to the kloof is about a mile away so my mother breaks into the fast walk-run that we use when we want to move quickly. Because elephants are so heavy, all four of our feet cannot leave the ground together the way those of a galloping antelope or zebra do. So we must depend on a very fast walk and long strides to move quickly

over the ground. And we can indeed move quickly. My father Nkosi can outdistance both uBhejane the Black Rhinoceros and the hunters of the Amazulu.

The fear that has driven my mother affects all of us. It is the fear of lightning. My mother knows that she cannot leave the herd standing under acacia trees on this exposed tableland. These isolated trees attract lightning strikes. A lightning bolt can come down a tree trunk and jump from it to any of us standing nearby. If the lightning leaping across from the tree strikes us in the head it will kill us. If it strikes us somewhere else on the body it can burn a great gash in our tough hide. This may not kill us right away, but such a wound is dangerous, for it immediately attracts flies, and they lay their eggs in it. Then it can go septic and be fatal.

The walls of the kloof are vertical and in places there are overhanging rocks. My mother leads us under one of these overhangs. Although it does not shelter us from the driving rain, it is good protection against lightning.

As the sky darkens and the towering clouds blot out the sun, we can see a rolling line of white cloud coming down the river valley. The cloud line seems to tumble slowly forward right down to the ground. Dust, leaves, twigs and even branches are swept ahead of it. As the dust cloud reaches us the trees and bushes around us begin to bend and break. The air becomes filled with choking dust and debris and we feel the icy blast of the storm in our faces. Thanks to my mother, we have reached shelter just in time, for very quickly behind this swirling mass comes the brittle crackle of lightning and the deafening crash of thunder. We can smell acrid fumes like those of basalt blocks crashing into each other when they plummet over the krans. Then the rain comes in billowing sheets, stinging our faces. We can hardly hear or see each other, and we huddle as closely together as we can. One flash of lightning has hardly faded before the next one lights up the kloof. The crash and roar of thunder rise and fall without pause. Rain mixed with hail pelts our bodies like the stinging yellow wasps in the figs lying on the ground along the Nyathi River. All the young ones, including me, want to run. Where we want to run to we don't know – we just want to get away from the storm. But my mother and aunts know better. They press in on us, keeping us against the wall of the krans and sheltering us from the worst of the rain.

A storm like this seems to last for ever, but in fact it usually starts to pass in about the same time that it took us to run from the acacia trees to the kloof, and before long we can see and hear that the lightning and thunder are receding down the valley towards the edge of the escarpment. After a few more bursts of rain, the noise of the storm fades into the distance and is replaced by the sound of rushing water. The little stream in the kloof is now a small river and water is pouring over the edges of the krans in small waterfalls. Shafts of light like the flashing of the Amazulu assegaais come through the clouds. Every bird for miles around seems to be calling. A bachelor herd of young impala that also sheltered in the kloof begins to run and leap for joy. Even the thorn trees with their leaves shining in the sun seem to be waving to each other.

My mother knows that this rain will bring plenty of new green grass and shrubs. She also knows that we must continue northwards towards Ndumeni to find the sweetest and best food.

When we come out of the kloof into the clear, crisp air behind the storm, the whole escarpment appears washed clean. The kranse of the Pumulanga Mountains glisten in the western sun, and waterfalls hang like silver ribbons over the rock walls. Ahead we may see egrets, Bateleur Eagles and Secretary Birds circling and landing in what looks like a cloud rising from the ground. Soon we can see that this cloud is really made up of termites swarming from their huge mound. After nearly six months of dry weather, they are leaving to form new colonies. The rain has softened the rock-hard walls of the anthill and the worker termites have broken through the surface with their powerful jaws. Now the winged males and females come pouring out of many holes and rise into the air on their fragile wings. Many lose their wings almost as soon as they have left the mound. Waiting for them are egrets, plovers and frogs who have gathered all around the mound. The termites make a great meal, especially for the frogs, who have been lying hibernating below the surface with nothing to eat ever since the beginning of the dry season.

Soon the place becomes as dangerous for the frogs as for the termites. Grass snakes and Mkulu the Python see the free meal and come slithering towards the mound. Bateleurs and egrets are also after the frogs and Mvusi the Meerkat with her new litter of kittens is soon feasting on both termites and frogs. Nungu the Porcupine and even shy Sambani the Aardvark join in the feast too. In fact just about everyone, including the Bateleur Eagle and the Secretary Bird, has to be careful that they do not become a meal for someone else. It will not be long before both Mpungu the Jackal and Insimbi the Genet also show up, and both of these animals are bold enough to try to surprise any eagle or secretary bird.

The only defense that the termites have is in their enormous numbers. There are so many emerging that no matter how many get caught and eaten, many more get away. Only a very few of these will mate and successfully establish a new colony. If a pair is able to establish a new termitary, the female will become the queen and the male the king. Other termites will then take on the tasks necessary to maintain the terminary. Most will become workers, with strong teeth called mandibles. They bring in all the food necessary to feed the termitary. Fungus beds are established and the coarse food brought in by the workers gets processed by the fungi. Some workers become builders and excavators who dig and build tunnels sometimes as deep as the height of the tallest yellow fever tree. They dig down until they find water. Then other workers carry this water drop by drop to the fungus beds and to the queen. Others act as air-conditioning engineers, building air passages from the deep water source to the surface. The air circulating in these tunnels keeps the fungus beds and the eggs laid by the queen at a constant temperature. The queen quickly becomes so fat that she cannot fly or even walk. Unlike all the other termites, she and her king have very good eyes and can see perfectly, but they never leave their chamber.

The rest of the termites develop into either workers or soldiers. The soldier termites must defend the termitary against attack, especially from Sambane the Aardvark. Each soldier is armed with a needle-sharp lance attached to its forehead, and in that forehead is a little sac of poison which the soldier can inject into anything through the hollow lance. When someone like Sambane with his powerful claws is able to break into the termite mound, the soldiers fend off the intruder. Then the workers with their strong jaws come to repair the break. They have special glands which produce a glue that binds the soil together like cement. Neither the workers nor the soldiers have eyes, ears or organs of smell. Yet they can detect light through two feet of hardened soil. When attacked, the soldiers make a "Tik-tik-tik" sound by quick movements of their throat plates. Somehow the workers, even though they have no ears, respond immediately to this call. They stop whatever they are doing and go straight to the place where help is needed. My mother says that the whole termitary functions like a single animal, with each group of termites functioning as one of the organs of the animal.

The path past the termite mound leads due north between the stream and the kranse of the Pumulanga Mountains. We have slowly been heading north since the moon was new. Now a half-moon hangs in the western sky. We have not stayed on the main path all the time but have gone into the kloofs along the kranse of the Pumulanga Mountains. Food is still not plentiful, but now that the first rains have reached this far south we will find more and more food as we head north towards Ndumeni, the Place of Thunder, and the Pass to the Unknown.

Chapter 2
Ndumeni and the Pass to the Unknown

As we head north towards Ndumeni my mother leads us up kloofs that run into the Pumulanga escarpment. This year, the day after the big rainstorm, she headed for a narrow rocky kloof with steep sides. There did not seem to be much to eat in this kloof and she seemed uncertain about going in. She stopped soon after we had entered and held her head high to listen. First we heard Ngede the Honeyguide calling "Vic-terr, vic-terr, vic-terr," over and over again. Then we saw Nsele the Badger hurrying into the kloof. Ngede saw him and began to fly frantically around him calling "Vic-terr, vic-terr." When she saw that Badger had seen her she changed her call to a clicking, rattling sound and flew from branch to branch up the narrow kloof. They had not gone far before we could hear the buzzing of bees. High up on the right-hand side of the kloof we could see a cleft in the rock face with bees busily flying in and out of it.

Ngede fluttered all around the entrance, calling and rattling to Nsele, who had stopped at the base of the rock wall. There did not seem to be any way up to the hive. But Nsele had done this many times before. He could already taste the sweet golden honey that he knew was in the cleft. Running up the kloof on his short legs, he found a ledge of rocks that slanted up towards the bees' nest. He went up the ledge and disappeared behind the rocks. Then he came into view again higher up, clinging to the rock-face with his heavy claws and inching towards the entrance to the hive. The bees had sensed his approach by now and were angrily swarming around him. But Nsele the Badger has very thick fur, and tough skin on his snout. He braved the bees and dug out great glistening combs of honey which he let fall to the rock floor. Some of the last combs he dug out were white with bee larvae. At last he had had enough of the bees' attacks and began carefully edging backwards down the ledge.

Ngede the Honeyguide was now hovering excitedly around the combs of honey. Nsele licked up the spilt honey and chewed into the whole combs. He left pieces of honeycomb as well as the comb with the larvae in it. Ngede knew this was her reward for leading Badger to the feast.

My mother had led us into the kloof for a different reason. Past the hive where Nsele and Ngede were still feasting on the honey, Ndlovu stopped, facing a grey-white band in the side of the kloof. This band rose from the floor of the kloof to the height of my mother's head. Holes had been dug in it in many places and the slick, shiny surface was streaked with brown. The ground along the white wall was trampled and there were the spoor of many animals in the sandy bottom. One could not tell who all had been there, but we knew that many animals had found this spot. My aunts joined Ndlovu at the wall and started scraping the surface with their tusks. One could see the great number of grooves that had been dug into the wall over many, many wet seasons. After scraping her tusks in a set of grooves, Ndlovu ran the tip of her trunk up the grooves and brought it to her mouth. We tried the same thing with our small tusks. The scrapings had a salty taste that was quite good at first, but soon the smallest ones, Mafutha, Ulambile and I, had had enough. We also began feeling very thirsty. Fortunately there was a small stream running down the kloof where we could drink. The bigger elephants spent a long time at the lick.

Like the strange-tasting soil that Ndlovu led us to on the Nyathi Plains in the dry season, this place in the kloof is an important one, my mother says. Even though we do not eat a lot of the salty lick and come here only once a year, it provides us with important minerals that keep our bones, tusks and teeth strong.

By the next day the kranse of the Pumulanga Mountains were closing in on the western end of the Balele Mountains. From Ndumeni we could see a wall of kranse and high rocky slopes ahead of us. There seemed to be no way through the mountains. Then, as we came around the final bend of the krans, we could see a cleft in the mountains. This, my mother knew, was the Pass to the Unknown.

A faint track led towards the pass, but my mother had never made this journey before. Both my father Nkosi and my oldest uncle, Amadala, had been north through this pass. This year they had gone through it nearly one whole moon before we reached Ndumeni. You could see that my mother and my aunts were listening for any faint sound from either Nkosi or Madala. They were nervous and stood very still with their heads held high facing the Pass to the Unknown. They knew of the dangers of thunderstorms and lightning in this pass. Once you started to go through it, it rose into a shallow rocky valley and eventually a bare saddle between the Pumulanga and Balele Mountains. In this shallow valley and on the bare saddle there was no shelter from lightning. If you were caught in a storm before you had finished crossing the pass, you would surely die.

Considering all the risks involved in crossing the pass, my mother did not know what had driven Nkosi and Madala to choose that route. She suspected that there were other elephant herds on the other side and that Nkosi and Madala were most probably seeking mates. The wet season is when mating takes place and also when the calves are born. Mathatau and Mabalel would soon be giving birth to new babies. Their youngest ones, Umphlope and Nyama, were already nearly eight and six years old. Unlebe, now nearly sixteen, would probably be ready to mate soon. My mother knew that other bulls besides Nkosi and Madala would be coming through the pass. There was lots of tension in the air and my mother and aunts kept on rumbling to each other. You can always see when they are getting excited and expecting visitors by the glands on the sides of their heads just above the level of their eyes. These glands start to run with a sticky liquid that leaves black streaks down the sides of their faces. By now, all the grown-ups had these streaks down their faces.

The male elephants were also likely to be in an excited state which is called musth. When they are in musth the big bulls become very aggressive and fights break out between them. They also charge others in the herd, so everyone has to be very careful when a musth bull is around. It was not clear to me why my mother had led us so far north and so close to the Pass of the Unknown. The valley had become very rocky and stony. All the acacia trees had disappeared and even the grass was thin and sour.

The path leading through the pass was only faintly visible on the stony ground. In fog or bad weather and at night this path would be very difficult to follow. My mother led us along it for some way before she stopped and listened again. There was nothing to eat and by now even the little streams and springs had disappeared. We were puzzled as to why we were there. The other younger elephants were milling around, anxious to leave this desolate place, but something told me that I should pay attention to my mother and to the surroundings. I tried to pick out the biggest of the rocky outcrops on the sides of the pass. These might serve as markers if I ever had to come through this pass. On the left I could see five rounded rock-faces, rather like the toenails of my mother's front feet, that marked the top of the Pass to the Unknown. We could just see the path swinging around the last of these strangely shaped rocks before disappearing downward into the unknown.

Clouds were beginning to form over the pass and the sky was

darkening to the northeast. Suddenly all was quiet. My mother stood very still in the middle of the path facing the pass, and we could tell that she could hear something. Then we heard it too. It was the deep rumbling of Nkosi. Dakiwe and Nkosana wanted to run forward to greet him, but my mother blocked their way and pushed them behind her. Just then Nkosi arrived in a cloud of dust. He was angry and trumpeting. My mother stood her ground and Nkosi came to a halt with his trunk stretched out towards her. We thought he was going to attack her with his huge tusks. She stood very still, rumbling gently to him. Slowly the tension went out of Nkosi's trunk and he and Ndlovu both began to explore each other's mouths and eyes and the black streaks down the sides of their faces. We could smell a pungent odor coming from Nkosi. He was in musth and very dangerous. Everyone stood perfectly still. Even our ears stopped waving and our tails hung straight down. Finally Nkosi moved past Ndlovu and through the herd. His trunk reached out to each of us as he passed but he did not stop. Even though he could have mated with Unlebe, he was much too closely related to her. He was going to seek a mate in another herd in the Balele Mountains.

As Nkosi's huge bulk swayed down the path my mother turned and gave a low "Let's go" rumble. Then she and the rest of our herd all followed Nkosi at a respectful distance. Not far down the path a track led off to the west between two peaks in the Balele Mountains. My mother led us westwards on this track into the Balele Mountains.

The sides of the valley rose in great waves of golden grass to the mountaintops that now enclosed us. Along the floor of this valley and up its sides, green grass and many succulents and sweet flowers can always be seen at this season. We are not the only ones to find all this food. On the slopes above us, standing on the crest of one of the billowing rises, we often see the black and white profile of Mplampale the Sable Antelope. The great curving horns that sweep over his back gleam like polished ebony. The jet black of his body glistening in the sun is highlighted by a brilliant white belly and patches of white on his face. The long hair of his tail streams out in the wind. When Mplampale is seen by Abantu women they ululate in praise of him, raising their voices in a high keening song which flows in harmony with his graceful running.

When attacked by Ngonyama the Lion, Mplampale kneels so that his great horns curve over his back. Then, swinging the razor-sharp horns back and forth across his back, he protects both his front and back from attack. Ngonyama knows that the tips of Mplampale's horns can slice him open from neck to tail. This knowledge is enough to stop Ngonyama from attacking any healthy Sable. Only if Mplampale is sick or very old will Ngonyama risk an attack.

We see herds of Mplampale much larger than our herd. The young are golden-brown and look more like their close cousins Ithaka the Roan Antelope. The horns of Ithaka are shorter and thicker but still they are powerful weapons. Ithaka's face is black and white, his body is a uniform grey and his long ears are tipped with dark brown tassels. Like Mplampale the Sable, Ithaka eats mainly grass, but is more often seen along the streams in the valleys rather than on the slopes of the mountains.

Along the streams in the valleys, too, we see herds of Phiva the Waterbuck. Phiva will also go into rocky places up the slopes of the mountains. Unlike Mplampale and Ithaka, only the waterbuck males have horns. Phiva will often run into water when attacked by Ngonyama the Lion. He will swim into deep water until only his nostrils are above the surface. Ngonyama will run into shallow water, but he does not like deep water, which enables Phiva to escape.

My mother says that once upon a time, long, long ago, Phiva saved Wenya the Crocodile from drowning. Wenya had been hiding among the roots of a tree on the riverbank, but some of the soil of the bank had been washed away, and without warning the tree fell on him, trapping him among the very roots he had been using to hide in. Phiva could hear Wenya calling for help but knew that the crocodile was a sly one and that this could very well be a trick. When Wenya saw the waterbuck he called, "O Phiva, you with the crescent horns, symbol of the healing moon, I am trapped in the roots of this fallen tree. Please help me."

"I see that you are trapped, O scaly one, but how do I know you will not clamp your jaws on my snout and drag me under the water?" asked Phiva the Waterbuck.

"O merciful one," Wenya pleaded, "I cannot move, and will surely die if you do not release me." Phiva approached the trapped crocodile with care and could see that, yes, he was indeed trapped. The soil binding the roots of a great acacia tree on the river's bank had been eroded by the flooded river and they were now a tangled mass. There was no trick about it: Wenya was held fast in this tangle of roots.

"Wenya, you with the half-closed eyes of morning, will you promise that if I free you, you will not now or ever hereafter harm me or any of my family when we enter your watery home?" asked Phiva the Waterbuck.

"O crescent-horned one with the plumed ears, I promise never to harm you or any of your family, from now on as long as you and your family are on this earth," pleaded the crocodile.

Waterbuck then agreed to free the crocodile and, placing his horns under the thick root that lay across Wenya's back, gave a huge heave. This was enough to enable the crocodile to slither out.

"Phiva," said Wenya the Crocodile, "from this day forward you and your crescent horns will be safe in my watery home. Because your wife and children do not have your great horns, I give both you and them a white ring to encircle you from behind. In this way I and my kind will always know and respect you."

And to this very day, as my mother says, you can find Phiva grazing in the shallow water and able to escape from Ngonyama into the deep water without being bothered by Wenya the Crocodile.

Chapter 3
Into the Balele Mountains

Two moons after we reach the Balele Highlands, it is time for my mother to turn away from the Pass of the Unknown and Ndumeni, the Place of Thunder, and lead us westwards into the deep valleys of the Balele Mountains.

As we reach the Balele Mountains the peaks close in around us. The purple horizons and sweeping vistas of the Nyathi Plains and the escarpment disappear. Often now in the mornings the clouds hang so low in the valleys that we cannot see the slopes on either side. On most days that begin like this, the clouds roll up the valley sides as the sun rises above the peaks. Soon only the tops of the mountains are hidden in cloud and sunlight slides over the sides of the valleys so that they shine and glow. On these mornings few sounds can be heard. Although in the cool of the early morning sounds travel a long way up and down the valley, there are no sounds to hear at first. Only after sunlight streams through rifts in the rising clouds do we hear the voice of Mfene the Baboon. Then other calls from Mbile the Dassie, together with the whistles of Lammergeyer the Bearded Vulture and Nxala the Reedbuck, ring up and down the valley.

The violent thunderstorms of Ndumeni and the Pass to the Unknown are replaced now by gentler rain. The valleys and slopes are thick with new green grass and lots of other plants which are good to eat. My mother finds patches of giant mushrooms called ikhowe. Some of these mushrooms have heads bigger than the print of my foot in soft sand. Along the stream on the valley floor we find sweet roots and thick clumps of new shoots coming up in the reedbeds. We spend much less time feeding and looking for food now than we did in the dry season on the Nyathi Plains. There is plenty of time to enjoy the pools in the streams. Here the games are not nearly as noisy as they were when all the herds gathered at Amamzintoti at the end of the dry season. Now everyone is content to have lazy swims and wallows and to stand in the sun dozing. My mother also leads us at a slower pace through the valleys of the Balele Mountains. It is easy to forget that the paths she follows among the branching arms of the valleys are not all that well marked. Yet she always knows where she is leading us, never hesitating when the valley divides in two. As when we were at the entrance to the Pass of the Unknown, I wonder whether I will be able to remember all the twists and turns we have taken.

One reason why the paths through the valleys of the Balele Mountains are not as well marked as along the Nyathi River on the plains is that three of the biggest makers and users of paths are absent from the Balele Mountains. Nyathi the Buffalo, uBejane the Rhinoceros and Mvubu the Hippo are not found on the escarpment. Only occasionally does an old Nyathi bull wander into these mountains. Mvubu sometimes goes on a long walk-about, but never into the mountains. So the wide paths that we find through the reeds and long grass along the Nyathi River are never found up here on the escarpment.

Even Idube the Zebra and Nkhonhoni the Wildebeest seldom come this far. The sweet grasses and succulent plants are left for us and the other animals of the escarpment.

Mbili the Dassie lives in the sandstone caves that nestle among the crests of the Balele Mountains around us. Dassies can be heard giving their warning call of "Gamfi, gamfi!" whenever they see Lammergeyer or Ngungulu the Bateleur Eagle. My mother says that the reason why Mbili hides in the rocks is that he is still a little ashamed of the fact that he does not have a tail, and also the fact that this lack of a tail is the result of his own laziness. This is how it came about.

Once upon a time, long, long ago, only Ngonyama the Lion had a tail. Ngonyama, as King of the Beasts, felt that all of his subjects should have tails. So he set to work and had tails of all shapes, sizes and colors made. He then called Mfene the Baboon.

"Come, Mfene," ordered Ngonyama. "I wish you to call all the animals to gather under the Great Indaba Tree. Tell all to come and choose their tails."

"I hear you, O powerful one. I will go and call all the animals to assemble under the Indaba Tree tomorrow before the sun sets over the Shonalanga Mountains," said Mfene.

Baboon then spent all day running through the plains, hills and valleys calling everyone to meet at the Indaba Tree before sunset the next day. After a lot of trouble climbing up a rocky slope he found Mbili the Dassie asleep in the sun.

"Wake up, Mbili. Come and get your tail from Ngonyama," said Mfene the Baboon. But Mbili was so comfortable sunning himself that he barely acknowledged Mfene's call. He felt much too sleepy to bother about going all the way to the Council Tree. Just then a troop of Vervet Monkeys passed on their way to get their tails.

"Come, Mbili, come with us to get your tail," called the oldest Nkawu.

"I'm too tired," yawned Mbili. "Couldn't you get a tail for me?"

"Yes, we can!" shouted the Vervets as they ran on their way.

By the time all the animals had assembled under and around the Indaba Tree, the sun had set and the light from the three-quarter moon shone dimly through the spreading branches of the tree. Lion, who was getting old and could not see too well at the best of times, made many mistakes handing out the tails. He gave the Ground Squirrel a huge furry tail, while he gave us elephants little ones much too short for our size. When all the tails had been handed out Ngonyama asked if everyone had a tail. Only then did the Vervets stop chattering and remember that they had promised to ask for Mbili's tail.

"O Great One, we are sorry, but we have forgotten Mbili's request."

"What?" roared Ngonyama. "Do you mean that Mbili was too lazy to come and get his own tail?"

"Yebo, Nkosi – yes, O King," squeaked the Vervets.

Despite Ngonyama's anger, he still wanted each of his animals to have a tail. So he gave the Vervets the last one available, a small furry white tuft, to take to Mbili. But Nkawu the Vervet Monkey is vain and full of his own importance: and the Vervets decided that they would teach Mbili a lesson by keeping the tuft of tail for themselves. So to this very day, as anyone can see, Mbili the Dassie has no tail, while Nkawu the Vervet has a long tail with a white tuft at the end of it.

We feel quite sorry for Mbili the Dassie, even though it was his own fault that he did not get a tail from Ngonyama. And here I must tell you another remarkable thing about Dassies. Amazing though it may sound, my mother says that if you go far enough back in time to the dim and distant past, you will find that we elephants are actually related to the little dassie. This we find very hard to believe, but coming from my mother, it must be so.

uFookwe the Rain Bird lives in the reedbeds along the rivers in the valleys of the Balele Mountains. We can hear him calling "Du, du, du-du-du," and sometimes he says, "Wafababa, wafamame, ngafa iszungu-nqu-nqu—my father is dead, my mother is dead and now I die of loneliness." When uFookwe's call tumbles down the musical scale the weather will be fine. If the call ascends the scale, rain will be sure to follow. We listen to uFookwe's call to guide us through the day. If uFookwe says the day will be fine, we go further up the slopes of the valleys to look for mushrooms and other succulent plants. If uFookwe says it will rain, we generally stay in the valley and graze along the riverbeds.

Isi-Kombazane, the Emerald-spotted Wood Dove, will also call like uFookwe with a "Du, du-du, du, du" sound which at the end goes quickly down the scale. My mother says that she is saying, "Whenever I lay eggs I am robbed of them, until my heart goes to-to-to-to-to."

Tegwane the Hamerkop and Hadeda the Ibis fly up and down the rivers in the valleys of the Balele Mountains. When he sees his reflection in the pools Tegwane often says, "Tegwane, Tegwane, I would have been a handsome chap, but I am spoilt by this and that and that." We have never found out what spoilt Tegwane's good looks. Hadeda, whose harsh voice you can hear for miles, flies floppily down the river bawling, "Ngahamba! Ngahamba! – I go! I go!"

The wife of Umabengwane the Wood Owl will mourn all night calling "Maye, maye, maye babo—alas, alas, alas my father," to which her husband answers "Yini, yini, yine, yine-nje—what, what, what is the matter?"

When the bullfrogs and tree frogs and crickets all decide to call at the same time they can make quite a noise. At night, if all the sounds suddenly stop, the silence that follows is deafening, and you begin to think of Ingwe the Leopard slinking through the wet grass or Ngonyama the Lion coming through the reedbeds. Then just as suddenly as the calls stopped, first one and then another starts up again until the whole chorus resumes. Everyone relaxes and goes on with what they were doing before.

Nungu the Porcupine, Ngulube the Warthog, Mpungu the Jackal and Logwaja the Hare all live in the valleys of the Balele Mountains. My mother says that once upon a time, long, long ago, Nungu the Porcupine was the handsomest of all the animals. He had a thick furry coat with black stripes along his back and a most beautiful tail.

Ngulube too was not bad-looking, but Mpungu the Jackal was the plainest animal of all. Nungu the Porcupine was quite vain and boasted of his good looks to the others. Mpungu did not like this and one day he decided to teach Nungu a lesson.

"Nungu," the Jackal said, "you are a handsome fellow. Would you like to have an even finer coat than the one you have now?" Porcupine, being vain, could not resist asking Mpungu the Jackal how he could get an even finer coat than the one he already had.

"You must take off your coat and go into that thorn bush with the long black and white thorns," said Mpungu. "Beyond that bush you will find Mutwa the Powerful Magician. He will give you a new coat."

"I do not believe you, Mpungu, you are always out to trick your fellow-creatures. What are you up to this time?" Nungu asked.

"Well, Porcupine," said Jackal, "it is up to you. I just happen to know that Mutwa can give you the most handsome coat that anyone has ever seen. Perhaps if you do not want it, I will go and get it for myself."

Nungu could not stand the thought of Jackal being better-looking than he was, so he said, "All right, Mpungu, I will go."

"Not so fast," said Nungu, "first take off your old coat and give it to me." So Nungu took off his fine coat and handed it to Jackal.

"Now go straight into the large thorn bush," said Mpungu. The porcupine, whose eyesight is not too good, went blundering into the thorn bush. Huge thorns stuck into him and when he struggled they broke off. He could not go forward at all, and when he backed out he was covered all over with long, sharp black and white thorns. "Oh dear! You'll never fit into your old coat now," said Mpungu. "It looks as if I will just have to keep it."

And from that day to this, Nungu the Porcupine has gone out only at night so that no one can see him. He makes his house in an old Aardvark burrow, and he backs into it so that when he is going in or out of his front door no one will see his back all covered in the thorns that have now become his quills. As I said, Ngulube the Warthog was once quite good-looking—but that was before the day long, long ago when he taunted Ngonyama the Lion a little too far, and Lion chased him until Warthog found safety by dashing into an old Aardvark hole. Ngulube did not know that this was Nungu's house, so he curled up down at the bottom of the hole and went to sleep.

Not long after he had fallen asleep, Nungu the Porcupine came home and backed in down his hole in his usual way—right into Ngulube's face. Ngulube could not get the quills out of his face, and to this day he has warts and growths where Nungu's quills are buried in his skin. So when it comes to looks, poor old Nungu the Porcupine and Ngulube the Warthog will always be pretty much at the bottom of the pile: but sly Mpungu the Jackal came out of all this with a fine coat with handsome black stripes down the back and a beautiful bushy tail.

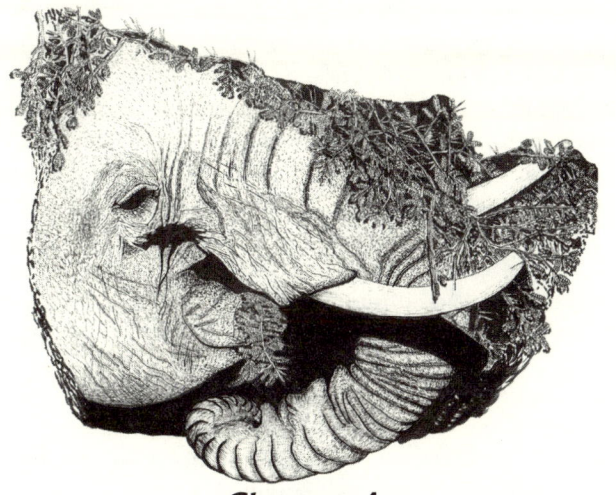

Chapter 4
The Thlabatini Forest

By now the moon has waxed and waned once since we left the Place of Thunder, Ndumeni. My mother chooses one of the valleys that run to the south out of the Balele Mountains and leads us into the Thlabatini Forest.

In the valleys running to the south, first small bushes and then bigger trees start to appear. We can also see bushes and trees on the stony ridges. My mother knows each of these trees: which ones are good to eat, when their fruit ripens, which ones are poisonous and which can help a sore tummy or a painful eye.

We soon find bright yellow Kei-apples and green and black Monkey Oranges along the river. The yellow Kei-apples are delicious and the leaves are edible as well. The green Monkey Oranges are much larger and the shells are quite hard to crack. We have to be very careful not to break open or swallow the large pips in the green Monkey Oranges as they can make us very sick. My mother shows us how to crack open the yellowish-brown Monkey Oranges that are lying on the ground. She stands on them, squashing them under her foot and getting to the pulp without eating the seeds.

Sausage trees also grow along the river banks. These trees bear a huge form of fruit that hangs down like the end of my mother's trunk. The fruit does not appear until later in the wet season. In any case, it is not really good to eat. The flowers, which are in full bloom, hang down in big chains as long as my mother's trunk. They taste delicious and we feast on them.

Fig trees, different from those we found along the Nyathi River during the dry season, grow in the river valley. Like the ones along the Nyathi River, these fig trees provide shade and attract many animals such as Mfene the Baboon and Nkawu the Vervet Monkey as well as Ngulube the Warthog and Nungu the Porcupine. On the rocky ridges of the valley sides we see other figs called rock figs, with very white trunks and large white roots. The roots squeeze into the cracks and fissures of the big boulders, splitting them open. The rock figs have red fruit with red leaves. They are not as sweet as the river figs and the red leaves are poisonous. My mother once used the white sap from some broken rock-fig branches to smear over a bad wound that Mafutha received when her foot slipped and a sharp rock cut her.

As we go further down the valley the trees thicken and spread out across the rolling escarpment. Haakdoring bushes with sharp hook-shaped thorns catch at our legs and tails. These bushes grow thickly on the edges of the forest. Spikethorn trees with long sharp white thorns also bar the way into the forest. My mother follows paths which twist and turn as we leave the valley and enter the Thlabatini Forest. Soon the thick bushes on the edge of the forest disappear and the forest floor clears into great pools of shade with shafts of sunlight coming through the leafy canopy to the ground. Giant iron- and yellowwood trees reach far above our heads into the sky. Silence reigns in the forest and brilliant blue-winged butterflies flash in and out of the shafts of sunlight. Now the going is easy and we can spread out and find different foods among the trees. Even so it is wise to stay near Ndlovu, who knows which food is best among the huge tree trunks hung with ferns and lianas. She soon finds a wild mango tree laden with fruit. Mangoes have a strong, strange smell that you have to get used to, but once you find the ripest ones they are very good. Near the wild mango trees, smaller bushes of mampoer berries grow in the shade of the larger trees.

Not long after entering the Thlabatini Forest we find that we begin to lose contact with each other. I stay near Ndlovu and Mabalel but can no longer see or even smell the others. This may sound scary but in fact we feel as though we belong here and as though the forest has always been our home. The soft rumbles of the grown-ups travel gently among the trees, replacing sight and smell, so even though you cannot see the rest of the herd you know where everyone else is.

My mother Ndlovu says that in the very distant past, when elephants were evolving from long-nosed animals called Proboscideans, the whole world was covered in forests. There were no plains like the Nyathi Flats where your eyes and noses can keep you in contact with each other. In the forest our ancestors could not rely on either sight or smell. Instead they had to use another sense: hearing. Now with all the trees in the forest, some sounds can travel only short distances—high-pitched sounds, like the ones that Ndlovu and

Amadala make at the water holes to chase off Ngonyama and his wives. But the low rumbling sounds that the grown-ups make in their throats and upper trunks are not affected by the presence of the trees. This low-frequency sound goes around the trees. Also, the cool air on the forest floor is capped by warmer air from the sunlight shining on the forest's canopy; and this layer of cold under the warm air traps the low rumbles, so that we can hear each other over long distances. This works best in a forest during the day, which is good, because that is when we spread out feeding. In the late afternoon and early evening, Ndlovu can gather everyone together from miles around in the forest. She makes sounds that we recognize as assembly calls telling us to come together. Other elephants from other herds may also make and hear these calls. Often our uncles Amadala, Nsimbi or Mfanyaan will hear and respond to these calls. Near sunset everyone gathers together. We stay together at night so that nothing will bother the youngest elephants in our herd.

The loud, low rumbles also bring males and females together to mate. Like Dakiwe, who is nearly fifteen, all the male elephants who are in their mid- or late teens are chased out of the herd. Each elephant herd is led by the oldest and most experienced female, such as my mother Ndlovu. She is called the herd matriarch. When the older females make the young males like Dakiwe leave, they get together with other young bulls from other herds to form bachelor groups. They probably do this because they feel lonely and sad that they have been made to leave their families. By joining together in a bachelor group they can have each other for company and feel much better. Once these males reach the age of about twenty-five, they are confident enough to leave the bachelor herd and go out on their own. Often a younger bull will join a mature bull as a companion, sometimes called an askari. Then you will see these two bulls wandering through the dry- and wet-season ranges of the other herds. Often they will recognize their old herd and rejoin it for a short time before wandering off again.

Young females in the herd like Indlebe, who is nearly sixteen, can have calves. They carry their calves for almost twenty-two months. After birth the calf will nurse for another twenty-two months. So it is only after nearly four years that the female elephant can become pregnant again. To become pregnant she must get together with a male. Her chance to do this lasts for only about four days. But she will not go off with just any male. She chooses the best, strongest and most handsome of all the males she can find. This ensures that her calf will be the best and the strongest.

The four-day period when a female elephant is ready to conceive again usually occurs in the wet season. This means that the calf will be born early in the wet season nearly two years later. The timing is important, because if the birth happens just before the start of a wet season it gives both the calf and the mother the best chance of surviving.

Soon after we entered the Thlabatini Forest this year, two exciting things happened. First, both Mathatau and Mabalel had new babies. Mathatau was the first to start making low rumblings different from any that I could remember hearing before. I did not know what they meant, but Ndlovu, Mabalel and Unlebe did. They all made low rumbling noises in sympathy with Mathatau, moving close to her side and standing and swaying with her. The glands on the sides of their faces were streaked with black shining liquid and everyone was getting agitated. Soon my mother led Mathatau away from the herd and into the forest. Mabalel stayed with us and stopped Mafutha and Ulambile from following my mother and Mathatau. The two of them stayed away all night. Then, as the first shafts of sunlight penetrated the forest, Ndlovu and Mathatau returned – with a tiny baby struggling on wobbly legs to walk between them. The baby's body was covered in red hair. Its little ears were pasted against the sides of its head and its tiny trunk dangled down nowhere close to the ground. The rest of us were all squealing with excitement. We crowded around and tried to touch and smell the new baby, but my mother rumbled warnings to us to stay back. She and Mathatau had difficulty keeping everyone at a safe distance. The little one was a baby girl and she was named Bomvu because of her very red hair. That day we did not move and most of the grown-ups did not eat much, simply staying close to Mathatau and Bomvu. My mother, in particular, never left their side. Bomvu soon learnt where her mother's milk was to be found and reaching up with her mouth between Mathatau's front legs was able to get plenty to drink. Because this was Mathatau's third calf she is a very good mother and knew how to help Bomvu.

By the next day Bomvu's legs were already stronger and she was not as wobbly as on the first day. Ndlovu led us towards one of the forest streams where there are thick stands of Boomcluster figs, wild camphor and white ironwood. She knew that in these areas insects like mosquitoes would be less bothersome, particularly to Bomvu. Two days later Ndlovu and Mabalel went off into the forest. Everyone was quite nervous because Mathatau was fully occupied with Bomvu, and the next oldest female, Unlebe, was not a lot of help. She was even more nervous than the rest of us, though we did not know why for another ten days. Dakiwe was no use either, because he was trying to boss everyone around, including Mathatau and her baby. Although he was two years younger than Dakiwe, Nkosana was much calmer. He helped to get everyone into a tight group with Mathatau and Bomvu in the center. Although we seldom encountered Ngonyama in or anywhere near the Thlabatini Forest, Ingwe the Leopard was a frequent visitor and could be heard coughing at night. Mfene the Baboon lived mainly on the southern edge of the Thlabatini Forest and along the cliffs of the Three Waterfalls. Even so we were not sure that he would not come this far into the forest. We had heard Mfene's barking, so we knew he was around, and it was not a good time for us to be anywhere near the Leopard's favourite prey. As it turned out, nothing happened during the night, but with daylight came a new worry. We had thought that Ndlovu and Mabalel would return with a new baby soon after sunrise, and they did not. The morning dragged on, while our fears rose, because we knew Mabalel had had trouble when Ukhanga was born. When the sun reached its highest point in the sky and the shadows in the forest were at their smallest we found it difficult not to go and look for Ndlovu and Mabalel. Just as the tension was about to break up the herd, we heard Ndlovu's gentle rumble. Then she and Mabalel appeared through the trees and we could see four little legs wobbling between them. Libele, which means "late", was bigger than her new cousin Bomvu and not nearly as red and fuzzy. She was soon suckling between Mabalel's front legs. Everyone was excited and very relieved that the two new babies had arrived safely.

In the middle of the Thlabatini Forest there are open areas, each one usually around a clear pool of spring-fed water. The trees that once stood in these open areas were pushed over by big elephants and have long since rotted away. Now the small bushes are kept low by the animals that browse on them. We stayed on the edge of one of these clearings for the next ten days.

Soon after the new calves arrived the second exciting thing happened in our herd. First Indlebe started to make very loud low rumblings, different from those made by Mathatau and Mabalel before Bomvu and Libele were born. These sounds were really loud and you could hear as well as feel them in your tummy. Soon after Indlebe started calling we could feel and hear replies coming from different parts of the forest. First one and then another huge strange bull appeared. Both were nearly as big as my father Nkosi, and both had large curved tusks. Udumo, "honor", was slightly larger than Shaya, "the one who strikes with his tusks". My mother knew Udumo and we remembered seeing him at water holes along the Nyathi River during the dry season. Shaya we did not know. He was darker and heavier than Udumo but not as tall. My mother said that Shaya had probably come from beyond the Pass to the Unknown. Both Udumo and Shaya wanted to lead Unlebe away from the clearing, but as soon as one got near her the other would come trumpeting in. This made everyone very nervous and upset, especially Mathatau and Mabalel with their small calves. My mother tried to keep everyone together under the big trees on the shady side of the clearing. Mathatau with little Bomvu and Mabalel with little Libele kept on the side of the herd furthest away from Unlebe and from where Udumo and Shaya were milling around.

It was not long before Udumo let out a piercing scream as Shaya had moved behind him and tusked him in the rear. Udumo swung around and faced his attacker. Both had their ears spread wide and their heads held high with their trunks curled up under their throats. Then with screams and clashings of their huge tusks they came together. Clouds of dust and debris rose around the two bulls so that at times we could not see the fight but only hear it. The ground shook as their huge combined weight was carried through their massive legs into the rocky surface. The thudding of their trunks echoed through the forest. As they drew apart and came back into view both had their trunks curled downward in front of them with their heads still held high. Their eyes flashed with fire and hatred for each other. It seemed impossible that neither was hurt, and we could not believe that both would survive this deadly battle. Time and time again they clashed and smashed into each other. The fight went on and on. Slowly the time between their charges lengthened, until eventually, after another such break, Shaya shook his massive head and ears, turned and left the clearing. The shade of the trees under which we gathered had not moved much. Time had stood still while the great battle raged.

Udumo seemed to have suffered little harm. His massive tusks were still intact and there was no blood on his face or head. The middle part of his trunk was red and his right ear had a gash which left the lower lobe hanging down. These were the only visible ill-effects of the mighty duel he had just won.

Udumo stood without moving for quite a while after the fight had ended. Then he slowly turned and, rumbling quietly, walked towards Indlebe. She stood still, allowing Udumo's trunk to trace gently over her body. Udumo towered over her and she looked terribly small next to him. Without any pushing or any other clear signal they both went off into the forest. We did not see them for four days. On the morning of the fifth day Indlebe came through the low mist that hung over the clearing and rejoined the herd as though nothing had happened. We did not see Udumo again until the next wet season.

Although most births and matings take place in the wet season, not all calves are born in the forest. I was born late in the wet season in the Hidden Valley. When this happens there is greater risk that the small calf will not be strong enough to make the difficult passage across the river above the waterfall and down the dangerous path to the Waterfall Pool.

During the days we spent in the clearing Bomvu and Libele grew a lot stronger. They stayed very close to their mothers but were soon easily able to keep up with the slow pace that Ndlovu set through the forest. I stayed close to Mabalel and helped her with Libele, keeping her between Mabalel and myself and making sure that she never strayed. Much of what I was doing reminded me of what Mabalel had done for me when I was small.

I still felt that I had to pay attention to where Ndlovu was leading us and to the places where the best fruit and sweetest leaves could be found. The herd especially needed to know where there

were Marula trees and when the fruit would be ripe. This small yellow fruit was a favorite fruit of many animals. It was equally important to learn from my mother which trees and fruit to avoid. The Tamboti tree, with its dark cracked bark like the skin of an old elephant, is very poisonous. The bark flakes off the tree and has a tempting spicy smell that you must resist. The Paperbark Thorn tree is also poisonous, especially the dry leaves and seed-pods which lie thickly and invitingly around the base of the tree. I already knew about the dangers of the red fig leaves and the poisonous seeds of the Monkey Orange.

Then there are other trees such as the Quinine Tree, which my mother knows is good for headaches and which can calm you down if you have become too excited. You also need to know which parts of the tree to eat, because the fruit, leaves, bark and roots can each have a different effect.

During a full cycle of the moon we have moved steadily southwards through the Thlabatini Forest. Now we follow a stream which leads out of the forest towards the Third Waterfall. It is strange to come out of the trees and see the distant horizon again. During the next cycle of the moon my mother will lead us along the escarpment where the streams tumble over the kranse onto the Nyathi Plains.

Chapter 5
The Kranse of the Waterfalls

Ndlovu leads us out of the Thlabatini Forest and down the stream to the Third Waterfall. Heading towards the sunrise, we are only a short day's walk from the head of the kloof of Mutwa the Magician. This brings us close to the path that led us up onto the escarpment more than three moons ago. The wet season is more than half over. Heavy rains have fallen from thunderstorms like the one that caught us on the way up to the Pass of the Unknown and Ndumeni the Place of Thunder. The rivers are full and we can hear the roar of the Third Waterfall long before we reach it.

Clouds rise like gigantic white tusks over the Nyathi Plains. From the edge of the escarpment we can see far out over a wide vista. Mabutu Mountain looms out of the haze of distance. The plains disappear in a curtain of dimness that hides the horizon. Only the memory of our dry-season wanderings reminds us of what is lost in the haze out there.

Families of Mbili the Dassie live both on the high kranse of the escarpment and along the rivers. We hear their sharp calls of "Gamfi!" warning of the presence overhead of Lammergeyer the Eagle Vulture and Ngungulu the Bateleur Eagle. With their soft padded feet, dassies are sure-footed and fearless of the heights on the kranse of the escarpment. They run along tiny ledges and do not hesitate to jump from one basalt block to another, even though any misstep may be their last. Igogo the Klipspringer, who is as sure-footed as Mbili, can be seen on the rocks along the ridges of the three rivers. Of course Ndlovu will not let us go anywhere even near to the edge of the cliffs, which drop many times the height of the largest trees to the Nyathi Plains below.

The kranse that form the edge of the escarpment are home to

Mfene the Baboon. Each of the three waterfalls defines the home range of a separate troop of baboons. Early in the morning after sunrise you can hear the booming "Booha!" calls of the alpha males echoing along the escarpment. The calls announce the presence of each troop and mark the boundary of its home range. Alpha males call to define their territory, for if they do not call the neighboring troop will come into their territory to look for food. The troops are not rigidly fixed groups, and single females and young males will sometimes leave one troop to join another. They are met with a lot of barking and get chased away at first, but if the newcomer persists and stays on the edge of the troop that it has adopted, he or she will gradually be accepted. Sometimes such a stranger can even rise in the ranks of its adopted troop and become a dominant male or female. The leadership of a baboon troop changes often, which is very different from how our herds work, but in other ways Mfene is just like us, for the wisdom of the troop resides in the oldest and wisest of the females and not in the changing alpha males. Wherever baboons live one is pretty sure to find Ingwe the Leopard. Ingwe finds the best dens in the rocky sides of the kloofs of the three rivers that spill over the escarpment.

My mother says that Ingwe the Leopard and Mfene the Baboon were not always enemies. Once upon a time, long, long ago, they were friends, but this friendship ended one day when Baboon lost Leopard's lunch. Ingwe had spent the best part of a hot morning trying to get near enough to Logwaja the Hare to catch him for lunch. Finally, as the sun was reaching its highest point, Logwaja went into a cool crevice in the big blocks of basalt along the river. Now Ingwe knew that there was no exit from this crevice, so creeping up the river in a low stealthy crouch, he got into position to spring to cut off Logwaja's exit. In one powerful leap Ingwe was at the entrance to the shallow crevice, and Logwaja was trapped. By now Ingwe was panting from the long hot chase and very thirsty.

Mfene the Baboon, who had been watching the last part of the chase, now came up to Ingwe. "Greetings, Ingwe, how are you?" he said.

"Greetings, Mfene, thank you, I am well," said Ingwe, but added, "I am very hot and thirsty. Would you watch this hare which I have been hunting all morning while I go and get a drink?"

"Yes, Ingwe, I will watch this hare that you have so cleverly trapped," replied Mfene. As soon as Ingwe had gone down to the river to drink, Mfene sat down in the shade at the side of the entrance to the crevice. Peeping out from his hiding place, Logwaja could see that Mfene was starting to doze and moreover was not blocking his escape route. Like a streak of lightning Logwaja sped out of the crevice and was up over the ridge and away.

"Where is Logwaja? Where is the hare?" shouted Ingwe on his

return.

"Oh my goodness! I don't know," said Mfene in a low and frightened voice.

"You stupid monkey!" shouted Ingwe. "I spent most of the morning catching that hare and you don't know where he is?"

Now a baboon does not like to be called a monkey. In fact that is the worst insult that you can offer a baboon. Shocked by Ingwe's insult, Mfene said without thinking, "You overgrown Mpaka," (which means, You overgrown wild cat) "I do not need to listen to that kind of talk!"

"You don't, do you?" snarled Ingwe. "Well, how about you being my lunch instead of that miserable hare?" And before Mfene could move a muscle, Ingwe had dealt him a blow with his powerful right paw. Caught off balance, Mfene tried to roll away, but this was a very bad mistake. Ingwe grabbed Mfene by the throat and it was all over.

So from that day to this, Ingwe the Leopard has been the mortal enemy of Mfene the Baboon. To make matters worse, when Ingwe first tasted baboon meat he realised that he liked it more than anything else he had eaten. So now Mfene is Ingwe's favorite prey.

One day, as Ndlovu led us along the escarpment edge towards the Second Waterfall, we witnessed a great battle between Ingwe and Mfene. The sun had just risen over the Pumulanga Mountains. The Third Waterfall baboons were sitting on rocks and in a big fig tree facing the sun and warming themselves. It had rained late on the previous day and drizzled into the night, and the baboons were cold and wet. Ingwe knew that they would be sunning themselves and would still be sleepy after an uncomfortable night. Smells and sounds are both difficult to detect in the rain. Because of this, Ingwe had spent a frustrating and unsuccessful night. He was tired, hungry and irritated. In this mood he was a serious threat to the baboons.

Ingwe targeted the baboons in the fig tree. He knew that the big alpha male sitting on the highest branches of the tree would be alert. Although this baboon looked as though he was snoozing, he was keeping a sharp eye out for leopards. Ingwe managed to reach a pile of basalt blocks which formed a little koppie between him and the big male lookout. Sidling stealthily around the koppie to the base of

the fig tree, Ingwe reached the tree undetected. Then with an effortless leap he landed in the fork where the two biggest limbs branched upwards out of the trunk, and slowly began climbing the right-hand limb towards the baboon at the very top of this branch. He was halfway up the branch when a young baboon saw him and screamed the alarm.

The alpha male plummeted down from his perch, but not knowing where the danger lay, landed up almost on top of Ingwe. The leopard, too, was taken by surprise, and failed to take advantage of the baboon's fright. The baboon was in mortal danger, for Ingwe was almost as agile as he was in the large fig tree. If Mfene tried to stay in the tree Ingwe would trap him in the highest branches. If he leapt from the tree Ingwe would be right behind and above him. If Ingwe was close enough he would be able to leap onto Mfene's back. There was no time to decide. Mfene chose to leave the tree. Ingwe tried to do exactly what Mfene feared – pounce onto Mfene's back as he left the tree. But Ingwe was not quite quick enough.

By now the chase had brought both the baboon and the leopard onto the level piece of ground where we were standing. Ndlovu had moved Bomvu and Libele into the center of the herd with their mothers. All the adult elephants except Mathatau and Mabalel were standing facing the fight.

As Mfene fled across the open space he seemed to decide that attack was the best form of defense. To the leopard's surprise the big baboon suddenly turned and charged towards him. Mfene's plan might have succeeded, for Ingwe skidded to a halt in a cloud of dust. But at this critical point Mfene's courage deserted him and he too stopped in his tracks. Almost obscured by dust, the leopard and the baboon were face to face. Mfene still had the advantage of surprise and could have panicked Ingwe into flight had he pressed home the attack. Instead he made the fatal decision to try once more to escape. Ingwe is far quicker off the mark than Mfene. With a surge of power from a standing start, the leopard accelerated onto Mfene's back and bowled him over.

Mfene has fearsome canines, but he had no opportunity to use them. As the dust settled we could see that the battle was over. Ingwe picked up Mfene as though he were no heavier than Logwaja the Hare and returned to the fig tree. With a single smooth leap the leopard carried the body of the baboon to the fork where the chase had started. Then he climbed the same branch that only moments before Mfene had been sunning himself on and lodged the lifeless body in a high fork.

It took a while before all of us calmed down after what we had just seen. Although we knew that this was the way leopards survived, most of us had never seen Ingwe or any other predator make a kill right before our eyes.

Baboons do not always lose their fights with leopards. The canine teeth of the alpha male baboon are as large as those of the leopard, and the backs of these canines have very sharp serrated edges. When the big alpha male fights, he tries to sink his canines into his opponent and uses his arms to push his victim away, slicing backwards with his teeth. This can inflict a fatal injury on his opponent. Often male baboons will band together to attack Ingwe the Leopard. If they catch him on a ledge of the kranse, they will attack from both his front and his rear. If the ledge is narrow Ingwe cannot easily turn to defend himself from both sides, and if he does manage to turn, it gives the baboon he has turned away from the opportunity to rush in. The danger to Ingwe is not only the fangs of Mfene but also the fact that he can easily lose his footing and plunge over the edge to his death on the rocks far below.

The oldest female baboons lead the way to begin the day's foraging. The big males stay with the females in the center of the group. The younger males and the females without young spread out on the fringes of the troop acting as scouts and sentinels. Baboons are omnivorous, eating meat when they find it, any insect, even a scorpion, and all edible fruits and plants. They turn over rocks looking for insects, and if they find a scorpion they deftly pull off its sting and then eat the rest of it with relish as a juicy morsel. Most of the time they feed in silence but every now and again a young baboon will get too close to an alpha male. The adult male will threaten the young baboon by raising his eyebrows to show large white patches on his upper eyelids. If the young baboon does not move away quickly enough the alpha male will charge it and smack it with his hand. Then there will be a lot of screaming and running before things quieten down again.

When baboons arrive at a favorite feeding place or at a water hole, the alpha male chooses the highest tree or mound to mount guard. Mfene have excellent eyesight and these sentries will warn the troop of any danger. They have special barks for different threats, a very loud bark for Ingwe the Leopard and a much softer bark for Nyoka the Spitting Cobra. A troop of baboons will often feed at the same place as we do, and once when we were feeding at a red fig tree on one of the ridges, a young male gave two sharp but soft barks. I did not pay attention until he barked again. Then I realized with a fright that this particular warning Mfene was giving was for a snake. I backed slowly away. Right there, coiled up under a rocky ledge, was a Spitting Cobra. Had Mfene not warned me at that moment, Nyoka could easily have blinded me.

Chapter 6
The Western Highveld

Over the next several days Ndlovu leads us along the edge of the escarpment to the First Waterfall. Then she turns and follows the stream of the First Waterfall back into the western edge of the Thlabatini Forest.

The trees on this side of the Thlabatini Forest stand alone or in small groups. Tall Mopane and wide-spreading acacias soon give way to open grasslands. Some fever trees, with their yellow trunks and light green tops, continue for a while along the streams that flow towards the waterfalls. Soon even the patches of low bush have disappeared and only waving vistas of golden-brown grass remain. The grass, which is in full seed, is thick and tall, reaching right up to my tummy, and in it we look as though we are wading through water. Deep into the grass there are green leaves. As the wind blows, waves sway across the veld towards the sunset. The veld seems to stretch on forever, disappearing into a purple-blue haze so that you cannot tell where the land ends and the sky begins. In the early morning the grass is so wet with dew that we are soaked up to our middles. Grass seeds with rows of dewdrops sparkle in the early sunlight. The nights are getting cold now, and walking through the wet grass we are glad to feel the warmth of the sun on our backs.

There are many different birds where the forest meets the veld. The tall fever trees are hung with weaverbirds' nests. The huge nests of the Sociable Weaver weigh down the thorn trees. These nests are as big as I am and have lots of entrance holes, each one leading to an individual nest. Sociable Weavers flash in and out of these openings, busily feeding their young. The nest of each pair is built into the underside of the large nest. In this way Boomslang the Tree Snake cannot get to the weavers' eggs or young ones. In the middle of the wet season the sun climbs directly overhead and there is little shade to be found even under the biggest trees. The thick layers of twigs and grass-stalks built into these gigantic nests provide shade and insulation from the fierce heat. Inside each small nest-chamber the eggs and chicks stay cool during the day and warm at night.

With their tails streaming out behind them, male Sakabula birds struggle to fly against the wind. They rise and fall as though held up by the waving grass. The sight of them reminds us of the time Dakiwe chased a Sakabula on the Nyathi Plains and nearly landed in serious trouble. Red and Yellow Bishop-birds have built their nests in the many little vleis that dot the veld. They like the reedbeds in these vleis, and draw two or three reeds together to anchor their nests, so that even long grass-snakes will not be able to reach them and rob them of their eggs and young ones. On the open veld Tinktinkies, the smallest of all the birds, rise straight up into the air calling their name and then dive back to earth. Their nests are very difficult to find. Tinktinkie and her mate draw the seed-laden grass tops together in a bundle and then build their nest down into the grass with the opening at the top hidden in the grass seeds. The inside of the nest is lined with silky strands which Tinktinkie pulls out of the tops of special grass. Her eggs and babies are nestled down at the bottom of this tube. When we get too close to a Tinktinkies' nest both parents will swoop around our heads making a "Zit-zit-zit" alarm call. We follow Ndlovu's lead and carefully avoid the nest. Big Gompous or Kori Bustards, as tall as the long grass, stand on termite mounds sunning themselves. They are the heaviest of all birds that can fly, so when they want to gain a little height it is probably less effort for them to walk up an anthill than to lift themselves on their wings. Korhaan call to each other with their loud, grating voices and rise and fall in flight like much bigger and clumsier versions of the tiny Tinktinkie.

Before we leave the edge of the forest we usually see Isikhova the Giant the Eagle Owl. With wings as wide as Ndlovu's head, he glides noiselessly between the trees and out over the veld. A concave circle of feathers on either side of his face helps to gather sound into Isikhova's ears, which can catch the faintest rustle of small feet in the grass. His big brown eyes are also very powerful, and he can see hares and field mice even in the dark. At night we hear his long-drawn-out whistles, like those made by Lammergeyer during the day. Then Isikhova will utter a series of grunts: "Hu-hu-hu, hu-hu", which can be heard deep in the forest.

My mother Ndlovu does not lead us far into the open veld. Instead we stay near the last stands of thorn trees, using them for shade in the middle of the day. The grass is sweet and tender but you have to know how to find the best parts. With their trunks my mother and aunts gather the grass stalks that have heavy heads of seeds

into a bundle. Then holding on to the bundle, they slide one of their tusks underneath it. Lifting with their tusks, they break off the nutritious seeds.

Each elephant is either left- or right-tusked. Breaking off the grass in this fashion eventually wears a groove near the tip of the tusk. My mother has worn a groove into her right tusk. Mathatau has a groove in her left tusk.

To get to the sweet green grass and succulent roots, we learn to grab hold of a bunch of grass with our trunks and pull up on it. We kick the grass and roots loose with the strong toenails of our front feet. After that we beat the bunch of grass against our feet to knock the soil off it before eating it. The sweetest grass grows in the shallow swales of the rolling veld. My mother leads us to the best places, where there are pools of water strung together by rivulets or damp ground.

This year Ndlovu led us deeper into the treeless veld. As we came over a rise we could see a stream in the swale with bright green grass on the other side. When we reached this grass we saw that the veld had been burnt, perhaps at the first full moon after we arrived on the escarpment. Green grass growing in the blackened clumps was already as high as my knees. The burnt stubble crunched under our feet as we kicked up the dust, and soon our legs were black. The grass tasted very good and we ignored the dust.

The Secretary Bird was also out on the burnt veld looking for snakes and other animals which had not been able to escape the fire. The Secretary Bird knows that grasshoppers and beetles as well as snakes will always return to a burnt area to feed on the new grass and other small creatures which are now easier to find there. This time we saw a pair of Secretary Birds with two young chicks about five moons old.

As we left the stream and headed for the crest of the rise we could see what resembled a low rolling cloud to the west. It looked like another fire, but my mother did not seem to be concerned. Soon we could hear a low rumbling, and despite Ndlovu's calmness we began to feel worried. A fire like the one on the Nyathi Plains when

Lamithi the Giraffe saved the Oxpeckers' chicks is bad enough, but up here on the open veld there is no Nyathi River to protect us. As the cloud got closer and the rumbling noise grew louder, however, we realised that what we were looking at was dust, not smoke. Then at the edge of the dust cloud we could see first hundreds and then thousands of Springbok antelopes. They were not coming straight towards us but were moving in a surging mass towards the north, and the rumbling was the noise being made by their many thousands of hooves. As the Springbok reached the burnt grass the dust cloud grew in size until it darkened the sky.

Then nearer to us we saw Nkontshane the Wild Dog. We couldn't see how many there were but my mother has told me that there can be as many as thirty to forty Wild Dogs in a pack. They follow the Springbok migrations for many days, preying upon any buck that fall out of the herd. Nkontshane can run almost as fast as Ihlosi the Cheetah, and what is more he can keep on running for a long time. When the pack leader selects a victim the adult dogs in the pack take turns at keeping pace with their target. In this way each dog gets a rest after a hard chase. Once the animal they are chasing tires, the Wild Dogs attack from all sides and the prey has no chance of survival. Cruel though this seems, the Wild Dogs are actually saving the weak animal from a slow and more painful death through sickness or starvation.

After seeing the pack of Wild Dogs we were not surprised to see Ihlosi the Cheetah and three nearly grown cubs. The migration of the Springbok is good fortune for a cheetah mother with three cubs, as she would otherwise have a very difficult time feeding them, and while following the Springbok herd she can also teach her cubs how to fend for themselves. That night we heard the "Wo-ooph, wo-ooph" of Mpsisi the Hyena, so we know that he too was following the herd.

The Springbok moved past us in an unbroken mass all that day and far into the night. All that time we could hear their continuous rumble, as well as other sounds like muffled bleating and the clicking of horns and hooves. By the next morning the dust cloud could still be seen to the northwest. As we moved westward closer to where the massive herd had passed we found only blackened earth, with not a blade of grass in sight. Giving her "Let's go" rumble, Ndlovu led us back towards the escarpment. For a time, she stayed on the green grass of the burnt veld.

By this stage of our yearly journey the veld has flattened into an unending sea of grass. There are no longer any trees and the small streams have disappeared. There are still small depressions or vleis with longer grass, some reeds and shallow water. Bishops and weaverbirds built their nests in the tall reeds at the beginning of the wet season, but by now the nests are empty and all the weavers are gathered together in flocks. As they rise into the sky they look like a swirling cloud which rises and falls over the veld until it suddenly dives into another wet patch of reeds.

Blue cranes with their flowing tail-feathers walk through the tall summer grass. They too are gathering in groups of both young and old. Like the weaverbirds, they will soon be leaving for the far-away parts of the world where they will await the coming of the next breeding season.

Ever since we had arrived on the highveld this year my mother Ndlovu had been less and less willing to put up with Dakiwe's increasingly bad behavior. In the Thlabatini Forest he kept on pushing Bomvu and Libele around, he would not give way to their mothers Mathatau and Mabalel, and he went on behaving like this out in the grasslands. One morning soon after the Springbok migration, when he pushed Bomvu into a muddy pool in a small vlei we were walking through, Ndlovu had clearly had enough. She gave a short sharp trumpet and with ears spread wide she moved sideways at Dakiwe. He knew by both the trumpet and her body language that she was serious, so he quickly cleared out of her way, expecting her to stop after a moment. But she did not stop. She kept on coming after Dakiwe. She had never before actually chased him, so he stood still. This was a mistake. Ndlovu first gave him a forceful thrust with her tusks and then thumped him hard on his rear with her heavy trunk. Dakiwe screamed in surprise and started to run, but he still expected Ndlovu to stop. Again he was wrong. Ndlovu kept after him, not stopping until both of them were well away from all of us. Only then did she turn back towards the rest of the herd. Dakiwe looked very puzzled. He stood still until Ndlovu was back among us. Then he started to come back to the herd. Ndlovu immediately spun around, trumpeting, and charged towards him. This time Dakiwe made no mistake. He ran. At first we thought this was some sort of game that Ndlovu was playing with him, but as the day wore on she continued to keep him out of the herd. It was obvious that the time had come for Dakiwe, now fifteen years old, to leave us.

For the next quarter of the moon Dakiwe could be seen in the open veld keeping within sight of the herd. Sometimes when we were drinking or wallowing in the shallow vleis, Dakiwe would try to sneak in. He had little chance of succeeding on the open Highveld. Ndlovu could see him begin his approach a long way off. She would let him know, by a few loud rumbles, that she knew what he was doing. This would be enough to make him stop. We felt sorry for Dakiwe, especially as all our aunts had taken sides with Ndlovu and joined her in keeping him away, but we knew that he would eventually find other young bulls or even an adult bull to join, and they would help him to grow up. Once he has matured Ndlovu will allow him to rejoin our herd for a few days at a time.

By the time we reach this stage of our journey each year, the first flights of Blue and Crowned Cranes begin passing over us on their way to places far beyond the Balele Mountains, and we see clouds of weaverbirds disappearing to the north. The vleis are now empty of birds, except for Tegwane the Hamerkop, who is still staring at his reflection in the water. The rain clouds of the wet season disappear over the north-eastern horizon and the nights are now clear and cold. The stars shine in the clear dry air like clusters of dewdrops reflecting sunlight. We can almost touch Mpofu's Constellation of Mbulwane's tears which rose to the heavens after the Eland saved Mother Earth. The full moon rising over the Pumulanga Mountains is a red ball as large as the sun. The wet season is ending, and Ndlovu turns us back to the Thlabatini Forest and the Hidden Valley.

Chapter 7
Back to the Hidden Valley

As Ndlovu turns and leads us back towards the sunrise and the Pumulanga Mountains, we can see the steep slopes and the top of Thaba Insimbi. Ndlovu knows that she must pass between Thaba Insimbi and the Balele Mountains. This will bring us to the head of the Hidden Valley and the path that will take us into the valley. Few animals come into the Hidden Valley during the wet season. The Ingagane River, fed by the rains over the Balele Mountains and the escarpment, changes from the quiet stream that we left many moons ago to a fast-flowing and dangerous river. We can no longer cross the river just above the Waterfall to reach the entrance to the Secret Path as we did at the beginning of the dry season. If you tried to cross the Ingagane there now, you would risk being swept over the Falls to plunge into the pool far below. During the wet season the waterfall is powerful and dangerous, and you can see and hear it from far up the valley. Clouds of spray rise high in the air and the waterfall pool that we swam happily in at the other end of the year is a foaming, swirling mass of water. And crossing the river would be only part of the danger. The Secret Path, which was risky enough in the dry season, is now doubly perilous. Water pours down the face of the krans onto and over the path. Water drips and runs everywhere. The stones of the path are green and slippery with moss. At the head of the Valley where Ndlovu now leads us, the path follows the river and is enclosed between the steep rock walls. During most of the wet season the river is too high to allow us to pass safely from the escarpment into the Hidden Valley, and we can neither enter nor leave the Hidden Valley.

By now it has been five moons since we passed through the kloof to the east of Mutwa the Magician's kraal in the shadow of the

Pumulanga escarpment. The flat top of Thaba Insimbi and the highest slopes are now white, and they glisten in the setting sun. The wet season's rains have ended. It will not rain again on the Nyathi Plains for the next five moons. Winter winds and storms will sweep across the Highveld and over the escarpment and Balele Mountains. Sudden storms will blanket Thaba Insimbi in snow. Ndlovu has watched and waited while the storms of the wet season have gradually retreated back beyond Ndumeni. There have been few storms during the past moon and the night skies over the Balele Mountains are no longer lit by lightning. Ndlovu knows that there is only a narrow window of time in which to return to the Hidden Valley. It is time to set out on the final stage of our year's journey.

A feeling of peace and quiet settles over the herd as we slowly wind in single file down the path into the Hidden Valley. We feel as though we have come home. Many of us were born here. All of us recognize the sheltering sides of the valley as they begin to rise steeply on either side of us. These walls will shut out the cold winds of the beginning of the winter on the escarpment. The seasons have completed another full cycle.

There are no animals in the Hidden Valley that we fear. Animals like Ngonyama the Lion and Mfisi the Hyena have not found their way into this place, nor can Wenya the Crocodile reach its small pools. With nothing to fear in the valley, we spend lazy days at the water pools. There is plenty of food: figs, marulas and sweet grass along the Ingagane River, berries and seed-pods on the slopes that rise up to meet the steep sides of the valley. We no longer have to walk many miles to find food and water.

This year, Bomvu and Libele took a while to join us in the water pools, for they had had a frightening experience earlier while we were still up on the Highveld. Up there by the end of the wet season the vleis have shrunk to shallow muddy pools. The two little ones had run towards a small pool of water surrounded by mud that had been trampled by many animals. Before they knew it they could not pull their legs out of the mud. They were unable to go either forwards or backwards. The more they struggled the deeper they sank. Only their fat little tummies stopped them from sinking deeper. Both were very scared and they squealed their terror over and over. Mathatau and Mabalel were trumpeting and milling around the edge of the muddy area, and they did not seem to know what to do. Ndlovu, who had been on the far side of the muddy pool, began making deep rumbles which quietened both the mothers and the calves. She came around to where Bomvu and Libele had gone into the mud and with outstretched trunk she tested it and then reached towards Libele. But she could not quite reach her. Mathatau and Mabalel were beginning to get agitated again and were trying to come in beside Ndlovu. She raised her head and swung it from side to side, rumbling loudly at them. This quietened them down again and they moved back out of the mud. Ndlovu then lifted her feet slowly and placed them carefully into the mud. However carefully she moved, she still sank in deeper with each step. Stopping and standing still, she reached out to Libele. This time she was close enough to just reach Libele's back. She first tried to grasp Libele's small tail, but although she got a good hold on it, she could not move her. The whole herd had now gathered on the grass behind Mathatau and Mabalel. Everyone's head was held high and our trunks reached out towards Ndlovu as though to help her. The air filled with rumbling and short anxious squeals and trumpetings. Ndlovu rumbled loudly to calm everyone. Then, slowly edging closer to Libele, she got her trunk down under the little one's right thigh. With all the strength that Ndlovu has in her trunk, she broke the suction of the mud and pulled Libele's back legs free. Wrapping her trunk around one freed hind leg, Ndlovu dragged Libele out of the mud and back towards Mabalel. Mabalel was beside herself with anxiety and did not seem to realize that her calf was free. With deep rumbles Ndlovu managed to calm Mabalel and got her to wrap her trunk around Libele's other back leg. Once Mabalel had a firm hold on Libele, Ndlovu released her hold and edged forwards to reach Bomvu. The effort to free Libele had sunk Ndlovu's forelegs deep into the mud. She was now in difficulty herself. The whole herd fell silent with fear. The sun stood still. Only low rumbles from Ndlovu could be heard as she continued to comfort Bomvu and keep her quiet. We were horrified to see Ndlovu's rear end sinking into the mud. Once all four of her legs were held by that sucking mud, she would be unable to move. We could only look on, helpless, our heads swaying back and forth in anxiety. With a great squelching sound Ndlovu pulled first her right and then her left foreleg out of the mud. With a tremendous effort she rose up on her hind legs and, straining every muscle, she stretched her body forward and slowly placed her forelegs onto the undisturbed mud. Then she rocked forward and slid her trunk under Bomvu. She lifted Bomvu right out of the mud and without turning, almost sitting down in the mud she pushed herself and Bomvu backwards to dry land. Libele and Bomvu were covered in mud and wobbly with fatigue and fright. With Mathatau and Ulambile helping Bomvu and Mabalel and Unlebe helping Libele, Ndl-

Bomvu

Ndlovu

ovu led them around the mud hole to a small ditch half filled with water. Sucking up the water in their trunks, first Ndlovu and then Mathatau and Mabalel washed Bomvu and Libele. For the next few days Bomvu and Libele had to be coaxed by their mothers to get close enough to water to drink. They would not go into the mud surrounding most of the pools. It was not until we reached the pools on the Ingagane River in the Hidden Valley that Bomvu and Libele forgot their terrible experience and lost their fear of water. But after that they were soon happily imitating the games that Mafutha, Ulambile and I played. We would climb on each other's backs and try to push each other over. Then we would go into deep water until only the tips of our trunks were above the surface and our feet barely touched the bottom.

The steep sides and cliffs of the Hidden Valley shelter us from the wind but also cast shadows across the valley which do not creep away until long after the sun has risen over the Pumulanga Mountains. The afternoon shadows soon follow as the sun drops behind Aasvoëlkrans. After the blazing heat of the open veld we welcome the cool days in the Hidden Valley. This year, early on the third morning in our sanctuary, we first heard and then saw an elephant come into the full sunlight on the eastern side of the valley. The noise of the river and the distant rumble of the waterfall masked his low calls, making them too indistinct to recognize, and the elephant was too far away for us to identify. The intruder waited on the slope for a long time before slowly walking towards us. As he began moving, Ndlovu and the rest of us recognized him as Dakiwe. He had followed us into the valley and was now trying to rejoin the herd. Everyone looked at Ndlovu, expecting to see her chase Dakiwe away as she had done on the Highveld. Instead she stood watching calmly as he came closer and closer. Then to our surprise she gave a low assembly call signaling to Dakiwe that it was all right for him to join us. He quickened his pace and we all ran to greet him. There was much trumpeting and greeting with outstretched trunks and rubbing of hides. Everyone, it seemed, and especially Dakiwe, was glad to be reunited. Even though this reunion that Ndlovu has allowed will last only until we leave the Hidden Valley for the Nyathi Plains, right now we are happy to have Dakiwe with us again.

Ntombi's Family Tree

(AGES) are at the end of Book 2. Female +. Male ↑.

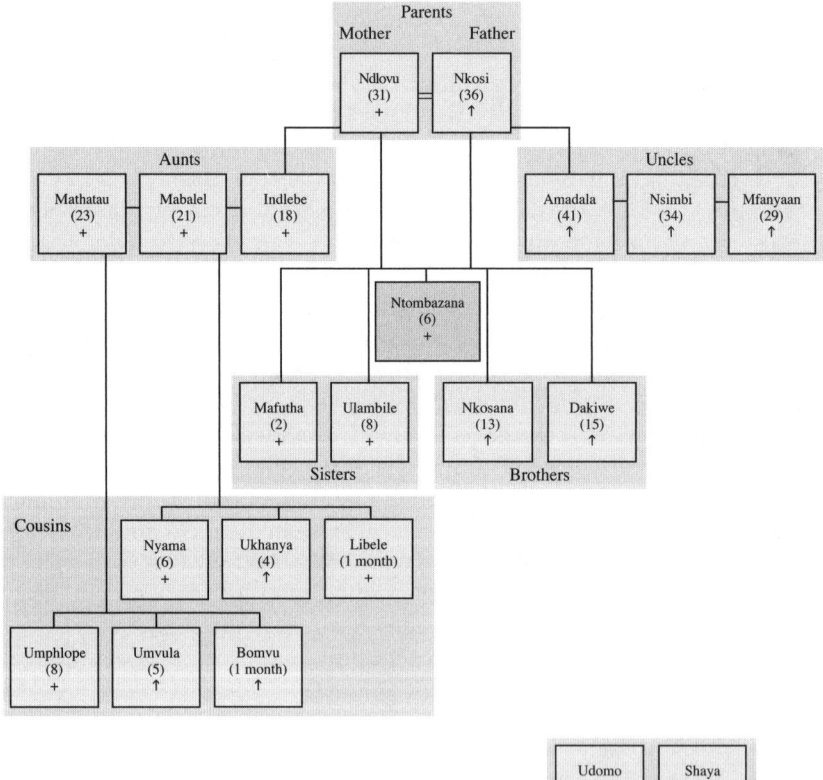

Book 3

Loss of our Home Ranges

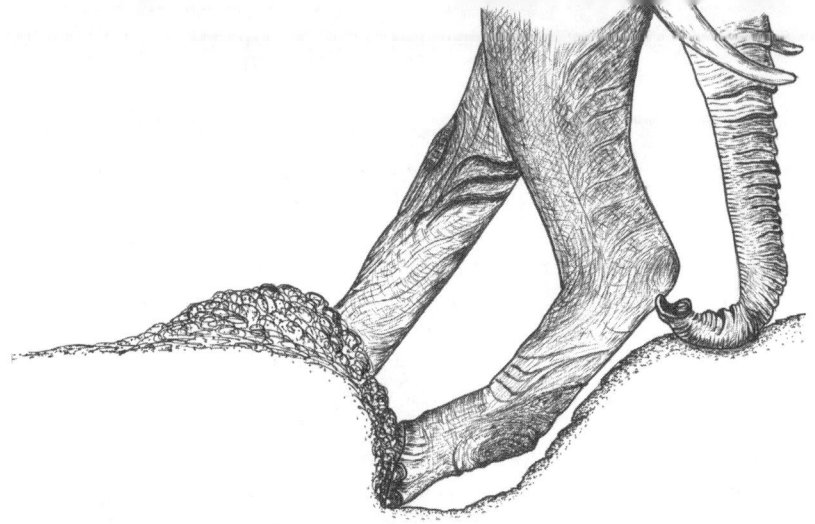

Chapter 1
A New and Dreadful Danger

Five dry and five wet seasons had passed in my life when I began telling you of my family and where we lived—of how we spent the dry seasons on the Nyathi Plains and the wet seasons on the escarpment and in the Balele Mountains; of all the animals we met and knew on the plains and on the Highveld; of their stories, of the San Bushmen and the Abantu people, the Zulus, and of Nkosi's fight with the Zulus. Much has happened since then. First, ten more quiet years went by (until I was fifteen years old) with the peaceful rhythm of our seasonal migrations going on as it had always done before. But after that, everything changed.

In those ten years—the last years of our old life, though we had no way of knowing this at the time—Ndlovu led us many times down the steep path next to the waterfall, onto the Nyathi Plains and back again through the narrow kloof to the Escarpment and the Balele Mountains. Little changed in the rhythm of our herd's life during these years. In some seasons rain fell in abundance on the Escarpment and over the Nyathi Plains. In others the rains failed to come. More than once the Nyathi River ceased to flow, no grass was left, and the thorn trees wavered and shimmered above bare, parched soil in the heat of the plains. In these droughts Ndlovu found water and food for us in the deep kloofs of the Shonalanga Mountains. She knew that the fig and amarula trees next to the shrinking pools of the Nyathi River still bore fruit. Often Ndlovu led us along the dry riverbed to places where she could dig for water. She would walk slowly across the hot sand until she detected a faint smell of water. She followed this scent until she knew water could be reached by digging. She never dug without finding water. No matter how thirsty we were, Ndlovu did not hurry. Instead she would stop to allow us to test the air, as she did, until we too were able to smell water. Then, moving very slowly across the sand, Ndlovu would make sure that we could sense that the smell of water was getting stronger and stronger until she knew it was within reach. Ndlovu used her huge front feet and strong nails to scoop out the sand. She did not use her trunk for digging but only to test the sand for signs of dampness. Once she had found water she would stop digging to allow it to seep into the hole. Then one by one each of us would take a turn to drink. The mother with the youngest calf in the herd usually led the way. Each one took only two trunkfulls of water, waiting between drinks for the water to return to its level in the hole. Everyone, even the smallest calves, kept away from the edge of the hole. Impala and Nyathi the Buffalo would be waiting for us to finish drinking. Then they would rush to the hole, collapsing the sides so that none of them got any water.

At these times hot winds carried clouds of dust across the plains and dust-devils spun and twisted over the dried-out mudflats of the Umzimkulu. Impala and Idube the Zebra would stand listlessly in small groups in the thin shade of the fever trees, and at the end of each day the sun would sink over the Shonalanga Mountains in a great ball of fire. It felt as if no animal could survive such a dry, dry season. Mvubu the Hippo and Wenya the Crocodile would already have left the Nyathi Plains, moving into the dangerous lands of the Amazulu in search of water. Mpisi the Hyena and the vultures of Aasvoëlkrans were the only ones to prosper. Just when the survival of the animals on the Nyathi Plains was hanging in the balance, the rains would come again. Towering clouds moved over the plains, riding on winds that spilled over the escarpment. Ndlovu would have to hurry us through the narrow kloof leading up to the escarpment before the rising river blocked the way.

Good rains in the wet season brought deep, sweet grass to the escarpment and filled the rivers and the Umzimkulu and Amanzintoti vleis. During those last ten years of our old life there were six wet seasons that had good rains. In those six seasons nine calves were born in the herd, which brought our number to twenty-five, not counting Dakiwe and Nkosana. I told you about Dakiwe's departure at the end of the story of our wet-season range, and Nkosana left two years after Dakiwe. Unlebe had two calves, Izolo, which means "yesterday" (because she was born a day late), and Umfazi, which means "old woman" (because she was all wrinkled and looked like an old woman when she was born). By our last year of peace Izolo was eight and Umfazi three. I had gained a little brother, whom my mother Ndlovu called Ubani, or "who" (because I was so surprised at his arrival and asked "Who is this?") Mathatau and Ulambile had five-year-old calves named Biza, meaning "come back" (because

Mathatau has to continually call her back to her side) and Bamba, meaning "to catch" (because he is always running off with Biza and has to be caught by Ulambile). Even though Mabalel already had two daughters, Nyama and Libele, and one son, Ukhanyaan, she had another calf called Fuma, meaning "wanted". Ukhanyaan was already fourteen years old and would soon be leaving the herd. Nyama was sixteen and had a calf of her own. Libele was ten and Funa four. Umphlope had Amafu, "the cloud", during a very rainy wet season, and Nyama had Ilanga, who was named after the sun because he was born in the next sunny wet season. In the middle of the most recent wet season Umvula had given birth to her first calf, whose name Jabula means "happy". Because of Ndlovu's wisdom and ability to lead, none of the calves born over the last ten wet seasons were lost. Ndlovu, my aunts and older sisters and brothers can still remember how Undlebe's calf Mhimbe was swept away and drowned when we were trying to cross the swollen Nyathi River.

Three other elephants also joined our herd from the outside: Khumbula with her calf Fisela, and Velapi, a much younger female. Khumbula, whose name means "to remember", came from a herd near the Shonalanga Mountains. Fisela's name means 'to wish for'. Velapi's name means "where do you come from", and there was something strange about her. She could not remember where she had lived, what had happened to her or how she had found our herd. Also, she always seemed very nervous and afraid, but we could not understand why.

Whatever it was that she feared, it could not have been the human beings we had known up to then: the Bushmen, and the Abantu people. We had known both of these kinds of people for as long as anyone could remember, and mostly they and we had got along together in peace, as long as we were careful. We could smell, hear and see the San Bushmen who lived in the caves of Mabutu and the Shonalanga mountains. Sometimes they hunted our kind, so we took care not to go near their camps. We could smell their small cooking fires from far away and in the early evenings and early mornings we could hear sounds of them preparing food and sometimes sounds of singing and chanting when they had killed Mpofu the Eland.

In the dry seasons the San Bushmen were the only people we knew who lived in the hills and mountains around the Nyathi Plains. They did

Umvula & Jabula

not stay in one place but favored caves and overhangs of sandstone which overlooked the water holes and paths used by the animals of the plains. I learnt from my mother and aunts over the years that elephants' knowledge of the presence of the San depended not only on seeing, hearing or smelling them. We knew of their presence through all these senses, of course, but we used many other signs as well. We could tell whether they were far or near, and whether they were just gathering roots and berries or hunting Mpofu the Eland. To be able to do this we learnt how to interpret many different signals that surrounded us. Ndlovu taught us that we could not rely on any one sense or sign alone. She might first detect only the faintest warning cry of a distant Go-'Way Bird or see the turn in the flight of a vulture high in the sky, but that would be enough to make her stand quite still. She would place her feet firmly on the ground. Turning towards whatever had alerted her, she would raise her trunk, head and ears. Then on the briefest breath of wind she might detect the pungent smell of humans. Ndlovu knew that the San could not suppress their excitement when chasing Mpofu the Eland. They smell different when excited than at other times. Mpofu's hooves would send subtle vibrations through the ground which Ndlovu could detect in her feet. She would know that it was Mpofu being hunted. She would also know whether Mpofu was heading for the hills or the Nyathi River. As soon as she was satisfied that she knew the direction the hunt was taking, she would give a low "Let's go" rumble and lead us away from the danger. Without Ndlovu's guidance we would not have known to stop and listen, feel, hear or smell. Nor would we have known how to find the meaning from not one but all of the signals together. Over time, each of the younger elephants began to follow Ndlovu's example and learn to interpret what they were sensing and how this created a continually changing picture of our surroundings. As we learnt from Ndlovu, we realized that her awareness of the world around her created a sense beyond sight, smell, hearing, taste and touch. And as we were to find out, she stored the minutest detail in her memory to use many seasons later.

As for the Amazulu, they lived in small groups in the rolling hills beyond the Nyathi Plains. In earlier times they were not called "the Zulu" but the "emaGladeni" or "those among the melons" for they grew melons in among the millet and sweet canes of Imfi – the sweet canes that tempted Nkosi into their fields, and nearly cost him his life, as I recounted to you earlier. By the time of Nkosi's fight, a chief named Zulu, the son of Mandalela, was the leader of the Gladeni clan. This clan adopted

his name, which means "the Heavens". The clan was proud of its title of "Amazulu": the "People of the Heavens". As the Amazulu prospered, their kraals spread over the grassy hills where the Nyathi River joins the Tugela.

There were other small clans neighboring the Zulus. Nandi, a strong-willed princess of one of these clans, gave birth to a son. She was not married and her son was thought to be the work of the spirit beetle called "iShaka", so he was called Shaka. Shaka grew up to be a great warrior and a mighty chief. He created a small but powerful Zulu army. He adopted a new short stabbing assegai, discarding the throwing spear previously used. He introduced new and larger rawhide shields, and made his soldiers throw away their oxhide sandals, since they could run faster barefoot. He formed his regiments into the shape of the head and horns of a bull. His most experienced warriors made up the head while the younger men and even boys formed the horns. The head made a frontal attack on an enemy while the horns encircled their foe. None of the other clans could withstand Shaka's ferocious attacks and he spread death and destruction far and wide. No kraals were left standing and whole regions were swept empty of people. As he destroyed the kraals and surrounding clans, Shaka gathered the young men of these clans into his growing army. He took the women and children captive to grow and prepare food for his army. All his enemies' goats and cattle were taken to swell his herds. The Zulu called this period of destruction the "Mfecane" or the "crushing".

We, of course, knew nothing about these things that were happening far from our dry-season range. At first all we noticed was that the few people who used to bring their cattle into the Nyathi Plains now disappeared. Even the San Bushmen silently left the caves in the Mabutu and Shonalanga Mountains, going we knew not where. For a number of dry seasons we saw no people on the Nyathi Plains at all. This absence of people was like the silence that descends over the escarpment before the first black clouds of the wet season roll down from Ndumeni, the Place of Thunder. For in the very next dry season, herds of Zulu cattle as numerous as wildebeest came to the grasslands along the Nyathi River. Only herd-boys accompanied the cattle, and they were afraid of us and ran away whenever we came near them. These herders did not spend many days in any one place but continually moved their cattle along the banks of the river. They hunted guineafowl and other birds, and whenever they could they caught Iphiti the Duiker and Logwaja the Hare in snares they set along the paths.

How could we have known that our old life, and the world that we had always known, were about to come to an end?

One day, when little Jabula was still only two months old,

we heard and felt faint rumbling sounds which we had never sensed before. Ndlovu stood still, listening and searching the air with her trunk. She could not interpret either the sounds she heard or the slight vibrations she felt through her feet. All she could tell was that
the sounds were sometimes sharp, like stones clicking and knocking together as they fell from a krans. The rumbling came from something that seemed as large as Nkosi. She felt uneasy, not knowing whether to keep us where we were or lead us away. Khumbula became agitated, and Velapi even more so: with her ears spread wide and her tail raised, she actually tried to run away from the herd. It was clear that both Khumbula and Velapi were very frightened of these strange sounds. After a long time Ndlovu chose to move into the thick bush along the Ingagane River. The river was running strongly, spilling over rock ledges and swirling around large boulders, and because of its noise we could no longer hear any of the strange sounds. Soon the rest of us were busy under a large fig tree, but I could see that Ndlovu and Khumbula remained alert. Every now and again they would stand still and raise their trunks to listen and test the air. That night Ndlovu continued to move up the Ingagane River towards the waterfall and the Hidden Valley. This puzzled us, as we had just come down the Secret Path and were following the river out onto the Nyathi Plains. Now we were retracing our steps. Ndlovu kept reassuring us with gentle rumbles and gradually helped our uneasy feelings to subside.

By the time the sun rose over the Pumulanga Mountains, with mist hanging in the still air over the Umzimkulu Vlei, calm had returned to the herd. We could hear the whistle of the Fish Eagle over the vlei. Then in an instant the peace was shattered by two crashes of sound in quick succession. Nohemu the Crowned Crane rose trumpeting over the vlei. These sounds were like thunder over the Highveld except that each one lasted only a brief moment: it echoed but did not persist like the rumble of thunder. Now Ndlovu had no doubt that these strange crashes were linked to the sharp sounds that she had heard coming from far away the day before. The two short thunderclaps seemed to have come up the Ingagane River from somewhere near the Umzimkulu Vlei, but from how far away Ndlovu could not tell. We all wanted to run away, but we had no idea where to run to, or what we would be running from. Ndlovu remained quiet and to our surprise did not move the herd for the rest of the day and all of that night. Instead she kept us in the deep cover of fig trees along the river. Soon after sunrise she turned and led us slowly back towards the Umzimkulu Vlei. It seemed as if she were leading us back into danger. We did not know that to cope with an unknown danger one had to seek it out. Only by knowing the source and nature of the danger would Ndlovu be able to find some way to deal with it. Now the only sound to be heard was her quiet rumbles. The thick bush along the Ingagane grew thinner as we entered the tall grass and reeds of the vlei. The hippo path we were following was broad and soft. A deep mat of reeds cushioned each step. No sound came from the feet of the herd, and our ears stopped flapping. Jabula kept close under Umvula's chest, staying perfectly quiet. Even the sounds of the vlei seemed muted. We did not hear the Fish Eagle's whistle or the rasping quacks of Idada the yellow-billed duck.

Without warning Ndlovu brought all of us to a halt. Only the arched tip of her trunk could be seen searching the air above the reeds. Although she was very alert, she was quite calm. She began moving ahead slowly until the path widened into a clearing. Here Ndlovu stopped with her head raised and her trunk curled under her neck ready to charge. She uncurled her trunk and stretched it out far in front of her. Now those in the front of the herd could see that the tall reeds on the far side of the clearing had been flattened. Two shapeless dark heaps showed above the crushed reeds. A smell of blood and death suddenly reached our nostrils. As if on a signal, two black clouds of flies rose buzzing about the shapes. Every nerve in our bodies tensed and tingled. Even from across the clearing the sound of the buzzing flies was loud in our ears and the smell of a freshly opened carcass filled our trunks.

With the herd strung out along the hippo path, only Ndlovu in the lead and Mathatau and I following her could see into the clearing. Mathatau backed into me. Moving out of her way, I was now next to Ndlovu. Ndlovu moved towards the dark shapes and I followed, not knowing what to expect. With outstretched trunks we simultaneously recognized the bodies of two hippos. But we could barely recognize them. Their feet lay scattered on the far side of the clearing and their teeth had been cut from their jaws. Spread over the crushed reeds in great red patches of blood were their insides. Their ribs, stripped of their thick hide, arched into the air like the branches of a dead fever tree. Little else of the hippos remained. Their great hides and massive rumps were gone. Trampled reeds smeared with blood showed that these parts had been carried back to the hippo path. We knew of no animal on the Nyathi Plains that could destroy Mvubu the Hippo in this way.

The herd was now milling around in confusion in the small clearing. Ndlovu had difficulty in bringing about some order. Without any clear instructions she led Mabalel, Unlebe and myself to the carcasses. There we gathered the dismembered feet and returned them to what was left of the bodies. Ndlovu then turned to the wall of reeds surrounding the clearing and began uprooting them. Then she took bundles of reeds in her trunk and spread them over the remains of the Mvubu. Following her lead we soon covered both hippos. Ndlovu emitted low moans that came from deep within her. We felt our throats constricting and unconsciously began to moan as well. These sounds stilled the rest of the herd who stood around nervously in the clearing. With a last touch of her trunk to the reeds covering all that was left of the two Mvubu, Ndlovu gave a low "Let's go" rumble, turned and led us back down the hippo path we had followed earlier that morning.

Once again Ndlovu led us towards the Balele Mountains and the Hidden Valley from which we had come less that one moon before. She did not know how the hippos had died in the small clearing. No animal could have torn Mvubu's thick hide from her back and left no trace of it. The poisonous arrows of the San could not penetrate Mvubu's hide. In any case we had not seen San Bushmen for many seasons. Only young boys tended the herds of Zulu cattle on the plains. They could not have done this. There was nothing in Ndlovu's long experience that could explain the terrible sight we had just seen.

All that Ndlovu knew was that she had heard sounds that she did not recognize, and that these sounds seemed to be linked to the death of Mvubu. To save us from the fate that Mvubu had suffered would mean a balancing act between gaining knowledge and running dangerous risks. She knew that for the moment she must keep the herd away from the Nyathi River and the surrounding plains. If she headed back to the Balele Mountains, Ndlovu also knew, there were only two passes leading to the escarpment: up the Secret Path to the Hidden Valley and along the kloof above Amanzintoti Vlei. In the dry season of winter the Secret Path could be icy and dangerous, while the kloof could be blocked by strongly-flowing water. If the evil that had killed Mvubu chose to come towards the Pumulanga Mountains, Ndlovu would have to make a choice between these two possible escape routes.

She had one other option, a risky one: to head across the dry plains to the slopes of Mabutu Mountain in the hope that she could identify this threat to her herd. Ndlovu chose to head for Mabutu Mountain. There she could look out over the plains and the Nyathi River. Any danger approach-

Ndlovu

ing Mabutu Mountain would have to cross the hot dry plain below. From the vantage point of Mabutu Mountain, you could faintly see the far side of the river. Once we got there, Ndlovu would have placed the river between us and the unknown threat.

To reach Mabutu Mountain we had to cross waterless bushveld. In the past Ndlovu had always led us to a bend in the Nyathi River which curved towards Mabutu. She had also always picked a time when the Bobbejaan-berry bushes were laden with fruit. Now our crossing of the dry plain would be longer and done without food or water. There was little shade to be found in the low bush of the dry plains. Ndlovu did not begin the journey on the day we found the dead hippos. Instead we circled around the Umzimkulu Vlei, crossing the Ingagane River but staying in the wet reeds of the upper part of the vlei. We spent the next day mostly in the shallow water of the vlei feeding on water plants and grasses. Ndlovu started out across the plain as soon as she felt the cool air of evening creep in behind the setting sun. We traveled as fast as the youngest calves could walk, with only a few short rests in the hours of darkness before the sky lightened over the Pumulanga Mountains. Ndlovu had allowed little time to find food because she knew there was little to be found: the acacia trees covering the plain did not bloom or sprout new leaves until the end of the dry season, and this early in the season the leaves were dry and tasteless and the thorns long and sharp. Soon after sunrise the blue and purple shades of dawn turned into the white heat of day. The horizon was lost in a shimmering heat-haze. The tops of the acacias detached themselves and floated above sheets of false water. We took no notice when shapes resembling Lamithi the Giraffe suddenly swam into view over the plains. Then all of a sudden a herd of real giraffe did take form in front of us. Their heads and long necks swayed not from the distortion of the heat-haze but from exhaustion. Two of the giraffe were barely able to stand. Dried blood lay caked on their shoulders and down their front legs. Terror shone dully in their eyes and we knew that whatever had come to the hippos had reached them too. They took little notice of us but continued to move in their swaying gait towards the rising sun.

Before this encounter with the giraffe it had seemed that Ndlovu was seeking a place to rest for the day. Now she pressed on towards Mabutu Mountain, which was lost in the heat-haze somewhere ahead of us. We had not had a drink since sunset on the evening we left the vlei. Nor had we had much to eat. Jabula and Ilanga were still nursing, and without water their mothers' milk would soon dry up. While the younger elephants in our herd had never gone without water for any length of time, Ndlovu and the older ones had often done so. Normally an adult drinks six or more trunkfulls every day. We could go without water for two days. If water were not found on the third day some members of the herd would begin to lose their senses. They would no longer follow Ndlovu's lead, but would rush off in a frantic search for water, only to stumble exhausted to a halt. Each desperate rush would drain the dwindling moisture from their bodies until they could no longer move. They would stand weakly in the fierce heat of the sun for a while, and finally they would collapse and die.

We continued without stopping until after sunset. Ndlovu then allowed us to rest. The small ones collapsed on their sides and looked as if they would never rise again. Most of us remained standing with our trunks resting on the ground. A number of times that night buffalo, wildebeest and other animals ran past us. They were all heading away from the Nyathi River towards the Pumulanga Mountains.

The sounds they made with their feet and voices were filled with fear, and their fear stuck to us like the glutinous mud of a drying water hole. Velapi, Khumbula, Fisela and some of the younger elephants in our herd were showing signs of breaking away and running with the buffalo and wildebeest. Only Ndlovu's strong grip on the herd kept it from breaking up. As darkness faded we could see Mabutu Mountain looming ahead of us. We did not know why, or even whether, this mountain was a safe haven. We only hoped that Ndlovu would soon find water in one of the shallow kloofs that cut into the mountain. The entrance of the kloof to which Ndlovu led us was obscured by a dense mass of haakdoring. The vicious hook-shaped thorns which grasped and grabbed at every part of us were impossible to get through. Yet Ndlovu found a shallow donga with walls free of the haakdoring. As I looked past her, all I could see was a tangled mass of thorns. It seemed that she had led us into a hopeless dead end. With the crush of the rest of the herd behind me, neither I nor anyone else could turn around in the narrow donga. Then I realized that Ndlovu had disappeared. Forced to press forward by those behind me, I suddenly found a sharp bend in the passageway. Once around it, I could again see Ndlovu ahead of me. No one who had not used this hidden passage before would have known that it was there and that it was the only way through the haakdoring and into the kloof. By the time that Ulambile and Isopho, who were the last in line, passed through the entrance, Ndlovu and I had emerged from the haakdoring into a narrow steep-sided kloof. Between its walls wandered a ribbon of dry sand studded with dry clumps of reeds and tambotie grass. Parts of the kloof were still in early-morning shade but the last of the cool night air was already draining out into the growing day. And then, from somewhere ahead, we sensed the unmistakable smell of water. It was all that Ndlovu and I could do to keep those behind us from pushing past and rushing up the kloof. Ndlovu, with a brief sideways motion and glances backwards, let the herd know that it was not to come past. Large flat sandstone ledges began to cross the floor of the kloof and pockets of green grass and ferns appeared. When the first pools of water appeared, Ndlovu did not stop. She let those behind us drink from these pools while she led me and the older ones to water holes higher up in the kloof.

The relief we felt in finding water and the feeling of safety in the kloof eased the stresses of the past few days. Water and rest were more important than food. Few of us fed on the grass and shrubs around the water holes or along the damp runnels of the streambed. The enormity of what had happened to us and the uncertainty of our future kept our hunger subdued.

How Ndlovu had known of this kloof was a mystery to me. In all the dry seasons that I could remember, Ndlovu had never led us past the hidden entrance to the passageway through the haakdorings. There were no clues in the featureless dry bushveld to tell us where we were. In any case, most of our journey had been done at night. Except for the brief time after dawn, even Mabutu Mountain had been lost in the heat-haze. We had seen no tracks leading through the bush and not even the spoor of the smallest animal had signaled the entrance into the haakdoring. Ndlovu had shown me that I had to be aware of what was around us. One had to recognize what was important and needed to be remembered, and ignore that which would serve no purpose. More and more I was realizing that Ndlovu was continually showing me things that were important and needed to be remembered. At times I was not sure what she was doing. Ndlovu used many kinds of information to enable her to find her way. As we had gone through our wet and dry season

ranges I had slowly seen that I too was aware of the stars and a subtle feeling of direction. It was only now that Ndlovu had led us to this one precise location without the help of any signs that I realized that something else must be at work here. Now that I was older, I was able to make and feel sounds that I had not been able to make or detect before. I could sense and understand much more in the very low sounds that all the older elephants were making. Below even the lowest sounds of the other elephants there was an uninterrupted background of sounds that I had previously ignored. This very low and faint rumbling did not come from Ndlovu or any of the other adults. Nor did it come from any other animal. It was a continuous sound coming from the earth itself. This sound never really stopped, although at some times and places it could be loud and at others almost undetectable. Because I thought that I heard these things, I have spoken of them as though they were sounds like the far-off deep booming calls of in-Singisi the Ground Hornbill. But they were not only sounds which you heard with your ears. Instead they were both sound and feeling: things that one felt in one's feet or perhaps deep in one's body. When we moved between the plains and the highveld these very low background sounds changed as the ground swelled into hills and mountains or flattened into level veld. In places like Aasvoëlkrans the sound was loud; in the plains it was soft and muted. It was as though one could see the shape of the land in pictures of sound as the earth breathed and its breath was gathered in swales and valleys or swirled up ridges and kranse. I could see the pictures even in the blackest night. You could pick out places that you knew and know where you were. This is what made it possible for Ndlovu to find her way to the entrance of the kloof hidden by the tangled thorns of the haakdoring. This was how Ndlovu always knew where she was, and how she could find the faint path across the Pass to the Unknown or recognize the valley that would take us into the Thlabatini Forest. Now I, too, was beginning to see the world around us without using my eyes.

After three days of rest in the kloof Ndlovu started up Mabutu Mountain. By sunset we had climbed through a narrow cleft in the sandstone to the top of Mabutu. We could see the distant purple wall of the Shonalanga Mountains and the plain stretching across the Nyathi River.

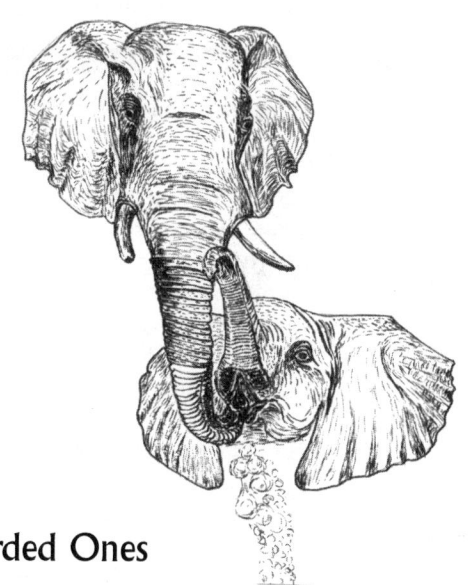

Chapter 2
The Arrival of the Bearded Ones

Ndlovu kept us in the upper reaches of the kloof in Mabutu Mountain for three days. By the end of the third day the little food that there had been in the kloof was gone. The gentle rumbles that were always present when we were on the Nyathi Plains or in the Thlabatini Forest had been replaced by long periods of silence. Even Bomvu and Ubani stopped their play and moved closer to their mothers. No one knew why we felt this vague sense of dread. We could neither hear nor smell any sign of danger. Each time the herd went silent, fear rose up through our bodies and the urge to flee grew in the stillness of the kloof.

As the kloof fell into deeper shadow Ndlovu led us up onto the top of Mabutu Mountain. The sandstone cap of the mountain, which looked so flat from far away, was actually crisscrossed by shallow swales and deep ravines. Little grass and few thorn trees covered the top of the mountain, but in the ravines and gullies the bush was thick. In the fading light Ndlovu led us along the top of Mabutu to the eastern end. She remained mostly silent, giving only occasional contact rumbles. The rest of us knew from her behavior that we should keep quiet. Yet it was not only the silence of the herd that we felt. The sounds of the bush had changed in some unknown way. Plovers and Korhaan called, but their calls were muted and of a different pattern. Instead of ringing out over the mountain, they seemed short and quick, as though in calling the caller did not want to be heard. The tension we felt in the kloof accompanied us to the top of the mountain. A feeling of fear was rising up from the Nyathi Plains.

Ndlovu stood quite still facing the Shonalanga Mountains in the purple distance across the Nyathi River. She held her head high and her ears were spread and still. Her trunk was raised and she swayed from side to side as though she was testing rather than smelling the air. Khumbula, who had joined the herd only a short while before, moved up next to Ndlovu. She too was listening and testing the air. It was then that I also detected the faintest of smells. A smell that was strange and unknown.

As the purple shadows of the Shonalanga Mountains turned into blackness, points of light like Mpofu's Constellation were being pricked out of the dark curtain hanging over the plains. A string of these lights stretched along the bend in the Nyathi River, which had now disappeared into the darkness. Darkness had also crept silently over Mabutu Mountain.

We had not been able to feed on the climb out of the kloof or as we crossed the mountain. Ndlovu now left the high ground which overlooked the Nyathi River and turned back into a wooded gully. In it a small spring rose, and thick grass and bush bordered the stream. Ndlovu clearly intended to spend the night here. Most of the herd spread out along the stream drinking and feeding. We needed to do this quietly, and when Bomvu let out a squeal to chase Ubani away from his clump of grass Ndlovu slapped him with her trunk. By the time the sky lightened over the Pumulanga Mountains everyone except Ndlovu and Khumbula had rested and fed. Most of the tension of the last few days had gone out of the herd. Ndlovu, Khumbula, Velapi and I were the only ones who had not slept much during the night. Soon after the first streaks of light touched the high clouds over the mountain, Ndlovu gave a low "Let's stay" rumble to the herd. Then she gently shouldered Khumbula and me as a signal that we should come with her. She led us silently to the edge of the mountain overlooking the Nyathi River. Ndlovu moved under a rock outcropping that had dense bushes at its base. She went in among these bushes so that the rock outcrop stood up between us and the rising sun. Then she stood motionless, looking towards the bend of the Nyathi River.

Small columns of smoke rose in the still cold air over the places where we had seen the points of light the previous evening. As the sun rose and light flooded the Nyathi Plains we could see many cattle like those herded by the Amazulu. With these herds were other animals of a kind we had not seen before. They looked like zebras without stripes, and were mostly plain brown in color. This was our first view of horses. Then we could see figures like the Amazulu gathering animals from the herd. Some of the cattle had horns that reminded us of Nyathi the Buffalo, and these were gathered in small lines like the termites that crawl from their mounds after the first rains of the wet season. Some of the figures climbed onto the backs of some of the horses. Then the string of animals moved off, followed

by what looked like the lost shell of Skilpad the Tortoise after it has been bleached white by the sun and rain on the veld.

Soon a long line of white shells, each with its own string of animals, was winding along the river. Following this long line were many more animals. Some of them, smaller than cattle, were of kinds we had never seen before. Most looked like half-grown Nyathi; some were as small as Iphiti the Duiker. All were going down the far side of the river, along the path we followed in the middle of the dry season.

Only after gazing across the Nyathi River for some time did we become aware of a growing strangeness. At first this seemed only to be because of what we were looking at across the river. Then each of us in turn realised that there was nothing else moving on the plain below us. Nor could we hear any sounds. We could not see a single giraffe browsing on the crowns of the tallest acacias. No herds of impala or zebra came into view in the clearings. No vultures circled above the plains, and we did not hear the clear crisp whistles of the Fish Eagles. A stillness blanketed the Nyathi Plains below us. It entered our minds like Mkulu the Rock Python slithering into a dark crevice in the rocks. The sense of fear that we had felt in the kloof was returning.

At this moment the booming "Booha!" warning call of Mfene the Baboon echoed from the shadows of the cliffs below us. Both Khumbula and I moved to run but a low rumble from Ndlovu held us in place. Then in the plain immediately below us, coming out of the shadow cast by Mabutu Mountain, bearded men, riding on horses almost the way Tokolosh rides on a baboon, emerged into the sunlight. As we caught sight of these men there was a crack of sound like the thundercrash that explodes when lightning strikes a basalt rock. It was the same sound we had heard in the Umzimkulu Vlei a few days before, but much louder and more frightening. At the same moment Mfene the Baboon uttered a piercing scream of pain, and then to our ears came the breaking of branches and dislodging of rocks as his body tumbled down the mountain. Grunts and calls came from the Bearded Ones, who then rode their animals back into the shadows.

Ndlovu stood motionless in the bushes below the rock outcrop. We knew, now, what had happened to Mvubu the Hippo in the Umzimkulu Vlei. We knew also why the giraffe and other animals had fled past us the night we were making our way to Mabutu Mountain. And why the plains had fallen silent. In all the years of our kind, in the world we had lived in for so many generations, there had been nothing like this to fear. San Bushmen had sometimes attacked the sick or old among us; Ngonyama the Lion and Mpisi the Hyena would kill any unprotected calf they could find; the Amazulu would chase and, if they could, kill those who raided their crops. But none of these were anything like this. Now we understood why Khumbula, Fisela and Velapi had joined our herd, why Velapi was so nervous and why Khumbula was so alert to the strange sounds we had heard. A new and terrible danger was among us: human beings who could kill Mvubu the Hippo despite his tough hide, and strike down dead Mfene the Baboon even while he sat high up on his krans, far beyond the range of any arrow or spear. We did not yet know the threat to our kind, but the caution and care Ndlovu had taken told us that she felt the Bearded Ones posed deadly danger to us.

Ndlovu waited a long time in the bushes below the rock outcropping until we could no longer hear sounds coming from the Bearded Ones where they had gathered around the dead baboon below us. As soon as she was sure that they had gone she led Khumbula and me back to the swale where we had left the herd. They too had heard the loud sound and Mfene's scream. Mathatau and Mabalel were having difficulty in keeping the herd in the swale and stopping the more disturbed ones from breaking away and running aimlessly. Velapi, who had probably some time in the past already witnessed what the Bearded Ones could do, was moaning and swaying. Ndlovu went straight to her, gently touched her trunk to Velapi's mouth and cheeks, and gave low reassuring rumbles to calm her.

Ndlovu kept the herd in the swale all day, waiting for darkness before leading us away from the Nyathi River side of Mabutu. There were no paths on top of the mountain. Towards the end of the night, when we reached the edge of Mabutu, we could faintly see the far-off outline of the Pumulangas. The Gramadoelas below were still shrouded in shadows. Where Ndlovu intended leading us was not clear. It was not yet the middle of the dry season. The escarpment and the Balele Mountains were deep in snow, and the kloof which we had taken many times from the Nyathi Plains to the escarpment might well be frozen and impassable. Winter storms would sweep over the escarpment for the next three moons. Without shelter and food Ndlovu knew that the herd would not survive on the escarpment.

With the coming of the Bearded Ones it seemed that we had lost the Nyathi Plain as our dry-season range. If we could neither stay on the Nyathi Plain nor reach and survive on the escarpment, there seemed to be no other choice than to turn towards the land of the Amazulu. Ndlovu knew that Nkosi and Nsimbi had gone far into this land. She also knew that Nkosi had almost lost his life while trying to escape from the Amazulu by crossing the Badlands of the

Gramadoelas. We could skirt the Badlands if we could find a way down Mabutu Mountain on the Nyathi River side. This route would take us back onto the Nyathi Plains and nearer to the Bearded Ones. If we crossed the northern end of the Gramadoelas and turned south along the base of the Pumulanga escarpment, we might reach an area not heavily settled by the Amazulu and far from the encroaching Bearded Ones. Ndlovu knew that none of us could go without water for more than two days. The young calves in the herd, and especially little Jabula and Ilanga, might not survive the Badlands. Three other calves, Amafu, Umfazi and Funa, were also still nursing from their mothers. Their survival depended on how well their mothers could take care of them.

More rain than usual had fallen in the first part of this dry season. The rivers and springs were running strongly and grass, shrubs, trees and other food were abundant. Perhaps this was what decided Ndlovu to risk crossing the Badlands. As we approached the edge of Mabutu Mountain it became obvious that she had decided to lead us around the Gramadoelas and southward along the foot of the escarpment. However, we did not leave the lower slopes of Mabutu Mountain. Instead Ndlovu took us to a strong spring emerging from the base of the deep sandstone band which lay over the entire mountain. There she kept us feeding and drinking as if nothing was amiss. Each evening, while the moon steadily grew in roundness, Ndlovu would stand quietly facing the Pumulanga Mountains. She gave no sign that she was thinking of moving. Then one evening she suddenly gave the "Let's go" rumble, and led us all down the mountain heading for the northern end of the Gramadoelas. The full moon rose soon after sunset so we could see the dark kranse of the Pumulanga Mountains ahead of us and the jumble of deep dongas of the Gramadoelas to the south. The air was heavy and did not cool as rapidly after sunset as happened on most dry-season nights. By morning we had reached the base of the escarpment. Here there were marshy areas with thick sweet grass and even some pools of water, and Ndlovu let the herd spread out and feed and drink all through the day.

In the evening clouds spilled over the edge of the escarpment together with a gentle rain that fell as softly as if we were being brushed by the wings of a moth. Ndlovu had been waiting for this rain. She immediately gave a loud "Let's go" rumble, calling the herd together, and headed towards the Badlands along the base of the escarpment. She had to move far enough away from the escarpment to avoid the large piles of boulders and smaller rocks which had fallen from the face of the kranse. Often these huge blocks of basalt were bigger than Nkosi. At first there was a faint path and in single file we kept up a walking pace as fast as the small calves could manage. By the time the moon was overhead the drizzle had stopped and the clouds had broken. Soon after this the easy going stopped and deep steep-sided dongas started to cut across our path. Ndlovu led us up along each donga to find its head so that we could continue to follow the base of the krans. We had barely dealt with one donga before we reached the next. In each successive detour up and around the donga the number of rocks and boulders increased. The small rocks were as bad as the large boulders. Still wet from the rain, they were slippery and painful to walk on. Soon more than one of us suffered cuts and twisted feet. A way around each large boulder had to be found. By sunrise we seemed to have made little headway. We could still see Mabutu Mountain to the side away from the escarpment. Our feet were sore and we were very tired. Our only solace was that Ndlovu had found the entrance to a kloof going into the escarpment A short way up it we found pools and sweet grass, and there we stayed all that day. The steep walls of the kloof kept the fierce sun at bay for at least part of the day. Despite this day's rest, no one was ready to resume our march when the sun set over the now distant Shonalanga Mountains. But Ndlovu would not wait. She led us out of the kloof and up and around the first donga of the night. One could feel the spirit of the herd weakening. When we had started out the night before many of the young elephants played games around the large boulders. Now no one was lifting their head. Each of us looked only at the ground and thought only of where to take the next painful step. By the time the moon had risen clear of the escarpment, there seemed to be no way that the calves and some of the older elephants could continue. Following in single file one saw rocks and stones stained with blood. Low moans, rising at times to cries of pain, were coming from those with injured feet.

    For most of the previous night and all of this one we had seen no sign of a path or an animal. During our day's rest we had heard the calls of Mbile the Dassie coming from the sides of the kloof. Vultures had crossed the strip of sky above us, but none had circled or landed. Now as we went down the slope next to another donga the rocks began to disappear and the spaces between them began to be filled with soft sand. Soon there were no more rocks, only a soft sandy surface. Our heads began to lift and the mood of the herd changed. At the time we did not know it, but we had cleared the last donga and from here the going was much easier. By morning we could no longer see Mabutu Mountain, and the escarpment of the Pumulanga Mountain was sinking and disappearing to our left. Slowly clumps of grass and small thorn bushes reappeared, but we could detect no sign of water.

Soon after sunrise Ndlovu allowed us to rest and find something to eat among the sparse vegetation. She knew well that it would not be long before the soft sand that had been so welcome would become burning hot and torture to walk on. The steep kranse of the escarpment had given way to rolling hills, often capped with sandstone like Mabutu Mountain. In the haze towards the bright rising sun it was difficult to tell how far away these hills were. Ndlovu, however, was firm in signaling us to continue. As the sun rose higher in the sky the low sandstone-topped hills grew clearer. By midday a sparse covering of grass and stunted bushes had appeared. For the first time since leaving Mabutu Mountain we saw some tracks of Mpungu the Jackal and Logwaja the Hare. Near us Gompou the big Kori Bustard rose with difficulty into the air, uttering its hoarse call and landing a short distance ahead of us. Not long after this we saw the deep tracks of Mpofu the Eland. There were no signs of the Amazulu and their animals. The presence of Mpofu and the absence of the Amazulu were both a relief and a puzzle.

Despite these favorable signs we were now in desperate need of water. We had had our last drink before leaving the shelter of the kloof at the end of the previous day. Now we had walked for a whole night and on through a day of burning sun and no relief from the heat. We had walked steadily since our brief early-morning rest among the thin stands of sour grass and small bushes, but by sunset the hills seemed as far away as ever. As the sun sank and the ground quickly cooled, Ndlovu finally brought the herd to a halt. However, little had changed. The grass was perhaps a little thicker, but it was still sour, and though the bushes were a little taller, they were dry and brittle. Adult elephants have a pouch in their throat in which they can store water. They can retrieve this water by putting their trunk down their throat and into the pouch. Those who were wise enough waited until the cool of the evening to do this, but those who had emptied their pouch in the heat of the day now had difficulty swallowing the dry grass and leaves. Umphlope and Unlebe had conserved this water, and they had milk for Amafu and Umfazi. But Nyama and Umvula, the mothers of our youngest calves Ilanga and baby Jabula, had drunk all their water by the time the sun was overhead. By evening Jabula was struggling to get milk from Umvula.

Once again Ndlovu waited until moonrise to give the "Let's go" rumble. Now our single file began to disintegrate. There were wide gaps between those with young calves and the other elephants. Umvula and Jabula in particular were lagging behind. Ndlovu, who was in front of me, stopped and stood aside, making it clear that she wanted me to lead the herd. She waited until Umvula and Jabula had passed her and then took up her position behind them. What I had learnt from Ndlovu immediately began to guide my actions. Since we were not on any path I had to choose the direction in which to lead the herd. Knowing that finding water was the most important task to accomplish, I followed what I had learnt from Ndlovu. Sandstone-capped hills like Mabutu were fractured and cracked. Rain falling on these broken hilltops ran into the crevices and down through the cracks in the sandstone. Here, deep in the mountain, the water accumulated and was not lost to the wind and air. This water created springs at the base of the sandstone: springs that would run even in the driest of dry seasons. Further, Ndlovu sought out dry sandy riverbeds coming down from the sandstone hills. In these sandy riverbeds she had shown us how to detect water that was close enough to the surface to be reached by digging. It was clear that Ndlovu had chosen a route which would lead to the nearest sandstone hill with a good chance for us of finding a streambed that came down that hill. So my course was clear. I kept the distant hills in sight, using both the light of the moon reflecting off the sandstone cliffs and the very low rumbling of the earth to guide me. These were the same earth sounds that Ndlovu had used to find the entrance through the haakdoring to the kloof on Mabutu Mountain.

By morning the veld was rising towards the slopes below the sandstone cap. Acacia thorn trees on these slopes formed patterns which told me the location of the dry and wet areas. Immediately ahead the thorn trees were concentrated in a dark line which twisted and turned up the slope. These trees bordered the course of a dry riverbed. If we were going to find water we would find it in the sandy bed of this dry river. Distances were deceptive and it was difficult to tell how far away we were from the streambed. Because I could not make out individual thorn trees, but saw them only as dense black blocks and lines on the side of the hill, I knew that we would not reach this streambed before the sun had risen high in the sky.

Since early light Umvula and her baby calf Jabula had been lagging far behind. I did not know how long it would take them to catch up if we stopped and waited. Even when they did, we had nothing to offer but an unknown further distance to an uncertain source of water. If we waited, the sun would only climb higher and the ground get hotter. I chose a course between waiting and going on. Calling Mathatau, Inlebe and Khumbula, I made the "Let's go" rumble while signaling the rest of the herd to stay where they were. Mathatau and Inlebe had to make Biza and Umfazi understand that they could not accompany their mothers and had to stay behind. Umplope and Ulambile understood what we needed and herded Biza and Umfazi away from us and into the middle of the group.

Being four adults, we could set a fast pace. Although the other three were all much older than I was, they had accepted Ndlovu's decision to have me lead. I knew that we were taking a huge risk leaving the herd in the hot sun and striking out in the hope of finding water. Yet I had no choice. Soon we could see individual thorn trees flanking a fan of white sand spilling into the veld. Small dry channels were visible in the sand. Water had recently been running in these channels since their outline had not been erased by the wind. Then to our further relief we found a well-trampled path leading straight towards the sand river. Once in the dry riverbed we slowed down, following the way Ndlovu had shown us to find water. We found where a pool of water had stood. Many tracks, as well as dry twigs and leaves blown into the depression, suggested that it had been dry for some time. We could detect no smell of water below the surface of this dry pan. Each of us followed a channel in the bed of the river. As the sand river narrowed and the banks on either side grew, Mathatau rumbled that she had detected water. Following her around a bend in the riverbed, we all came to the same place. Khumbula started digging near a steep bank. I started a hole further into the streambed. Both of us reached out wet sand at the same time. Soon we had four holes all collecting small pools of water. Without any signal from me, the other three filled their pouches with water and started back towards the herd. We each gave loud low rumbles that we had found water and even though the herd was a distant smudge on the veld, they heard us and started towards the sand river. All except Umvula with Jabula and Nyama with Ilanga, and with them Ndlovu, passed us before we were halfway to the small calves. As soon as we reached them we drew water from our pouches and fed it into the mouths of Jabula and Ilanga. Ilanga was able to take most of the water given to her, but Jabula seemed unable to swallow, and most of the precious water spilled out and vanished into the dry soil. Ndlovu pushed Nyama and signaled her to take Ilanga to the water holes. Mabalel,

Nyama's mother, went with them. Mathatau, Umvula's mother, tried desperately to get the remaining drops of water she had into Jabula's mouth. But again Jabula could not swallow, and now she sank to her knees. Ndlovu and Umvula tried to lift Jabula onto her feet with their trunks and tusks. As they lifted her onto her front legs her back legs gave way and she collapsed and rolled onto her side. Despite frantic efforts by her mother and the rest of us, we could not lift Jabula back onto her feet. Her legs were too weak to support even her little body. Ndlovu gently shouldered Umvula away from Jabula's body. Mathatau went to the other side of Umvula and she and Ndlovu stood gently swaying Umvula between them. Umvula now ran her trunk slowly over the still form of Jabula, lingering at her mouth and eyes. Ndlovu and I found small acacia branches from the few trees near us. We brought these branches to cover Jabula. At first Umvula removed the branches but eventually she too gathered some until Jabula was completely covered. Even though Mathatau, Umvula and Ndlovu were desperately thirsty they remained standing very still. Only Umvula faced Jabula's body. Mathatau and Ndlovu seemed to be looking far beyond the horizon. No one moved for a very long time. Then Umvula moaned softly and ran the tip of her trunk over the pile of acacia branches for the last time. She turned slowly and started to walk towards the sandstone mountains. Without a sound Ndlovu, Mathatau and I followed her. In the long walk up the slope to the sand river Umvula never changed her pace. Even as the smell of water reached us her slow strides did not quicken.

By the time we had quenched our thirst the rest of the herd had spread along the banks of the sand river and were feeding on the grasses and acacia leaves. They were sweeter and less dry than those we had found earlier. Ndlovu kept the herd in the sand river for the rest of the day and that night. As dawn approached she led us out of it and around the slopes of the sandstone hill. Sparse bushveld dotted with sandstone-capped hills stretched as far as we could see towards the rising sun. Once we were around the hill the land to the south took on a darker hue with larger hills rising on the horizon. Ndlovu turned towards these hills, and all day we walked towards them. By the end of the day they seemed no nearer, but at least we had seen small herds of zebra, wildebeest and impala. Birds, too, had returned and we could hear the haunting call of the Emerald-spotted Wood Dove. For a while two Bateleur Eagles rose and fell as though linked by an invisible cord in the blue sky overhead.

The tension and fear that we had felt since leaving the Umzimkulu Vlei many days before had diminished but not vanished. The sadness of Jabula's death had spread through the herd. Umvula could not stop the low moans which welled up in her throat, especially as her breasts swelled with milk again. Nyama brought Ilanga to her and after a while she allowed Ilanga to nurse, which seemed to help her a great deal.

The strangeness of the land and our lack of knowledge of the place we were in bothered Ndlovu and the herd. It was vital to find more reliable water sources and better food, but Ndlovu was uncertain just where the Amazulu might be. However, since our need for water and food was greater than our fear of the Amazulu, Ndlovu chose over the next few days to move further and further into the wetter hills to the south.

As the days passed the grasses thickened and we found more and more food trees. Water remained scarce, but luckily we were able to find at least some each day, so we never had to go for a whole day without any. Then finally we came upon a spring feeding a small stream. Fig trees were growing along the banks of the stream, the first we had seen since leaving the Nyathi Plains. But our joy at finding permanent water and better food was short-lived. Ndlovu came across clear signs of Zulu herds, then old fields and places where the Zulu had lived. Once again fear rippled through the herd. We could go neither forward nor back to the Nyathi Plains.

Ndlovu kept us within a day's walk of the spring and stream. Everyone expected to hear or smell the Amazulu. But none came. It was not until many moons later that we discovered why these homes and fields of the Amazulu had been deserted.

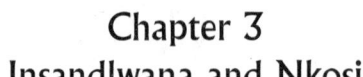

Chapter 3
Insandlwana and Nkosi

We did not know of the coming of the Bearded Ones to the Nyathi Plains until Ndlovu, Khumbula and I saw from Mabutu Mountain their moving white houses and their many animals following the Nyathi River. Nor did we know that more Bearded Ones were coming north to meet those descending the Shonalanga Mountains. These Bearded Ones began grazing their large herds across the Nyathi River, on land where we knew the Amazulu were increasingly bringing their own herds. The Amazulu and the Bearded Ones each began claiming the Nyathi Plains for themselves. It made no difference to them that the Nyathi Plains were home to many animals and had been our dry-season range for as long as anyone could remember. Humans do not settle their differences by loud calls as we and Ngonyama the Lion do. Instead they gather together in large numbers and attack, wound and kill each other.

The lands which we found deserted beyond the Gramadoelas were empty because, some time before, the chief of the Amazulu had called all his people together to resist the Bearded Ones. At a dark mountain which the Amazulu called Insandlwana, a mountain shaped liked the stomach of a beast, the Amazulu met the Bearded Ones. The Amazulu knew this mountain and the hills and gullies around it. Even though they did not have the power that had killed Mvubu the Hippo in the Umzimkulu Vlei and Mfene the Baboon on the cliffs of Mabutu Mountain, they killed very many of the Bearded Ones, and the rest they chased across the Nyathi River.

The Bearded Ones, licking their wounds in shame and thirsting for revenge, gathered together a huge number of men. In a great horde stretching far up the Nyathi River, the Bearded Ones crossed the river where the Ingagane joins the Nyathi. They continued past the Umzimkulu Vlei and made a great camp around the Amanzintoti Vlei. There they put up many white shells like those we had first seen moving down-river. From here the Bearded Ones sent many men mounted on horses to hunt and kill all the animals they could find. They hunted as far as the forests along the Ingagane River below the Hidden Valley and Waterfall.

Dakiwe had joined Nkosi nine dry seasons after he had left our herd. Older bull elephants often have younger bulls with them. The younger bull serves as a look-out and guard for the older one and in return for this service the older male teaches his young companion the lessons of survival. Amadala and Nsimbi were good friends and they were often seen together. Amadala was now fifty-one years old, Nkosi forty-five and Nsimbi thirty-three. All three had deep knowledge of the ways of the Amazulu, and each had been wounded by Zulu assegais. They and Dakiwe had come down the Secret Path next to the Waterfall and the mouth of the Hidden Valley just before Ndlovu led us down to the plains for this dry season. Amadala and Nsimbi were now somewhere on the Nyathi Plains. All four bulls must have seen or been close to the Bearded Ones as they came onto the Nyathi Plains. Nkosi and Dakiwe had immediately turned back to the Ingagane River to seek shelter in the thick bush and forest which stretched right up to the Hidden Valley Waterfall. While these forests offered food, water and shelter, they were not large, and hunters soon found the spoor of Nkosi. We did not yet know that the Bearded Ones valued our tusks above almost anything else. These hunters could see from Nkosi's spoor that he was a very large bull. They suspected that he carried the largest tusks of all the elephants on the plains.

At first only one or two hunters from the camp around the Amanzintoti Vlei tried to find Nkosi. They were not very skilful and Nkosi and Dakiwe easily detected their strong smell and heard their noisy movement through the bush. Nkosi would use the Ingagane River and rocky places to hide his spoor. He and Dakiwe would find stands of Tamboti grass and dense acacia thickets in which to shelter. The dry Tamboti grass was the same color as their skin and Nkosi's massive body would vanish in the deep shadows of the acacias. He and

Nkosi

Dakiwe would stand so still and silent that the Bearded Ones would pass close by them without seeing them.

Nkosi and Dakiwe quickly learnt the ways of the Bearded Ones. They had the strong sour smell of rotting Marula fruit. Their passage through the bush was often as noisy as that of uBejane the Rhinoceros. They chattered like Nkawu the Vervet Monkey when they became excited. Every so often sharp cracks as from lightning broke the silence of the bush. Nkosi and Dakiwe found blood spoors left by Nyathi the Buffalo and Phiva the Waterbuck, and along the edges of the Umzimkulu Vlei they also came upon mutilated carcasses of Mvubu the Hippo like those we had discovered. Nkosi and Dakiwe could no longer feed or even move during the day. They climbed higher up in the bush around Aasvoëlkrans so that they could look out over the plains during the day. At night they would work their way silently down to the Ingagane River to feed along its banks. Before dawn they would return to the slopes below Aasvoëlkrans.

As the moon grew in the clear skies of the dry season, the night became almost as bright as the day. Now moving at night was almost as dangerous as in the daytime. Nkosi knew that he and Dakiwe had to get away from these hunters. Nkosi also knew that they had only one real option. They could not go back to the Nyathi Plains, which were swarming with Bearded Ones like angry bees. Moving in either direction along the base of the escarpment would be dangerous and would not lead them to safety. The only choice was to risk their lives by climbing back up the now icy Secret Path next to the Waterfall. Not only would they risk injury or death on the path but they could not be sure that they would get through the Hidden Entrance and across the river into the Hidden Valley. Once in the Hidden Valley, they had the choice of either staying there or trying to get onto the escarpment through the narrow passage leading from the Hidden Valley. Even if they could make their way safely up that route, their difficulties would not be over. The escarpment might be covered in snow, difficult to negotiate and devoid of food. If they made it up onto the escarpment their best hope would be to reach the Thlabatini Forest and try to survive the winter in it.

One morning the decision was made for Nkosi and Dakiwe. On the plain below there appeared a party of Bearded Ones who had brought Amazulu trackers and their dogs along with them. Faintly but clearly through the still air came the yelping and barking of the dogs, who knew that a hunt was about to start. The hunters had already found Nkosi's tracks the previous evening, and now they were preparing to follow these tracks, which would lead them right to where Nkosi and Dakiwe were at that moment standing in the bush below Aasvoëlkrans. Without hesitation Nkosi swung around and set off towards the Waterfall Pool and the bottom of the Secret Path.

He kept in the bush along the base of Aasvoëlkrans. The sun rising over the Pumulanga Mountains flooded its light across the Nyathi Plains. The bush at the foot of Aasvoëlkrans was in full sunlight. The rays of the sun were still low and threw long dense shadows across the faint path that the elephants were following. As they went from dark to light the alternating pattern of light and shadow disguised their movement. The hunters had not seen Nkosi and Dakiwe leaving their dense patch of bush, and the Bearded Ones and their Zulu trackers were not hurrying to get started. Only the dogs with increasing excitement were straining at the rawhide riems with which they were tied to the thorn trees. The hunters clearly thought that they had Nkosi trapped on the slopes of Aasvoëlkrans, for to them there seemed no way of escape. If Nkosi and Dakiwe were to come down the slope they would be confined to one or two tracks leading between the boulders that had crashed down from Aasvoëlkrans. If they tried to move either to the left or right along Aasvoëlkrans they would be in full sunlight and in thin bush. The hunters did not believe that Nkosi would leave his thick patch of bush before they found him.

As Nkosi and Dakiwe pushed on, the yelping of the dogs which had signaled the start of the hunt slowly faded. The hunters were climbing straight up the slope towards the hiding place that Nkosi and Dakiwe had just left. They had not seen that the two elephants were moving away quickly towards the Waterfall. Nkosi and Dakiwe reached the dense bush of the Ingagane below the Waterfall before the shadows had left the kloof of the Waterfall. They could hear the faint rumble of the water falling. The sound of the falls smothered the yelping of the dogs. Nkosi and Dakiwe had been moving at a very fast pace across the sloping rough ground. Despite being careful where they placed their feet, they had dislodged a number of rocks that had crashed down the slope, knocking more stones loose and starting minor avalanches. They could not tell whether the hunters or their dogs had heard these noises and turned in their direction. They could only hope that their pursuers had not heard and were continuing up the slope. They knew that in the end the hunters would find their hiding place and locate their tracks that led towards the waterfall. Because the secret path along the steep side of the krans headed for quite a long way back in the direction from which they had just come, they needed all the head start they could get. Nkosi knew that climbing up the Hidden Path would be a slow process. If they were not high enough above the river before the hunters arrived, they would be seen and, like Mfene the Baboon on Mabutu Mountain, they would be killed from down below.

The roar of the waterfall meant that so far the winter on the escarpment had not been severe, for the river was not frozen. If there was no ice on the path the climb would be much less dangerous. Nkosi and Dakiwe reached the start of the Secret Path next to the Waterfall Pool without knowing how far or close behind them the hunters were. They began the slow climb up the side of the waterfall krans back in the direction from which they had just come. Soon they needed to focus all their attention on the task of keeping their footing on the path. Although there was no ice, the rocks and red clay of the path were wet and slippery. In places there was barely enough room between the edge of the path and the walls of the kloof for Nkosi's large body to squeeze by. Yet climbing up the path was easier than coming down. Dakiwe was having less difficulty than Nkosi and easily kept up with him. They had just reached the place where the path turned back on itself and started its climb to the top of the krans when they heard the barking and yelping of the dogs above the noise of the waterfall. Then Dakiwe caught a brief glimpse of the hunters in the bushes below. He and Nkosi had been close to hunters along the Ingagane River and he felt a ripple of fear at the thought of being trapped on this path. The hunters were no longer keeping silent and their shouts rose up the krans. Nkosi and Dakiwe could not leave the path: they could only go forward and upward. They could hear the Bearded Ones running with their dogs toward the start of the path. The steepness of the krans for the moment shielded Nkosi and Dakiwe from the hunters climbing below them, but this would last only until these pursuers reached the switchback in the path. At that point they would appear behind Dakiwe. Nkosi was climbing steadily and deliberately, and Dakiwe was right under his hind legs, wanting to go faster. As they approached the top, icicles hanging from the ferns growing in the rock-face broke into splintering pieces. Then Dakiwe heard the jingling of the collars around the necks of the hunting dogs. On the narrow path he could neither look behind him nor turn around. He felt teeth rasping at his heels and kicked out hard. There was a yelp and crashing of bushes as his hind foot caught a dog squarely in its chest and sent it flying over the edge of the path. A second dog yelped as its lower jaw was broken by another kick from Dakiwe. Then came two crashes in quick succession that echoed across the kloof, rising above the noise of the waterfall. Dakiwe felt no pain as his hind legs gave way beneath him. He slid backwards and sideways and then over the edge of the path, crashing down through the trees that clung to the side of the krans. It was as if all other sound, including even the booming of the waterfall, suddenly ceased in a moment of stunned silence. Then the roar of the waterfall and the frenzied barking of the hunting dogs rose again. Nkosi knew Dakiwe was gone, and he could feel the dogs snapping and biting at his heels and legs. He had no time to kick or defend himself as he was rounding a large boulder which almost cut the path off. Dirt flew over his head and stones and debris fell on his back as he heard a loud crash and something whined like a hornet past his shoulder. In the next moment he had rounded the boulder. He was nearly at the top and behind the protruding boulder the path widened. Now he could turn and face his tormentors. In fury he swept two of the remaining three dogs off the path and into the abyss. The last dog turned and fled down the path. Nkosi drove his tusks behind and underneath the protruding boulder and with his powerful neck and shoulders lifted it from the face of the krans. As the boulder crashed over the edge, soil and rocks gave way and a section of the path collapsed into the waterfall pool far below. Swinging around again, Nkosi heaved himself to the top of the path and waded into the water channel that led into the narrow cleft separating the krans from the columns of basalt standing above the lip of the waterfall. The river was full and the water tore at his legs as he emerged from the cleft and began to cross the river. For a moment it seemed as if he would lose his footing and be swept over the edge of the waterfall. He stood still, feeling with his feet for a secure purchase. The water boiled and foamed up to his chest and under his hindquarters. Again he slipped, and his great frame shuddered like a tree in a flood. Then, one step at a time, he slowly came out of the river and entered the Hidden Valley.

The hunters had no choice but to turn back down the Secret Path. Where the boulder dislodged by Nkosi had been, the path had disappeared, leaving only a yawning gap and a sheer cliff-face. The hunters would not be able to follow him into the Hidden Valley either now or at any time until the snow on the escarpment melted. He was safe in the Hidden Valley until the arrival of a new wet season.

Nkosi did not know where Amadala and Nsimbi or Mfanyaan and Nkosana were. He feared that Amadala and Nsimbi were trapped on the Nyathi Plain, their escape route blocked by the Bearded Ones around the Amanzintoti Vlei and the broken pathway up the Waterfall Krans into the Hidden Valley. Mfanyaan and Nkosana had often been seen together after Dakiwe had joined with Nkosi. Nkosi knew that in some dry seasons, elephants that had crossed through the Pass to the Unknown had not returned

Umadala

to the Nyathi Plains. Mfanyaan and Nkosana might have stayed beyond Ndumeni, the Place of Thunder.

Nkosi felt an emptiness deep inside his huge body. He knew that whether he stayed in the Hidden Valley or tried to shelter in the Thlabatini Forest, it was going to be a hard winter. Now it would be a very lonely one as well. He did not try to stop the deep moans that welled up from his chest. Perhaps Dakiwe could hear him; no one else could, he thought. But in this Nkosi was wrong. He soon found that there were many animals in the Hidden Valley. He saw a tribe of baboons silently slinking among the rocky crags of the valley, with never a booming warning call to be heard from Mfene. The shadows of Nyala and Phiva the Waterbuck, who before had seldom been seen in the Hidden Valley, vanished into the bush. All that Nkosi found were their spoor in a few of the sandy places along the river. Like him these animals were the remnants of the many that had been on the Nyathi Plains before the coming of the Bearded Ones. Now they were full of fear. Nkosi wondered if any of them would ever run free again. Although he had mostly roamed alone across the plains and on the escarpment beyond the Pass to the Unknown, he had always returned to Ndlovu's herd. In recent seasons he had come to rely on the near presence of Dakiwe. He stood with his head bowed and his heavy trunk resting on the cold rock of the Hidden Valley.

If Nkosi was going to get out of the valley and into the Thlabatini Forest he would have to act quickly. Each day that passed increased the risk that the river would rise further, closing the pass for the rest of the winter. Even with the unusual numbers of animals in the Hidden Valley, there was more than enough food to last through the winter. In fact, there was probably more food available in the valley than in the Thlabatini Forest. But the valley was cold. Its steep sides allowed the sun to reach its floor for only a short time before and after midday. Cold air from the escarpment above spilled over and down the kloofs to fill the valley with a deep chill during the night and early hours of the morning. The short time each midday when sunshine reached the floor of the valley was not enough to warm this deep pool of cold night air. But these things, though important, were not what concerned Nkosi the most. What concerned him the most was that the feeling of being in a trap was already growing upon him. He had seen enough of the Bearded Ones to know that their burning obsession with the tusks of his kind would not let them rest until they had found a way into the Hidden Valley. If they did succeed there would be no escape for Nkosi. He would rather take his chances in the Thlabatini Forest.

Nkosi set out on the path that led out of the Hidden Valley as soon as the mist hanging in the cold air over the river lifted. By midday the rays of the sun were dancing on the water of the stream.

The valley was narrowing as its walls closed in on each other. They pressed in ever more closely, until the stream and the path became one, and Nkosi began wading knee-deep against the current. Soon the water was foaming and pressing against his chest. Forward progress was slow and a number of times Nkosi lost his footing, sliding backwards and coming close to being swept downstream. Even his great strength would not last long against this onslaught of rushing water. A slight bend in the river, where the walls of the valley swung in unison to vanish into the escarpment, sent the water rushing against the western wall. Over eons of time, grain by grain, the rock wall had been cut away here, and the water rushed and boiled through the hollowed-out channel. Countering this accelerating water, a back-eddy formed a whirlpool which swept water upstream against the opposite wall. Nkosi struggled against the suction of the whirlpool that would spin him into the water rushing through the undercut rock. In some previous flood the remains of an ironwood tree had become wedged in the rocks away from the whirlpool. Nkosi reached out with his trunk and was able to grasp a limb of the ironwood tree. Using the great strength of his trunk, he freed himself from the grip of the whirlpool and squeezed past the wedged tree to emerge onto the escarpment.

He stood there for a long time with the tip of his trunk curled back and resting on the ground. It was a good while before he realized that the ground under his trunk was covered in snow. Snowfields stretched across the escarpment and the white mass of Thaba Insimbi was catching the slanting rays of the setting sun. He could see the dense trees of the Thlabatini Forest not far above him. The forest was black even though snow clung to the trees. A cold wind which he had not felt in the valley was strengthening. Exhausted by his struggle against the rushing river, Nkosi started slowly towards the forest. He entered it as the last light of the short winter day faded. It was already dark in the forest, and the swaying tops of the trees reduced the wind to calm down at ground level. Nkosi pushed deeper into the forest until he found the heavy limbs of a White Stinkwood tree drooping close to the ground. A thick bed of hairy leaves and velvety small twigs covered the ground under the tree. Nkosi rested his heavy trunk on a low branch and slept for the first time since leaving the slopes of Aasvoëlkrans.

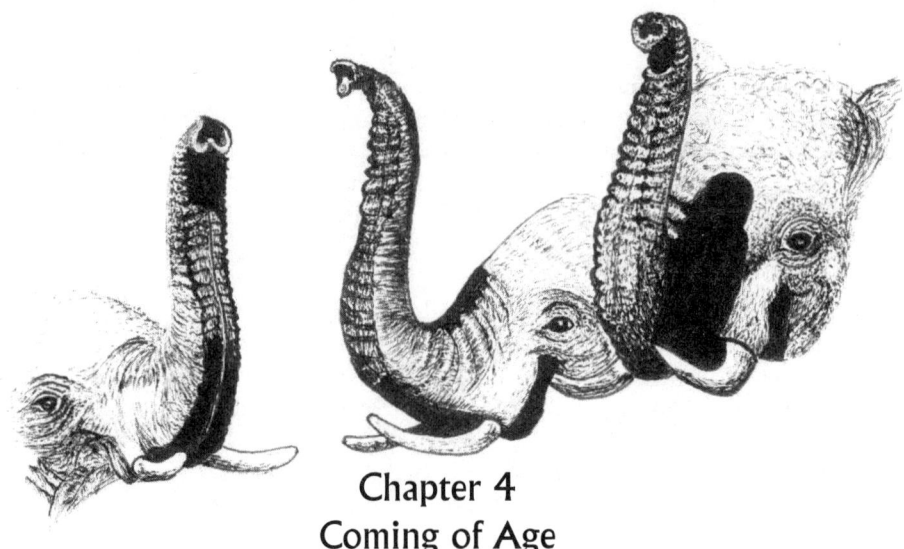

Chapter 4
Coming of Age

Now that we were in the new territory that Ndlovu had brought us to, she would lead the herd short distances into the valleys of the sandstone-capped hills to the east and north. She always brought us back to the spring and the stream, never staying away from them for more than a few days. She was allowing a picture of the bush and hills and sounds and smells of this new place to take shape in our heads. But this increasing knowledge of our surroundings did not comfort me. Instead a void grew within me. It was not only the loss of our dry-season home and the death of little Jabula, but the realization of the enormity of what had happened to us. The knowledge which had been formed in our beings over generations had become like the bones of Idube the Zebra when these are scattered across the plains by Mpisi the Hyena. Just like the bones, our precious knowledge had taken years to form; now, just like the bones, it was broken up, cast to the wind, lost, finished, meaningless. In the sun-bleached dry bones, no traces were left of the brightness of Idube's eyes or the unique pattern of black and white stripes that had once bound mother and young one together. Much more was lost than the flesh that had once covered these bones on the veld. Like a dead creature our entire being had been dismembered. It felt as though the coils of Makulu the Python were tightening around my chest and I could not breathe.

I saw that all the stories which Ndlovu had told me over the years, and all her teaching of things like what to eat, where to find it, how to search for water, and how to lift water in my trunk from a deep hole in the sand, were not just separate pieces of knowledge. When all the parts were assembled they formed a whole. With this realization I was crossing over, without knowing it, from calfhood to adulthood. I could now see that we did not view the world around us simply through our eyes and ears, the sounds we could make, the touch of our trunk or the faint smells we could detect. As a very young calf I could see, but I did not know what I saw; I could hear, but I did not know what I heard; I could smell, but I did not know what the smell meant. Now, when Ingwe the Leopard moved silently through the Tamboti grass, it was not the leopard that we saw but the flight of a weaverbird disturbed in her nest. It was not the leopard that we smelt but the sour scent of fear from the baboon who knew that he was the prey. Nor was it the sound of the leopard moving through the grass that we heard, but the warning call of the Kwêvoël. By themselves each of these happenings meant little. Taken all together, they meant life and death to Mfene the Baboon and to us.

Like an unhatched tadpole within the egg of Ixoxo the Frog, I was surrounded by a transparent shell of sounds, smells and images. The touch of my trunk or the increasing number of sounds which I could make were part of the envelope. Within the sphere surrounding us, Ndlovu could hear, smell, see and feel what we could not. Each of her senses drew into her being the happenings around her. Since far back in the mists of time, the ability to intercept every sign carried in the air and on the earth had been passed from mother to daughter. Was it really possible that Ndlovu could hear everything from the faintest rustle of Nyoga the Spitting Cobra sliding through the grass to the roar of Ngonyama the Lion? Or smell everything from the slightest trace of smoke from a fire beyond Mabutu Mountain to the stench of Mpisi the Hyena feeding on a rotten carcass? Or feel everything from the lightest tread of Ingwe the Leopard to the beat of the hooves of a thousand buffalo stampeding on the Nyathi Plains? Or see the shadow of a chameleon amongst the colored leaves of a Mopani tree as well as the bulk of Nkosi coming out of the shadows into the bright light of the sun? Yes, Ndlovu could do all of these things and more. She chose, from all that she heard, saw, smelt and felt, only those signs which formed a whole picture. Like Mfene the Baboon she not only found the seeds of the Marula tree in the sand but knew the shape of the pod that contained those seeds. The shapes that formed continually in Ndlovu's head guided her every action. At first these actions led me to believe that my mother had a sense which I did not possess. Often in the past I had been puzzled by some course of action that she had decided upon. She might choose, for example, to leave the last waterhole remaining at the end of a terrible dry season, in order to cross a plain devoid of water. Now I knew that this was because she had detected and interpreted what we had not: the faint rumblings made by distant clouds. She knew that only clouds that were raining produced such sounds. She also knew that this meant water and fresh food.

Now it was dawning on me why Ndlovu had insisted on showing me, again and again, so many things that had seemed unimportant at the time. Slowly I was becoming aware of all that was coming to me from my surroundings: what I should pay attention to and what I should let pass, and how in the end all that I retained must be drawn together to form a coherent whole. I had to develop the same awareness of my surroundings that Ndlovu had, and the same ability to bring together all that I could sense. This was what she could do and I still could not. It was not a sixth sense that Ndlovu possessed but a total comprehension of the world which surrounded us.

The deep anxiety that had made its way into my being was because I was no longer in the center of a world I knew. My ability to survive depended upon the knowledge of my surroundings and all that was impinging upon me from these surroundings. This knowledge had been lost when we left the Nyathi Plains. I no longer recognized what I saw, smelt and heard. I no longer knew where the paths were, or where they might lead. Returning again and again to the spring, Ndlovu was slowly fixing in us the patterns of our new surroundings. She was creating the time needed to recognize new sounds and smells and know what they meant. We could not know what warning might travel ahead of the returning Amazulu. Would it be the blowing of the wind and a faint smell of smoke, the flight of Amajuba the Dove or Imbabala the Bushbuck, or some combination of an unknown group of signals? On the Nyathi Plain we had known such things for many generations. Now we had to depend upon the knowledge stored in Ndlovu's being and used in this new environment to regain our balance.

Ndlovu was spending more time in the sandstone hills to the north of the spring. We heard the calls of Ivukutu the Rock Pigeon being repeated over and over again. Naka the Reedbuck whistled from the slopes below the sandstone cliffs, and Mbili the Dassie called from the tumbled piles of fallen rocks. Yet a basic silence reigned in the absence of the calls of other elephants. In the Nyathi Plains we could almost always hear the low rumbles of elephants we knew coming from across the river or from deep in the vleis. We knew many of the callers and recognized the calls of Nkosi and the other bulls of our family. Here, where we now foraged, all was still. Yet in this stillness the low rumbles of the earth reflected off the slopes of the hills and cliffs, creating a picture of our new surroundings. The dry season was ending and each afternoon we saw dark clouds building up over the distant escarpment of the Pumulanga

Mountains. When the first rains of the wet season arrived, Ndlovu set off to lead us deeper into the hills, leaving the spring behind us. She did not seem to be listening to the changing weather as carefully as she used to do before we left the Nyathi Plain. Instead she remained in the folds of hills which now seemed to be our home for this wet season.

Mfanyaan and Nkosana had, as Nkosi expected, gone beyond the Pass to the Unknown and not returned until well into the dry season. They had not returned to the Hidden Valley. Instead they headed for the kloof that we had taken to the Balele Highlands. Although the cold of winter had settled on the escarpment, the river into the kloof was not frozen. Mfanyaan and Nkosana easily descended into the kloof and were emerging from the narrow upper part when both suddenly stopped in their tracks. They stood still, with ears spread and trunks testing the air above their heads. Neither of them could tell what had stopped them so suddenly. With the steep rocky sides of the kranse still pressing in on either side of them, there was no shelter and no place to hide. The rushing stream masked all other sounds and there was no wind to carry scents. Mfanyaan stood close to the wall of the krans. He moved slightly forward so that Nkosana could stop behind him. Just ahead of where he now stood, a large overhanging bush in the wall of the krans cast a dappled shadow across the path. He and Nkosana moved silently into the shadow, their wrinkled grey skin blending with the lichen-covered walls of the krans. Only patches of light falling on Mfanyaan's massive tusks gave any hint of his presence. Mfanyaan was now in his fifty-second dry season. He had survived clashes with the Amazulu, and had been the first to come face to face with a hunting party of the Bearded Ones, even before our herd had seen them for the first time from Mabutu Mountain. He had outwitted this hunting party in the deep bush along the Nyathi River by deliberately stampeding a herd of buffalo into the Bearded Ones. The next morning vultures were circling over the bend in the river where he had stampeded the Nyathi. He had heard the crashes of the Bearded Ones' weapons and their shouts and screams, but he did not know if any of them had been injured or killed. He knew from tracks of blood which he found later that day that buffalo had been wounded. He did not know how the Bearded Ones killed their prey. He only knew that the crashing sounds they made brought injury and death.

Now as he and Nkosana stood with their ears held still and flat against the sides of their heads and their trunks curled up under their mouths, a flight of rock pigeons burst from the kloof wall ahead of them. Mfanyaan realized that it was such a flight that had alerted him and Nkosana in the first place. He could see the forms of two Bearded Ones leading their horses up the kloof, one behind the other.

Mfanyaan could not tell how many others there might be. These two were careless of the noise they were making and were unconcerned about their surroundings. The leading Bearded One walked steadily up the kloof, his eyes fixed on the path in front of him. Mfanyaan did not even think of flight. He knew what he was going to do. The leading Bearded One had come within three body-lengths of Mfanyaan when his horse jerked backwards, letting out a high-pitched scream like that of Idube the Zebra. A deafening roar of anger rose in Mfanyaan's throat as he curled his trunk below his throat and charged. The first Bearded One's horse had knocked down his companion in his wild flight down the kloof. As the first Bearded One struggled to unsling his weapon from his shoulder Mfanyaan's left tusk went under his arm and his curled-up trunk hit him squarely in the chest. Like Insimba the Genet playing with a fieldmouse, Mfanyaan caught the Bearded One by the leg and threw him in a high flailing arc onto the rocks of the stream. The form of the second Bearded One lay still on the path where the fleeing horse had knocked him down. Mfanyaan stretched his trunk out towards the form but did not touch it. With a shake of his great head that raised a cloud of dust, Mfanyaan turned to face Nkosana behind him. He nudged Nkosana aside and scraping past him with his rough hide, Mfanyaan started back up the kloof.

    At the head of the kloof Mfanyaan and Nkosana faced a choice: they could head for the Thlabatini Forest, or they could turn into the Pumulangas. Mfanyaan had been down the Pumulangas, remaining on the escarpment. He knew that eventually the towering kranse of the Pumulangas sank into rolling sandstone-capped hills bordering the land of the Amazulu. Mfanyaan also knew that when the horses of the two dead men returned to their camp around Amanzintoti, many of the Bearded Ones would come to hunt Nkosana and himself down. Although the Thlabatini Forest would give the two elephants some shelter, they would be trapped on the escarpment and sooner or later the Bearded Ones would find them. The Pumulanga Mountains were rugged, with many steep-sided valleys and steep kranse, but Mfanyaan knew a path through them. He and Nkosana needed only to turn at the head of the kloof towards the rising sun. Yet Mfanyaan did not do this. Instead he headed straight towards the Thlabatini Forest. He kept this course, taking little care to hide his tracks, until he had crossed the stream leading into Mutwa the Magician's kloof. Then he headed for the nearest tongue of trees stretching out from the Thlabatini Forest. Just before he reached these trees Mfanyaan swung abruptly away over stony ground. He and Nkosana then walked parallel to their course of the early evening, back towards the Pumulanga Mountains. It was clear to Nkosana what Mfanyaan was doing. But neither knew that by laying this false trail they were leading the Bearded Ones to Nkosi's hideout.

When dawn broke over the Pumulanga Mountains, Mfanyaan and Nkosana had reached a point north of where they had started the previous evening. Both knew that with this same dawn the Bearded Ones would be starting up the kloof to hunt them down. Mfanyaan had followed this route across the escarpment of the Pumulangas only once before. His memory was hazy but as he concentrated on the images being formed in his head by the low rumbles coming from the earth's crust, he could recognize the rounded shape of a high mountain. The path he had traveled before had been flooded at dawn by the light of the rising sun. He knew that the path was on the side of the rising sun and that he must pass this mountain on that side.

They found the path late in the afternoon as the shadow of the mountain crept across it. Not knowing whether their plan to deceive the Bearded Ones had worked, they did not stop. They had been walking steadily since the previous sunset, stopping only to drink from the streams they crossed. Except for some mouthfuls of grass gathered at these streams they had eaten nothing. The path was faint and difficult to follow in the darkness before moonrise. Once it was above the surrounding hills, the moon cast enough light for them to see the path. As dawn broke the mountains were receding and before them were the rolling sandstone-capped hills of the land of the Amazulu.

Their fear of the Zulus was less than their fear of the Bearded Ones. They had seen the Bearded Ones and the Amazulu clash on the Nyathi Plains. They did not know that the Amazulu had inflicted great wounds on the Bearded Ones, who were now bent on revenge. As the shadows shortened and the sun climbed higher, the valleys below them broadened and they could see rivers bordered by bush. There was no sign of the Amazulu. No smoke from their fires rose in the still morning air. There was no lowing of cattle or whistling of herders. An unusual silence filled the valleys. Mfanyaan and Nkosana continued downhill towards water. Once they had reached one of the silent valleys they stopped to quench their thirst and to feed. By evening they had recovered and were standing quietly in a clearing along the river, which was much like the Nyathi River of their dry-season range. Then, at the same moment, Mfanyaan and Nkosana heard a sound, and this time there was no doubt about its source. It was the voice of Ndlovu calling up the valley in the stillness of the evening. Mfanyaan and Nkosana answered together. There was a pause before her strong call of recognition sounded up the valley. Despite the dull feeling of fatigue in their legs Mfanyaan and Nkosana broke into a run. Ndlovu and the herd were further down in the valley. It was dark before the pair finally found them. Then there was a great commotion of trumpeting, rumbling and squealing. Each member of our herd touched the streaming temporal glands of Mfanyaan and Nkosana. Trunks sought out mouths and intertwined. Tusks clicked and thudded and rough bodies rasped together raising clouds of dust. There was a great shaking of heads and a loud clapping of ears. The young elephants in the herd did not fully understand the reason for celebration and raced around with their tails curled over their backs, trumpeting shrilly and charging bushes. Gradually the excitement subsided into gentler rumblings. Mfanyaan still leaned against Ndlovu's side and Nkosana twined and untwined his trunk with mine. For the moment we had regained our world and were content.

Chapter 5
The Return of the Amazulu

Ndlovu accepted Nkosana even though he had left the herd soon after Dakiwe many seasons before. Mfanyaan stayed aloof from the herd, often keeping to himself. Yet he was never out of hearing of the low rumbles that rippled almost continuously through the herd. He would respond to Ndlovu's assembly call as she gathered us near sunset to go to water. We would all be aware of his steady and measured approach, each of us giving way as he reached the water. One day soon after Mfanyaan and Nkosana joined us, I saw Bomvu run towards Mfanyaan, then sit down on his haunches with his back feet thrown out behind him and lower his trunk to Mfanyaan. This was unexpected since Bomvu was one of the most rambunctious of all the young males. His mother Mathatau often had to curb him as he mock-charged everything from the other young elephants to bushes. He would squeal and trumpet, throwing dirt and twigs in all directions. He would charge Mpungu the Jackal if that scavenger came near the water hole, and he would even run at innocent egrets and guineafowl.

Ndlovu stayed in the sandstone hills all of the remainder of the wet season and through the next dry season. Rain-clouds had just begun forming in the late afternoons over the Pumulanga Mountains, heralding the coming of another wet season, when one evening we heard on the still air the lowing of cattle. This meant that the Amazulu had returned, and that night Ndlovu moved us further into the sandstone hills. We did not know how many of the Amazulu had returned but it became clear over the next few days that they had come back to their old homesteads which we had seen near the spring. The valleys between the sandstone hills where Ndlovu had taken us were narrow and steep-sided. There might be enough food to last this wet season, but there was not enough to carry us through the next dry season. Only Mfanyaan and Nkosana knew the path to the north. Neither of them was used to leading the herd. It was a new and strange situation for Ndlovu and the rest of us.

The urgency to leave was heightened over the next few days. On each day Amazulu hunting parties were seen in the valleys and on the slopes of the hills. They were seeking out and killing everything they could find. We did not know that these Zulus who had returned to their kraals had been defeated by the Bearded Ones. Now they were impoverished and starving. Without crops, and with only a few animals that were nothing but skin and bone, they were living off what they could find on the veld and in the valleys. At this early stage of the wet season there was no fruit or berries. Along the moist banks of the streams in the valleys lush grass had sprouted. There were also roots and bulbs of plants that we pulled out or dug up with our feet. The Zulus were gathering these same plants. Not only were we using the same food, but to the famished Zulus we were also the meat that they hungered after. If they could kill any one of us they would have food for many days.

Ndlovu led us to a valley running into the Pumulanga Mountains. Its entrance was narrow and strewn with boulders. We had difficulty squeezing between massive sandstone blocks which had tumbled into the valley from the steep rim above. Ndlovu may have hoped that the Zulus would lose our spoor and fail to see that we had turned northwards towards the Pumulangas. Mfanyaan just managed to get his massive body through the narrowest passages. He seemed to know this valley and stayed with the herd all that day. Everyone in the herd was nervous, feeding with little interest, often standing in disarray with a front foot swaying as though they were uncertain of where to stand and whether they should take a step or not. The sounds from the herd were muted. Everyone seemed to be waiting for a signal to move. Mfanyaan stayed close to Ndlovu most of the day. Even though she was large, he towered over her. While Ndlovu gave no sign that she was intimidated by Mfanyaan, she was much quieter than usual. She did not feed much and stood for long periods facing back to the entrance to the narrow valley.

The place was in deep shadow when Ndlovu rumbled for us to leave. With Mfanyaan she set off up the valley. Already narrow, the sandstone cliffs of the kloof quickly closed in on us. Over countless wet seasons the stream had scoured and undercut the cliffs on either side. Only a narrow strip of sky was visible above our heads. Soon the sandy floor of the kloof turned to stone. Great holes rather like those we had dug in search of water were strung along the sandstone channel like figs on a branch. Stretched out in single file, we carefully worked our way around these potholes. At last a steep ledge of sandstone lying across the kloof floor marked the top of the sandstone cliff. Above the sandstone ledge the valley ended with heavy bush spilling down the sides to enclose the stream. We had just cleared the kloof when shrill trumpetings of fear echoed up the kloof. We knew that these screams came from Inlebe and her two calves, Isopho and Umfazi. Earlier Umfazi had slipped into a pothole. Inlebe and Mabalel had quickly helped her out. Umfazi was not hurt, only frightened, but Inlebe had to spend a little time calming her down. By this time the rest of the herd had crested the sandstone ridge.

What had happened was that as Inlebe and her two calves crossed the ledge, Amazulu hunters suddenly burst from the bush on either side of our track and, roaring their warrior calls, dragged a fence made of vines and poles across the narrow kloof. As the two groups of Zulus met in the middle they lashed the poles of the fence together with their rawhide ropes, cutting Inlebe and her calves off from the rest of us who had already gone ahead.

At the sound of the first scream all those at the back of the column rushed forward, carrying the rest of the herd with them. Ndlovu, Khumbula, Mfanyaan, Nkosana and I swung around, all with our heads and ears held high, trumpeting in answer to Inlebe. It seemed to take forever to free ourselves from the surging mass and get back to her. Mfanyaan was in the lead and so was the first to see the barrier of the fence before him. Standing in front of the fence banging their assegais against their shields and shouting were seven Zulu hunters. Their dogs were with them, barking and yelping at Inlebe behind the fence and at us in front of them. Mfanyaan curled his trunk under his chest and thundered towards the hunters with his huge tusks thrust forward. The three hunters in the center stood their ground but the other four fled back into the bush where they had lain hidden. With a single sweep of his tusks Mfanyaan flung two of the Zulus screaming into the air. As he crashed through the fence the third Zulu thrust his spear into Mfanyaan's side just below his left shoulder. Ndlovu behind Mfanyaan, blocked by his great body, brought her huge trunk crashing down on the hunter but not before he had speared Mfanyaan. Ndlovu slid to a halt with the hunter sprawled on the ground before her. Without hesitation she knelt on him with her massive knees. Out of eyes filled with fear the spirit of the Amazulu hunter left this world. Inlebe was still making desperate alarm calls which panicked her calves back towards the sandstone ledge. Ndlovu made a powerful rumble that quieted Inlebe and brought Isopho and Umfazi to a halt. Nkosana and I reached Inlebe's calves and shouldered them roughly around.

Squealing in panic and not knowing why we seemed to be attacking them, Isopho and Umfazi desperately tried to reach their mother. Khumbula and Ndlovu got on their other side and between us we headed the calves towards the top of the valley. There the rest of the herd was milling around in confusion, trumpeting, rumbling and flinging their heads from side to side. A huge cloud of dust hung over them. When they recognized us some of the trumpeting ceased and, bunching together with the calves behind them, they faced us with outstretched ears and trunks as we came out of the valley. Without waiting for us to reach them they swung around and, with tails and necks outstretched, went into a stiff-legged run. Velapi, with no mother or aunt to help her, ran panic-stricken into the thick bush. Ilanga and Amafu had run ahead of Mabalel and Umphlope, but now they stopped in confusion and started back towards the kloof. Mfanyaan, who was following behind us, frequently slid sideways as he looked over his shoulder back down the kloof. Ndlovu was rumbling loudly but without any effect on the herd. Trumpeting at their calves to stop them from running back, Mabalel and Umphlope tried to head them off and turn them in the direction of the fleeing herd. I followed Velapi into the bush and found her thrusting herself under the branches of a fallen tree. By the time I had calmed her down and persuaded her to follow me the herd had disappeared over the crest of the hill. I could still see the bulk of Mfanyaan as he too reached the top of the rise. A strong sweet smell rose from the new grass crushed by the running herd. I would have no difficulty in following them. Then, as I urged Velapi up the wide path of flattened grass, the same smell that had met us when we found Mvubu in the Umzimkulu Vlei filled my trunk. As I slowed Velapi down to a walk, the smell grew stronger and soon I could see white flecks on the grass and bushes. The flecks soon grew to patches of foam run through with pink streaks like the feathers on the breast of Kholwane the Flamingo. Then I saw Mfanyaan standing just beyond the crest of the rise. His ears were flattened against his head and his trunk hung down so that the curl at the end rested on the grass. He was calm and at peace, very different from the panic and fear that could still be felt in the air. Coming up on his right side I saw that his long eyelashes lay down over his eyes. I thought that he was asleep. Then I saw that the foam I had seen on the track was welling out of his mouth and trunk. Moving around and behind him, completely forgetting about Velapi, I was horrified to see bright red blood streaming down the back of his left leg. The spear of the Amazulu was still deep in his chest, the shaft angled down to the ground and dripping blood. The sound of his breathing was like that of a cold spring welling up from the base of a sandstone cliff.

    I had neither seen nor heard the return of the others. First

Ndlovu, then Nkosana came up to where Mfanyaan and I were standing. Ndlovu gently ran her trunk up Mfanyaan's, stopping at his mouth but not touching him. Then she moved closer to him and leaned her head against his so that their ears rasped together. Ndlovu and Mfanyaan stood like this for a long time. By this time darkness had fallen and the herd stood in silence around us. Except for low sounds coming every now and again from Ndlovu and the occasional scrape of an ear against the side of a head, the silence was complete. The frogs in the stream were quiet and Isikhova the Owl made no call. And so we remained, all through the night.

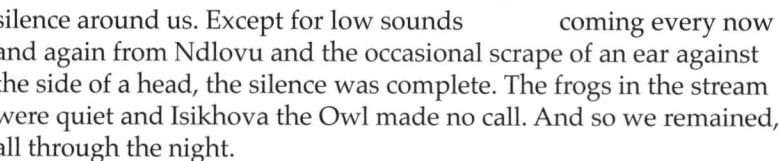

The approach of dawn was signaled by raucous "Krracker, krracker" calls from Nkakalo the Korhaan as the sky over the Pumulangas turned from black to grey. When we became visible to each other in the early light it seemed that no one had moved. Velapi and Fisela were leaning against Khumbula. All the other calves were gathered in the center of the herd behind their mothers. All were facing Mfanyaan. At last the unmoving stillness was broken. Mfanyaan took a step towards the rising sun; then he sank to his knees and rolled over on his right side. Fear rose in us again as ears extended and trunks were stretched out towards Mfanyaan's massive form stretched out on the grass. Ndlovu and Nkosana immediately tried to help him to his feet. From either side they slid their tusks under his head. I too felt an overwhelming urge to help him. With Mathatau and Ndlovu we raised Mfanyaan to a kneeling position. He could not keep his head up, and as soon as we stopped lifting him he rolled back onto his side. Despite this none of us could stop trying to lift him. Then Ndlovu stepped back and stretched her trunk out to touch the foam-flecked tip of Mfanyaan's trunk. She held her trunk there for a long time; then, turning and facing the sun, she stood without moving until the sun cleared the ridges to the east. Then she turned back to Mfanyaan and, digging her tusks deep into the ground, broke large pieces of earth free. She gathered the clods of earth in her trunk and tossed them gently over Mfanyaan's still form. Automatically some of us started doing the same thing while others went towards the surrounding bush and broke off branches. They brought these branches to Mfanyaan, piling them on and around him. I joined in and we covered his body until only a huge mound could be seen. Slowly individual members of the herd stopped covering Mfanyaan and started to walk away to the north. Almost all had gone as the sun rose high above us. Only Ndlovu, Nkosana and I remained. After some time Nkosana and I slowly walked in the direction that the herd had taken. Still Ndlovu remained next to Mfanyaan. Then, laying her trunk on the pile of brush and dirt for the last time, she turned and followed us.

The loss of Mfanyaan, who had been only a few seasons younger than Ndlovu, hung over us like a dark pall of smoke over a bush fire. We had no fear that the Amazulu would pursue us. In earlier times we had seen their weak attempts to run Imbabala the Bushbuck to ground, and now we had killed four of their best and bravest hunters. Our fear was once again of the unknown. Nkosana was now the only one of us who had crossed the Pumulanga escarpment. But he had relied upon the knowledge of Mfanyaan. They had come down a faint path with the hills, mountains and valleys before them. Now he had to guide the herd back in the opposite direction. Going back was never as easy as following the same path a second time. The indecision in Ndlovu that we had felt in the narrow valley disappeared as she shouldered Nkosana into the lead. Nkosana was reluctant to lead off, and at first stood uncertainly facing towards the Pumulanga escarpment. We were now above the sandstone hills and the slopes ahead of us rose steeply to the high kranse of the southern Pumulangas. Deep kloofs, dark with bush, sliced into these cliffs. All the kloofs that we could see ended at the foot of an impassable wall. Towering buttresses flung ahead of the kloofs blocked the view and the way to more favorable routes. Yet, with Ndlovu urging him, Nkosana seemed to regain confidence and set off along a path that ran to the west and away from the most formidable barriers of the Pumulangas. The path neither rose nor fell but followed the sweep of the slope into and out of each kloof. After walking all of this day we could look back across the valley and see the place where we had started. Ndlovu allowed Nkosana to continue along this path into the next kloof. There, where an arm of the bush below us reached up to a small trickle of water, Ndlovu let us stop for the remainder of the night. Sleep came only fitfully to all except the young calves. The events of the day were still too vivid in our minds to allow us to either feed or rest. None of the older ones lay down to sleep. For much of the night we stood silently, our trunks resting on the ground.

During the next two days and nights we wound our way through kloofs which varied only in their depth and the distance we had to cover to get around the ridges that pointed down to distant valleys and sandstone hills. On the third day, with the sun climbing overhead, Nkosana stopped at the head of one of these kloofs. Bush cascaded down the sides and a small waterfall tumbled over the rock ledges where the path turned back away from the escarpment. Another path, a faint one, led upwards to the side of this waterfall. It was not as steep or as high as the Secret Path down from the Hidden Valley. The herd, which had turned at the head of the countless kloofs that we had traversed over the past few days, milled around impatient to continue. Ndlovu, however, rumbled for us to stay. She looked steadily at Nkosana, watching his ears and the arch of his trunk. She watched his trunk waver across the faint path that led into the bush on the side of the kloof. What she saw I did not know, but she gave the "Let's go" rumble and nudged Nkosana up this path. At the top of the waterfall we could see the path going on up towards the ever-present kranse. Nkosana and Ndlovu continued up the path for some distance and then stopped where it crossed a small gulley. Green grass and sweet acacia bushes filled the gulley, yet it was not the food that interested them. With trunks searching just above the ground, Nkosana and Ndlovu moved towards a particularly green patch of grass. Again they made no attempt to gather this grass into their mouths. They were now rumbling quietly. Suddenly their rumbles had a meaning. Despite the passage of time, they had realised that the roots of this patch of green grass were feeding upon what remained of a pile of dung left here by Mfanyaan three wet seasons before. Both Nkosana and Ndlovu had detected Mfanyaan's imprint. There was now no doubt that this was the path that Mfanyaan and Nkosana had come down more than three dry seasons before. The recognition rippled through the herd, lightening the burden that had weighed us down since leaving the valley behind and below us.

Now all the adults who had known Mfanyaan and Nkosana could verify the path we were on. Confidence grew in the herd, with contact calls returning and young ones playing again. It took the remaining part of that moon to reach the top of the kloof where Mfanyaan and Nkosana had first turned into the Thlabatini Forest and then reversed their tracks to come down the Pumulanga escarpment. Even though the wet season was ending, Ndlovu did not go down to the Nyathi Plains. None of us had forgotten the presence of the Bearded Ones on the plains. We could only hope that they had not penetrated the escarpment and the Balele Highlands. Like Nkosi before her, Ndlovu chose the shelter of the Thlabatini Forest and the chance that in it the herd could survive the winter.

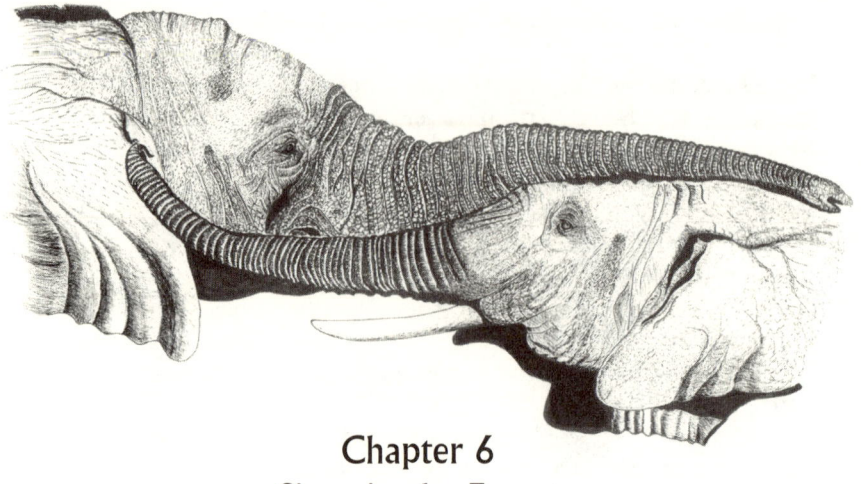

Chapter 6
Signs in the Forest

On the morning after Dakiwe's death the slanting rays of the rising sun struggled through the canopy to reach the forest floor beneath the heavy branches of a White Stinkwood tree. Nkosi stood with his trunk resting on a large branch that bent under its own weight to the ground. He had slept standing as he usually did, in short spells, waking every so often to test the air and to listen to any break in the silence of the forest. Even when he was properly asleep the slightest change in the air or snap of a twig would awaken him into instant alertness. He had slept well after the violent exertions of the previous day, but while the world awoke around him his feeling of comfort drained away, for the events of yesterday returned in full force and hard, painful emotions welled up in his immense body. The two crashes of the Bearded Ones' weapons had been followed by an eternity of silence before he had heard the terrible splintering and breaking of branches even above the roar of the waterfall. It might have been better had Dakiwe screamed. At least then Nkosi would have known that he had been struck. But the silence between the crack of the weapons and breaking of tree limbs filled Nkosi with uncertainty. Was Dakiwe really dead? Could he have helped him? Why had he, Nkosi, not turned around immediately and faced their tormentors? He knew the answers to all these questions, but it did little to lift the heavy sorrow pressing down on him. If he had been able to touch and feel Dakiwe's body, cover it with soil and branches; if he had had time to know that Dakiwe's spirit had departed and what was left no longer bound them together, he could have grieved in peace. He did not know whether he could overcome the loss of both his companion and his family. What he did know was that he was filled with a deep hatred of those who had brought this upon him. Perhaps this burning anger would ease the pain, though he knew that it could not erase it.

He stood silent for a long time, not moving his ears or trunk. He was not consciously listening or testing the air, yet every sense in his body was alert. Nkosi did not expect the Bearded Ones to follow him into the Thlabatini Forest. They could not cross the gash left in the path where he had dislodged the huge boulder. Yet he did not doubt that as the storms of winter left the escarpment, they would come to seek him out. The prize that they had glimpsed would lure them on as surely as the stench of carrion lured Mpisi the Hyena.

Nkosi spent the next many days gradually working his way through the Thlabatini Forest towards the Pumulanga Mountains. The icy winds that swept over Thaba Insimbi and the Balele Mountains did not penetrate the dense forest. With only Imbabala the Bushbuck, Ipithi the Duiker and a few other animals in the forest, there was ample food. He recognized many of the signs left by the herd in earlier wet seasons in the forest and easily found the paths they had followed. One day he was on a well-marked path leading to the stream that fell over the Third Waterfall into the Nyathi Plains when he heard the faint snap of a twig and the rustle of a dry leaf. The sounds were not those of Ngundwaan the Fieldmouse, who took shelter in the forest edges during winter. The air on the floor of the forest was moving away from Nkosi down into the kloof of the Third Waterfall. His probing trunk found only the sweet scent of taaibos. Then a single sharp "Kwek" from a Grey Lourie set every sense in his mighty frame on edge. Without a sound Nkosi slid into the thick taaibos bordering the path and vanished like water into a dry riverbed. A moment later two Bearded Ones passed within a few steps of him. Their heads were crowned with a strange crest something like that of the Hamerkop and their skins hung in folds around them like the bark of the False Thorn Tree. They moved silently, searching for signs on the path. Luckily it was deep in rotted leaves and droppings from countless elephants that had passed that way. The dry leaves and droppings, moistened by rain and dew, had been trodden into a surface as soft as the underbelly of Ihlosi the Cheetah. They found no tracks in the path.

A careless step must have snapped the twig that Nkosi had heard. The air barely moved the leaves of the taaibos which hid him. Now it brought the smell of the Bearded Ones to his trunk. Anger rose within him and his eyes flamed as red as coals of smoldering iron-

wood. It would take no more than three strides for him to bring his massive tusks cracking into the back of the second Bearded One, and an instant later a sweep of his trunk would bring the leading one crashing to the ground. Neither of the Bearded Ones would even know what was thus suddenly ending his time on mother earth. Yet Nkosi did not move. He heard again the sound of the Bearded Ones' weapons on the path of the Waterfall and the breaking of trees as Dakiwe's body fell to the Waterfall Pool. He did not know where Ndlovu and the herd had gone or whether either Amadala or Insimbi was still alive. The Nyathi Plains were lost to him and all his kind, and now the Bearded Ones were seeking his destruction on the winter vastness of the escarpment. In the moment between detection and death Nkosi saw that the Bearded Ones did not deserve to die quickly and unaware, with no more than a moment's knowledge of what was happening to them and no realisation at all of why it was happening. No: before they met their fates, their bodies needed to feel the slow grip of fear and their hearts the loss of all hope. He would bring to these two Bearded Ones the salty taste of the tears that had fallen in the sands of the Nyathi Plains.

The single warning call of the Kwêvoël had saved Nkosi's life. He had not expected the Bearded Ones to come looking for him so soon. He did not know that it was the false trail laid down by Mfanyaan and Nkosana that the Bearded Ones were following. These two were not the same ones who had pursued him and shot Dakiwe. Two of their kind had been killed by Mfanyaan and it was revenge as well as greed that had sent these Bearded Ones onto the escarpment in midwinter. Mfanyaan and Nkosana had escaped. By a twist of fate Nkosi and these Bearded Ones had unknowingly become each other's prey.

Nkosi had little difficulty in shadowing the two hunters. Without dogs, he knew, the Bearded Ones were not skilled enough to detect his presence should the light winds on the floor of the forest change suddenly and bring his scent to them. He knew the forest and its daily changes well. At night one could faintly hear the wind above the canopy. Only occasionally during the darkest hours would gusts of wind penetrate the dense cover of trees and spill through the branches to the floor of the forest. When the sun was high there was seldom any movement of air across the forest floor. Nkosi had to be careful at these times, for it was the smell of the Bearded Ones that he depended upon to bring him warning, and the air movement could change and carry that smell away from him. Then there was the danger that he would get too close to them. Times of rain and sleet tested his skills. The sounds of dripping water and rustling winds from the storm above the canopy masked all other noises and then Nkosi could not hear his prey. The wet forest floor dulled all sound and the birds took shelter and offered no warning calls. The damp air hung sullenly below the trees and carried no message to him. On these days Nkosi would retreat away from the Bearded Ones and remain quietly feeding until he could once again seek them out and follow them. Without showing himself he left clear signs of his presence in clearings ahead of the hunters. He led them deeper and deeper into the forest as he played upon their driving urge to find him.

Nkosi had watched the Bearded Ones in the clearings where they spent the nights. At first only one of them slept while the other watched by the fire. Soon, however, they tired of watch-keeping and both slept. There came a night when Nkosi waited until their fire had died down to ashes. Then he moved silently closer to the sleeping forms and, stepping carefully over their bodies, crushed under his feet all he could see and feel on the ground. Some objects cracked like dry branches under his feet, and using his trunk he flung other things off into the surrounding darkness. As the hunters awoke and leapt up in terror Nkosi silently disappeared into the forest. He stayed among the trees around the clearing for the rest of the night, every now and then breaking branches so that the Bearded Ones would know that he had not left. The Bearded Ones sent crashing sounds which flew into the branches above him. These sounds seemed to be of two kinds. One was large and tore branches and leaves from the trees. The other sound was weak and caused only a plopping sound like ripe fruit falling. Nkosi recognized the loud sound as the one that he had heard with Dakiwe and he knew this was the sound to be feared.

When day came the Bearded Ones turned and headed along a path leading back to the place where they had entered the Thlabatini Forest. If they were lucky they could clear the forest in two days of walking. But Nkosi had no intention of letting them do so. All that day he followed the hunters, taking little care to be silent and often coming perilously close to them. At first they let off sounds in his direction, but soon they ceased and tried to move more quickly. On all the other days that Nkosi had followed the Bearded Ones, they had rested when the sun was at its highest. Today they did not. By evening their pace had slowed. They sought out another clearing, and this time they built a large fire, which they fed all night with ironwood. Neither hunter slept, for Nkosi let them hear and feel his presence. The sour smell of their mounting fear hung in the air like green slime on the surface of a tainted waterhole. In the gloom of early dawn the hunters left the clearing. Nkosi could see that things that they had been carrying lay strewn around the fire. He approached

Nkosi

the fire without fear and trampled to destruction everything they had left.

Nkosi caught up with the hunters well before the rays of the sun had filtered through the trees onto the path they had taken, and by-passed them without their knowing it, going on unseen ahead of them into a thick stand of spike-thorn interspersed with large red-leaved fig trees. The path had narrowed, with dense spike-thorn on either side. Nkosi chose a fig tree leaning over the path. He curled his trunk under his chest and with his tusks on either side of the leaning fig-tree trunk, he pushed the tree across the path. Half of it now blocked the path, while half remained standing. Then he turned back into the spike-thorn and moved quickly through the dense forest in the direction from which he had come. He swung onto the path, quickly testing the surface to make sure the hunters had already passed. His bulk filled the narrow path and he broke into a fast walk with his head held high and his ears held flat against it. He caught up with the hunters as they met the broken fig tree across the path, and with a full-throated roar of fury he charged them. Their only hope of escape was to frantically climb that part of the fig tree that remained standing. In their desperate panic they dropped all their remaining equipment. Nkosi soon found and destroyed the only weapon that had survived his attack on their camp. Both hunters were just out of reach of his outstretched trunk. Their skins were torn and they had lost their head-coverings. Hair like that of their beards hung in strands around their glistening faces. Their eyes stared wide like those of a baboon facing a leopard. With deep rumbles that sounded like those of Ngonyama the Lion, Nkosi waved his outstretched trunk below the feet of the Bearded Ones. They tried to scramble higher but could not. Nkosi's eyes were red with anger, black streaks streamed down his cheeks, and with his ears raised to form a line his massive head looked twice as large. Turning from the hunters towards the weakened main limb of the fig tree, he wound his trunk around the limb and with one shuddering shake whipped the whole fig tree from side to side. Both hunters screamed, and with flailing legs and arms one of them flew out of the tree like a startled pigeon trying to escape from a hawk. The other had wrapped his legs and arms around the branch he was on. Nkosi pushed through the thick spike-thorn bush towards the fallen one. Caught in the thick thorns of the spike-thorn tree, the hunter could not reach the ground. Nkosi grasped him by one ankle and threw him in a high arc into the low branches of another fig tree. Then, leaving this man's now limp form hanging from the branches of the tree, Nkosi returned to the remaining one. He made no further attempt to reach the terrified hunter or dislodge him from the red-leaved fig tree. Instead he stood motionless below the tree for the whole of that long day. Only once did he move away, to stretch out his trunk to the body hanging in the other fig tree. Then, satisfied that that hunter would move no more, he returned to his position below the clinging form. The hunter had wedged his legs in the fork of the branch he was on. With his arms he clasped the limb to his chest. He dared not release his grip for fear of sliding down the tree. He had no need to look down, for he could hear the low, threatening rumbles coming from below. With the coming of evening the weak rays of the sun were soon swallowed by scudding cloud. Streamers of snow hung below the dark clouds like the plumes of the tails of Sakabula birds struggling against the wind. Soon snowflakes were settling on Nkosi's long eyelashes as he looked up at the Bearded One locked in his deadly embrace with the limb of the red-leaved fig tree. As night fell, heavy snow was gathering on the limbs of the trees and shrubs. Nkosi did not leave his post until the storm abated late the following day. Then, finally, he moved on; but the hunter in the tree moved no more.

Nkosi knew that many Bearded Ones had come to the Nyathi Plains. He had seen Bearded Ones on the Highveld beyond Thaba Nsimbi coming to the margins of the Thlabatini Forest to destroy the trees. At the beginning of his third wet season in the Thlabatini Forest, he sensed that his only escape lay through the Pass of the Unknown. He knew there were vast lands which were still free of the Bearded Ones. They were the lowlands beneath the great escarpment that formed again beyond the Balele Mountains. And because they were home to Umiyane the Mosquito and the Tsetse Fly, in these lowlands none of the animals kept by the Bearded Ones could survive.

Nkosana recognized the arm of the Thlabatini Forest stretching out to the kloof of the Third Waterfall. He could see the faint path into the forest and knew that this was where he and Mfanyaan had turned back to the Pumulanga Mountains after laying the false trail to mislead the Bearded Ones. Nkosana had not come face to face with the Bearded Ones since the day that he and Mfanyaan had met them in the kloof going down into the Nyathi Plains. That had been three wet seasons before. He did not know whether the pungent smells of that day had remained with him or not. Ndlovu, Khumbula and I had been close to the Bearded Ones on the western end of

Mabutu Mountain, but not close enough to smell them.

Ndlovu followed Nkosana into the Thlabatini Forest on the path that he had found. Both moved slowly into the forest with the tips of their trunks swinging from side to side along the path. Nkosana rumbled softly, indicating that he had picked up an old trail of the Bearded Ones. None of us could find any new trails. We soon began to detect evidence of the last time that we had moved down that path. Confident that there was no danger and sure of where we were, Ndlovu led the herd into the Thlabatini Forest.

She was moving quickly and I knew that she was heading for a large clearing where we would spend the night. I let the rest of the herd pass me on the path so that I could be sure that the young calves, who did not know the forest well, would not stray off the path. Soon after settling into my place in the rear I heard a sharp alarm-call from Ndlovu up ahead followed by trumpeting and squealing from the others. A ripple of fear ran down the path, with some turning and others backing up. Ndlovu did not follow her first alarm-signal with any other call, so it must have been triggered more by surprise than by an immediate threat. Mabalel was at the back of the herd with Nyama and Ilanga. I rumbled to her to stay put and then moved up the path to where Ndlovu and Nkosana stood. The remains of a dead fig tree lay across our path. Old pieces of trampled stick-thorn branches were under the part of the fig tree that was still standing. Then, almost at the same moment, my nostrils were struck by a sharp stinging smell like that of Qaga the Striped Polecat, and ahead of Ndlovu's outstretched trunk I saw what I thought were the remains of Mfene the Baboon. But Nkosana's distressed rumbles told me this was no baboon. The remains were those of a Bearded One. Broken pieces of things that had belonged to it lay hidden in the leaves below the fig tree. From the other side of the fig tree Mathatau gave an alarm-call which sent another shudder through the herd. She held her ground and soon we found what she had discovered: the remains of a second Bearded One still caught in the branches of a smaller fig tree. Then Ndlovu gave a rumble of recognition. She was standing under the first fig tree with her trunk swaying over bright green acacia seedlings. As soon as I tasted the smell above the seedlings, I knew that Nkosi had been there. Without showing any further interest in the remains of the Bearded Ones, Ndlovu turned the herd around and headed out of the Thlabatini Forest. As so often before, this was exactly the opposite of what I had expected her to do. I knew that her purpose now was to find Nkosi. It seemed clear that he was in the Thlabatini Forest and that we should therefore go into the forest to find him. Instead, Ndlovu left the forest and turned towards the Balele Mountains. The escarpment here was gently rolling grassland with only scattered acacia trees. Ndlovu was able to set a rapid pace, which she kept up until the sun disappeared behind Thaba Nsimbi. She rested the herd in a shallow depression, allowing us to drink and feed for a short time. Then with a sharp "Let's go" rumble she set the herd in motion again. A full moon rose over the Pumulanga Mountains behind us. Now Ndlovu went even faster than she had done during the day, and the mothers with small calves were soon strung out far behind us. She kept up this unrelenting pace while she led us along a route that slowly curved around the Thlabatini Forest towards the Balele Mountains. I knew from the outline of the Baleles as the moon began to sink over them that we were heading for the path we had followed regularly for many wet seasons. This path led out of the Baleles and into the Thlabatini Forest. Had we stayed in the forest, its paths would have taken us into the interior before we could have found our way to the Balele Mountain path. We would have taken all the next day and part of the night before reaching the place where the path from the Baleles entered the forest.

In the cool air of the dawn, well before we were within reach of the Balele path, Ndlovu began making strong low rumblings. She rumbled at regular intervals, silencing the few of us who had stayed with her and listening for a reply. She did not stop walking to listen but kept up her pace. Our long shadows slanted out in front of us. Suddenly she stopped and rumbled loudly. She stood very still and erect as though her feet were planted in the red soil of the escarpment. Her head was held high and her ears were raised and spread. Long moments passed while she stood motionless facing the spot where the path from the Balele Mountains entered the Thlabatini Forest. It was after her third rumble that she heard a faint reply, though I did not hear or feel it. Ndlovu rumbled again and again a weak reply wavered to her senses in the cool air. At once she set out with even greater determination than before. We had crested a small rise, with the sun now warm on our backs, when she stopped again and repeated the sequence of rumbling and listening. This time there was no doubt: we all heard a reply. Ndlovu's temporal glands glistened and fluid streamed down her cheeks. She knew the reply was coming from Nkosi.

Nkosi had left the Thlabatini Forest at first light, heading up the path to the Balele Mountains, when he thought he heard the call of another elephant. He had not heard an elephant's call for three seasons. He stopped, turned and listened, but heard nothing. Hesitantly he was turning to make his way further towards the mountains, when once again he felt the slight tremor. This time he turned and began walking back towards the Thlabatini Forest. He had not gone far before he was certain that it was another elephant's call. With the disk of the sun rising above the Pumulangas, he knew it to be Ndlovu's call.

Ndlovu and Nkosi greeted each other not loudly but with deep low moans. They touched each other's eyes and mouths with the tips of their trunks and then, standing quietly, each laid their trunk over the other one's head. They stood like this for a long time. Nkosi then quietly greeted each of us in turn. By now the rest of the herd was approaching. They came with outstretched trunks and tails raised over their backs, squealing and trumpeting. Nkosi stood without moving or calling a greeting. He touched the tips of the trunks of the young males and clanged his tusks against those of Khumbula, whom he did not know well. He touched the backs of the females and rumbled quietly as Mabalel and Mathatau greeted him. For the first time in many seasons ripples of joy ran through the herd. But in Nkosi's presence the young ones were subdued in their play. You could see Bomvu glancing sideways at Nkosi and carefully keeping out of his way.

The herd milled around on the edge of the Thlabatini Forest waiting to see whether we would go back into it. Ndlovu stood facing Mathatau and Mabalel while I stood to the side and slightly behind her. Nkosi and Nkosana stood near a small pool of water that had a thin skin of ice on it. No one had taken a drink from the pool. Inlebe with Isopho and Umfazi began feeding towards the edge of the forest. The others hesitated, waving their trunks towards the green acacias that Unlebe and her calves were browsing on.

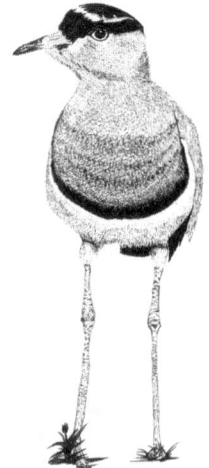

Nkosi was the first to move. He began walking slowly, his massive body swaying in a gentle rhythm, up the path away from the forest towards the Balele Mountains. Nkosana followed him. Ndlovu did not move but shook her head with loud clapping of her ears producing a cloud of dust around her head. Two Blacksmith Plovers rose making loud clicking "Kick-k-k-k, kick-k-k-k" calls. Nkosi and Nkosana were slowly drawing away from the herd. Ndlovu shook her head again. Then she gave a loud "Let's go" rumble and followed them up the path leading to the Balele Mountains.

Chapter 7
Ndlovu's Toenails

The trees of the Thlabatini Forest slowly disappeared behind us, and the next morning we entered the first of the deep valleys of the Balele Mountains. The rains of the wet season had come early and the sides of the valleys were deep in sweet grass. Golden-yellow puffs of flowers with new green leaves showed on the scented thorn trees along the streams and succulent leaves were springing from bulbs on the banks. The morning mists that hung in the valley soon lifted to form lines of white cloud over the hilltops. All our memories of previous wet seasons in these valleys flooded back to us. The tensions which had ebbed and flowed through the herd ever since we had left the Nyathi Plains weakened. But they did not disappear, for the silence that had descended on our world remained. We did not hear the high fading whistle of the great Lammergeyer as he soared over the ridges. Nor did we hear the call of the Mountain Reedbuck. Even Mbile the Rock-rabbit was silent.

Instead of the Lammergeyer we saw the vultures of Aasvoëlkrans sweeping in wide circles high in the sky. On all of our migrations through the Balele Mountains we had never seen the vultures of Aasvoëlkrans come this far north. It took only one more day to show us why they were here now. A short distance up the slope from the path we saw a mass of vultures flapping and squabbling over a carcass. Many more flapped heavily across the slope, and others stood with hunched wings and drooping heads. Then we saw that there was not one carcass but many. They had no skins, horns or tails. In many cases even the hooves were missing. With outstretched trunks and ears flattened against their heads Nkosi and Ndlovu examined the nearest carcasses. They were those of Mpofu the Eland and Mpalampale the Sable Antelope. There could be no doubt that this was the work of the Bearded Ones. A shiver of fear went through the herd again, and any joy we had felt at being in the valleys of the Balele Mountains fled from us.

Ndlovu and Nkosi did not linger or hesitate. Although the valley was already deep in shadow they gave an emphatic "Let's go" rumble and headed past the slaughtered animals and onwards. That night, with only a few stops to feed and drink, Ndlovu led us steadily into the Balele Mountains. She had taken over the lead from Nkosi, who now followed her. Near dawn Ndlovu swung out of the valley in which we were and led us up its steep side and over a ridge into a new valley. I soon recognized this as the one we had taken into the Balele Mountains many times before. The direction Ndlovu was following led to the place where the path from the kloof and the Nyathi Plains met the path to the north and to the Pass of the Unknown.

Everywhere there were signs that the Bearded Ones had also been in this valley. We could see their tracks and smell their recent passage. Their spoor told us that it had been only a day since they had passed that way. The tracks of their horses and of the house that they took with them showed their number to be small. Accompanied by their dogs, they were clearly a hunting party and extremely dangerous. Fear began to grip the herd as Ndlovu continued toward the meeting of the paths. The valley was widening and I knew that its entrance was not far ahead. We could now see up the path to the north, and we were startled to realise that from that direction a wall of black cloud was rolling towards us. In our fear of the Bearded Ones we had not noticed the darkening of the sky and the approaching storm. The storm was almost upon us when the first flash of lightning lit up the rolling clouds. In the blazing glare of the lightning we suddenly saw ahead of us the white shape of the Bearded Ones' home on the path at the entrance to the valley. A moment later a violent rush of wind filled our eyes with dust and our trunks with the sharp polecat smell we had smelt once before. As the first sheets of rain came hammering down fear overpowered the herd and turned it in wild, headlong flight. Caught up in the same terror, I ran with the rest as thunder cracked around us and rain slashed at our backs. It was not until the rain slackened and the sound of thunder rolled away down the valley that I came to a stop. Night had fallen as suddenly as the storm had come and gone. The dripping of water and the rushing of the stream were all that I could hear. Then around me I could feel as much as hear the presence of some members of the herd. I recognized Mathatau and Bomvu, and then Mabalel and her two calves. Contact calls drew some of us together, and a group formed with the younger calves tightly packed in the center. At first fear prevented anyone from calling loudly. I could not hear the firm voice of Ndlovu or Nkosi's deep rumble. With louder calls, more responses came. I did not know how far we had run and how much distance we had put between us and the Bearded Ones. The night was black and a light rain fell steadily on our backs. I knew that in this rain our calls did not travel very far. Even so, something was needed to dispel the fear that had the herd in its power. Strong, loud assembly calls brought more replies. Recognition calls were needed to determine who was missing, so by rumbling continuously I found out who were huddled together. Ndlovu, Nkosi, Khumbula, young Velapi, and two calves, Fisela and Ilanga, were missing. The four oldest females, Mathatau, Mabalel, Inlebe and Ulambile, were all present. Mabalel and Nyama were very agitated at not being able to find Ilanga. They kept on trying to break out of the circle but did not know where to look. Fisela and Velapi, with their previous experience of the Bearded Ones, had probably run much further than we had. Since stopping no one had heard any sound from the Bearded Ones. This was not very comforting, but it was unlikely that they would come looking for us on a night as dark and wet as this. Velapi and the missing calves would have a better chance of finding us if we remained in one place. Although I was uneasy about Ndlovu, Khumbula and Nkosi, I knew they could take care of themselves.

The rain had not stopped when daylight began slowly to return. Mist hung in the valley and tendrils of clouds clung to the slopes. Ndlovu's determination to reach the Pass to the Unknown remained with me. Despite my fear of the Bearded Ones, I began leading the herd back towards the crossing of the paths. Mist hid us and our feet made no sound in the wet grass. The rain masked our scent and the air was still. I stopped the herd many times as we approached the place where we had seen the house of the Bearded Ones the previous evening. We were all silent and tense. At each stop we faced the place where the paths crossed and listened for long intervals. We searched the air constantly for any hint of the Bearded Ones, but found none. Suddenly the mist parted to reveal to us that we were right on top of their camp. We all froze in fear. Yet nothing moved where the camp had been. After a long, tense pause I went forward with Mathatau. The rest of the herd remained

stiff-legged in place, trunks stretched out towards the camp and ears held still and flat. Tails were raised over backs and the young calves stood under their mothers' chests. As we approached we saw that the camp was not empty. What had been the Bearded Ones' house lay shattered and scattered over the trampled grass. Piles of skins of Mpofu the Eland, Mpalampale the Sable, Nyala and others lay strewn over the ground. Heaps of horns from the same antelopes were tangled together like the broken branches of dead acacia trees. Then we saw the white and yellow shapes of tusks lying amongst the chaos. Mathatau and I were led by an unknown force to touch and smell these tusks. With deep grief in our throats we found that the largest belonged to Amadala and Nsimbi. Circling the scattered camp I found first one and then two more bundles of unrecognizable skins. The smell that caught in my trunk was that of the Bearded Ones. Then two mounds became visible through the mist that still hung over the stream. They did not move. By smell I could tell that they were the bodies of Fisela and Velapi. In their panic they must have run with Ndlovu, Nkosi and Khumbula straight into the camp of the Bearded Ones.

Blood and trampled grass led from the camp onto the path to the south. The blood was not that of a single individual or kind. The blood that was streaked on the branches of the thorn trees and smeared by the rain seemed to be that of Nkosi. Other streaks were the blood of the Bearded Ones. Both trails led away from the camp southward down the path to the kloof and the Nyathi Plains. Of Ndlovu there was no sign. Nor was there any sign of the remaining Bearded Ones.

Mathatau remained with the tusks of Amadala and Nsimbi. She carried them away from the wreckage of the camp into the thick Buffalo-thorn growing along the stream. Here she tore a trench in the soil and into the roots of the Buffalo-thorn. Then she laid the tusks in the tangle of the exposed roots. When I reached her she was covering them with soil and thorn-tree branches. The rain was washing the soil into the trenches. The tusks' hiding place was already vanishing into the thick stand of Buffalo-thorn.

I do not know how long we spent in the destroyed camp of the Bearded Ones. I had no idea where they were. Gradually the wisdom of what had seemed to be a foolish act on the part of Ndlovu and Nkosi began to dawn on me. The Nyathi Plains were lost to us. We could never return there. The Amazulu had returned to their lands in the south and east and the Bearded Ones had entered the escarpment and penetrated the Thlabatini Forest. Escape through the Pass to the Unknown was our only hope of finding sanctuary. Only Nkosi knew whether this sanctuary was a reality. He had worked with Ndlovu to open the possibility and had distracted and led the Bearded Ones away from the path to the Pass of the Unknown so that the herd might escape. I wondered if I could achieve the end that he and Ndlovu had placed within my grasp. I wondered too whether, if I succeeded in leading the herd into a sanctuary, I would ever accumulate the depth of wisdom that had dwelt in their great beings.

We had stayed too long at what remained of the camp of the Bearded Ones. Their greed would bring back those still alive to claim what they had plundered. The rain had stopped but the mist still lay heavily on the track to the north. The herd vanished into this low-lying cloud like Mvubu the Hippo sinking below the surface of a deep pool. The blackness of night came early as we began the slow ascent of Ndumeni. Thinking back through past years I could recall only one time when Ndlovu had led me up Ndumeni and the Pass to the Unknown. Even in the fog I knew this to be a desolate place with no vegetation and no place to hide from the fierce storms that often rage over the Place of Thunder. The stony path reminded me that it would soon become almost indistinguishable from the stones of the mountainside. To keep on the path I would have to call upon all the powers that Ndlovu had instilled in me. I had to use to the utmost every sense that I possessed. The feeling in my feet had to replace my eyesight. I had to know instantly the difference between the rounded pebbles on the path and the sharp-edged stones of the mountainside. I had to sense the width of the path with the tip of my trunk and pick up from the rain-scoured surface the faintest of smells locked in its crevices and cracks. I had to see in my mind the patterns of the earth's low sounds being reflected from the sides of the mountain around me. I had to recall the shapes and sequences of rocky outcrops on the sides of the pass that I could not see with my eyes but only sense in my mind.

The slope of the path changed imperceptibly. We were approaching the unseen crest and I searched in my mind for a pattern of rocks that marked the turn of the path at the top of the pass. An image of the strong toenails on Ndlovu's feet wavered before me. I sensed a series of rounded rock-faces embedded in the topmost cliffs of Ndumeni. As dawn broke behind them the rounded rock towers rose out of the darkness of the abyss. Clouds like the fingers of Mfene the Baboon reached into the kloofs and valleys and then spread outwards to be lost in the dark shadows below. When the mists of the night lifted, a vast lake of cloud lay below us. To the north and west the escarpment fell into the cloud-filled basin. The path descended sharply and turned out of sight into a kloof which cut deeply into Ndumeni. We had crossed over the Pass to the Unknown.

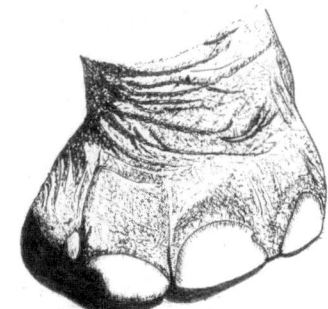

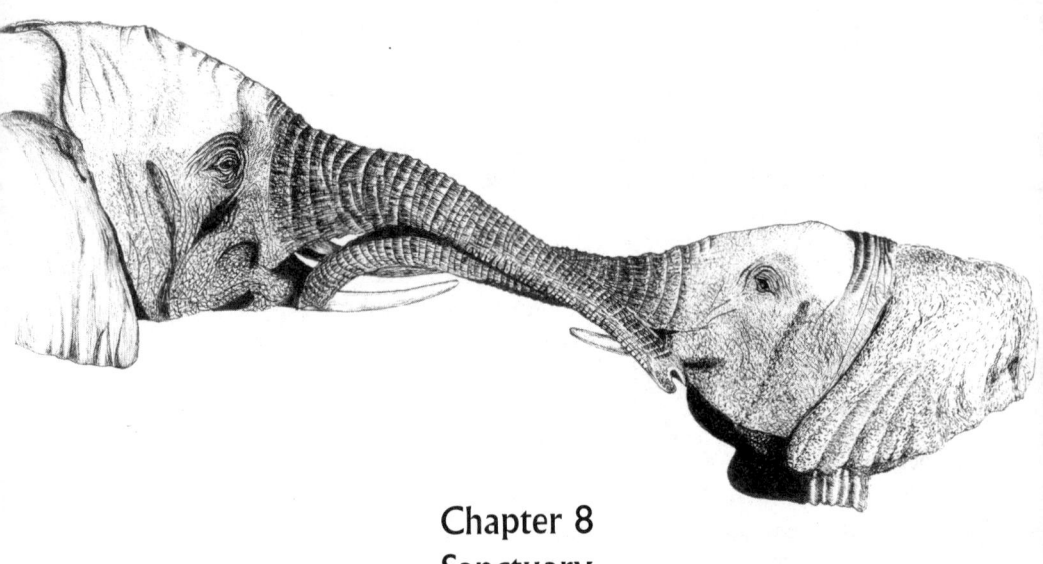

Chapter 8
Sanctuary

The path led us deep into the side of Ndumeni before it turned and began running below the buttressed columns that had marked the entrance. The sun was high by the time we rounded the last buttress and the cloud that had filled the vast basin below us had lifted into long lines like egrets flying home at sunset. Only the occasional glint of sunshine reflecting off a bend in a river broke the unending expanse of bush. Except for rounded domes of rock that rose out of the bush to the south, the surface was flat and featureless. No sounds rose to greet us and no bird wheeled below us.

Shadows of the western escarpment had spread far across the bushveld before the dry stream we were following joined a flowing river. The bush, which from above had looked to be low and dense, now grew in stature and parted before us. Along the streambed and river stood towering yellow fever trees and spreading acacias. The river that we had reached ran in many channels. Thick reeds lined its banks and covered its islands, and dense tamboti grass kept the trees at a distance from its banks. There were no signs of paths made by Mvubu the Hippo through the reeds and tall grass. No sandy spits were occupied by Wenya the Crocodile, and no kingfishers hovered over the deep pools or flashed like arrows down the channels. Except for the running water the place was silent. The air was heavy and warm, but the water was cool and sweet. It had been many moons since we had had waded deep into water. We had not stopped long at runnels crossing the path as we came down from Ndumeni, so we drank deeply from the river. When the herd came out of the water many were black and glistening all over. Some had their bodies divided in half by a sharp water-line running all around their middles. We found little grass and few bushes and trees that were familiar to us, but fed quietly on whatever we could eat. A group of tall fever trees stood in a moist green swale near the river. I drew the herd together among their bright yellow trunks to spend our first night in this strange new land.

During the night we heard no deep reverberating call from Ngonyama the Lion. Nor did we hear the cough of Ingwe the Leopard, the whooping of Mpisi the Hyena, or the drawn-out yipping cries of Mpungu the Jackal. The silence of the night was not broken by the dawn. The rays of the sun did not awaken isi-Kehle the Francolin with his harsh and repetitive call. No plaintive whistle of "Come back, come back" or stuttering "Kek-kek-kek" alarm-calls came from Impangele the Guineafowl. The silence of the previous day, which we had been too tired to notice, now pressed down upon us.

Over the following days, as we moved deeper into the bush, we did not find any clear paths or the spoor of a single animal. We crossed old paths that were overgrown and abandoned. Although many animals must once have used these paths, small bright green acacias sprouting underfoot showed that none had done so for the last two wet seasons.

The herd had not yet recovered from our clash with the Bearded Ones at the place where the paths crossed. Our escape into the lowveld and our unhurried progress through the empty bush had restored some life among our young ones, but fear hung close below the surface in all the adults, especially Nyama and Mabalel. Their bodies were tense and their movements guarded. The bush had closed about us and we had lost the horizon. The escarpment to the west had long since disappeared into a haze of heat and distance. Each day the blueness of the morning was soon consumed by the white heat of the sun. Hot air surrounded us as if we were among the smoldering ashes of a bush fire. No movement of our ears could dissipate the heat. Only cool mud and water thrown between our legs and over our backs could challenge the fierce assault of the sun. Against the heat of the day I sought the solace of water and the shade of the camelthorn trees. For several days we found no river, only shallow pools of stagnant water. Each day thunderheads rose as the sun slanted towards the escarpment. But each day the promise of rain faded away in the low rumbles of distant storms. The fever trees and the acacias had disappeared and only the sparsely branched limbs and meager yellowing leaves of the Mopani offered any shade. Then came a day and night in which we found no water, only drier and drier bush. There was little choice but to turn back towards the escarpment.

We did find water the next day, however, and that night, without sensing that the ground was sloping westward, we reached the bank of a river. When daylight came we could see that, like the first river we had found, it was wide and ran in many small channels. Reedbeds and tamboti grass covered its many islands. Fever trees lined the banks and clumps of grass and ferns grew in their shade. There was no sign of any other animal and the grass and shrubs were untouched. On the morning of the third day of following this river, we reached a place where an unmistakable track came down and crossed it. The track was old and overgrown, and had not been used for at least the last two wet seasons. We crossed to where it climbed out of the riverbed and up a sandy bank. The bank had been trampled down over the years and the path passed through a shallow depression to reach the far side. As I reached the top of the bank fear cut through me like an icy winter wind on the escarpment. The bones of many animals lay there, some piled in heaps and some strewn across the sand. It was the work of the Bearded Ones, of this I was certain. No animal that we knew would have gathered together so many bones. I wanted to turn and run but the rest of the herd were coming up the bank out of the river. Panic set in as each one, breasting the bank, saw what I had come upon. The screams of alarm threw into confusion those who were still crossing the river. The whiteness and the absence of smell soon told me that these were old bones. More calm now, I approached the pile and tested the air above it. There was only the smell of bones bleaching in the blistering sun. I could find no bones of our kind on the surface of the pile. Whatever was hidden below the surface was masked by the smell of those in the sun. I could recreate no image of the living from the faint traces of past life that my searching trunk found. Only a mountain of unknown death lay before us. There were furrows in the old path like those I had seen back at the crossing of the paths. These were the tracks made by the houses drawn by the Bearded Ones' animals. They had gathered the slaughtered animals here and taken their meat and hides away in their houses. There were many branches of the thorn trees lying on the ground. The Bearded Ones must have spread their meat on these branches to dry in the sun as iLunga the Shrike impales his food on the spikes of a thorn tree.

  The Bearded Ones had been here before us and our paths had crossed again. I rumbled quietly to the herd and after some time they calmed down. Then I led them back across the river and along the old path returning to the other side of the river. Here we found signs of the Bearded Ones' camp and bones of their animals. Mounds of stones carried laboriously from the streambed lay in heaps and rows below a thorn tree. The air above the mounds of rocks had a faint smell of the Bearded Ones. It seemed that these mounds were the last resting place of some of them. I led the herd away from the camp and rejoined the river. The Bearded Ones had been here and had left, leaving some of their dead behind. We knew now that death stalked the lowveld that we had entered. We had seen the devastation wreaked by this new tribe of men on the Nyathi Plains. They had brought the same fate to the lowveld. But here they, too, had suffered. The swarms of mosquitoes that live along the rivers and in the vleis during the lowveld's wet season had brought sickness to them. And the Tsetse Fly had attacked their animals with the deadly Ngana sleeping-sickness. Perhaps for these reasons the Bearded Ones had fled the lowveld. But why had they destroyed all those animals? Moreover, they could not have destroyed all the living things of the land, the air and the water: but where were those that had escaped? These were questions we could not answer.

    I kept the herd grazing along the river for the remainder of the wet season. The rains ceased and the skies cleared. The sun, unobstructed by clouds and free of the cooling rain, beat down on the bush with as much fury as in the wet season. Yet the nights were cool, even cold, and the mornings fresh and full of light. Moving down the river we came one evening to a point nearly opposite the dry riverbed that had led us down off the escarpment. The sun had dropped almost below the escarpment and the air was crisp and still. Often, as night crept over us, I would recall the feeling of comfort that Ndlovu had brought to the herd and wish I could do the same. Her gentle and reassuring rumbles had seemed always to be there. Now I felt as if I could still hear her low calls vibrating within my being. The sensation of her long-lost voice was so strong within me that I almost responded to it with a call of my own. But even as I stopped myself from answering the calls of her spirit I was jarred into consciousness. I had heard her call! Tensing my whole body and turning with ears spread in the direction of the path down the escarpment, I heard the call again. It was Ndlovu! It was not a spirit dream! I rumbled an answer with all the power within my being. My call brought the herd rushing out of the reeds of the riverbed, pounding and struggling up the steep sandy bank. I did not wait for them, nor did I hear them behind me. All I could hear were the answering calls from Ndlovu. She had heard me and knew who I was! I did not see the trees and bushes in my path, nor did I collide with any of them, yet I felt as though I was running through the sucking mud of a spent waterhole. I could see Ndlovu but I could not reach her. My legs felt too weak to carry me. Would she dissolve back into the spirit world where I had until this moment believed her to be? Then she was before me, her trunk and rumbles joined with mine. Our tusks clunked together in a deep-throated greeting. Dust from our flapping ears formed a halo in the rays of the setting sun. Joy at Ndlovu's return from the lost radiated into the herd. They spun around, clasping trunks, rubbing against each other and rumbling and trumpeting. Every cheek was glistening wet with fluid pouring from our temporal glands. There was no doubt that it was mixed with tears of joy. The return of Ndlovu lifted the gloom of the herd like a Lammergeyer soaring into the blue of the heavens. Unlike other occasions when the spirit of the herd had been lifted only to fall again, this time I knew that Ndlovu had brought hope back to us to stay.

Ndlovu did not resume the leadership of the herd. She had passed it to me and the herd had accepted this. Yet her presence united the herd as I was unable to do. Somehow the knowledge of what she had endured and what she knew reached all of us. At the place where the paths crossed, on that night long before on the escarpment, she and Nkosi had formed their plan in the few moments it took for the hunters' camp to loom out of the mist. With terrifying force and complete surprise Nkosi had smashed the house of the Bearded Ones and thrown its contents across the camp. In the instant of time between his scream of rage and the horror of recognition that gripped the Bearded Ones, Ndlovu charged through the startled group who had risen to their feet around their fire. Nkosi and Ndlovu had not known that Khumbula would join in the charge, but join it she did, choosing as her target the kraal of the Bearded Ones and killing or scattering their animals. Within a few heartbeats the Bearded Ones had been thrown into utter disarray.

Nkosi and Ndlovu had correctly guessed that our herd would turn and run and that I would take charge. All that remained was for them to lead the Bearded Ones away from the herd in a futile chase down the path to the escarpment. They did not know that Fisela and Velapi had panicked and run after Khumbula into the hunters' camp. Khumbula's action had crippled the Bearded Ones' ability to follow Nkosi and Ndlovu. He and she had intended to leave a clear trail to ensure that the pursuers would follow them and not go after the rest of the herd. The trail they left was clear but not what they had planned. In the wild shooting at the camp at least one bullet had struck Nkosi in the chest, while Khumbula had sustained multiple wounds and was bleeding badly. The trail of blood left by both Nkosi and Khumbula lay red across the path. It was not long before Khumbula was unable to go on. Against all their instincts Nkosi and Ndlovu had to leave her.

Nkosi and Ndlovu headed towards the escarpment and Thlabatini Forest. If their luck held they could shelter briefly in the forest

and then circle back the way the herd had gone to the Pass of the Unknown. But this was not to be. Nkosi's wound was too serious and his loss of blood too great. Shortly after dawn Nkosi shouldered Ndlovu off the path and directed her across the veld towards the Thlabatini Forest. He did not step off the path but gave Ndlovu to understand that she must not follow him. Ndlovu had last seen his massive form swaying out of sight as the path to the escarpment dipped into the river that ran through the kloof leading to the Nyathi Plains.

Ndlovu had spent little time in the Thlabatini Forest. Sounds of the Bearded Ones encroaching into the forest from the west came closer each day. As the few animals of the forest fled ahead of the intruders, Ndlovu learnt that these humans were now fighting amongst themselves. Great numbers of them had flowed back and forth across the escarpment and the Highveld. As with the Zulus before them, their crops had been destroyed and their animals killed. Now they were surviving in the far reaches of the Balele Mountains and down in the lowveld. The Bearded Ones who fled killed whatever living things they could find so that they could eat and survive. The Bearded Ones who pursued them destroyed any living things that were left in order to starve the fleeing bands they were chasing. Two wet seasons before we reached the bushveld the Bearded Ones had left it, starving and suffering from the sicknesses of the lowveld.

Gradually tranquility returned to the herd. As days and then moons passed without threat, the river and the bush on either side of it became our home. The changes in the seasons in the lowveld did not bring with them any need to travel long distances to new home ranges. I led the herd towards the escarpment in the wet season and deeper into the lowveld during the dry. In the dry season the sun rose over mountains far distant from the river. The river flowed southwards before turning to the mountains of the morning. The low rounded hills of rock that we had seen from the path down the escarpment grew and closed around the river in the south. We found new foods as well as ones that we knew. As the wet season ended there was an abundance of wild figs, Marula fruit and nuts and Mopani leaves.

I never led the herd far from water. In the heat of the lowveld we learnt to cover our bodies with mud. When there was no mud, we threw dust onto our wet bodies. In the short while that we had moved up and down the river, grass and acacia seeds that we ate were spread up and down our routes. The piles of droppings from the herd spread many seeds across the bush. In some places Ndlovu, Nkosana and I pushed trees over to reach fresh green leaves and flowers. In these newly opened spaces grass began to grow.

One day early in the dry season as we were moving down the river I saw Ndlovu stop and move her straightened trunk carefully back and forth across the path. I knew from her body that she had found something of importance. Going over to her and searching over the same ground, I felt my shoulders tighten as fear that I had forgotten rose again within me. The scent was that of a horse: the animal that the Bearded Ones ride. It had followed our tracks of the previous day for some time before swinging away towards the river. There on a sandy bank we could see where the Bearded One had dismounted and where both he and his horse had drunk from the river. Away from the bank we found the ashes of a small fire where he had slept. He had not resumed tracking us. This puzzled Ndlovu and me, for we had learnt that once the Bearded One was on your trail he would pursue you until he found you. Yet this one had not done so. Instead, his tracks crossed the river and continued into the bush. He had headed into the dry bush, but we knew that he would soon return to the river, so I led the herd quietly away from it on the side opposite where we had found the signs of him. We climbed the slopes of one of the huge rounded rock domes and in the shade of two large White Pear trees stood silent and still. From here we could see the Bearded One on his horse. For many days after this we followed and watched him as he crossed and re-crossed the river. He seemed to be looking for tracks and signs of other animals as he worked his way slowly up the river. We knew from his body language that he knew we were watching him. We saw him examine our spoor many times, looking carefully at the footprint of each one in the herd. The fear we had felt when we first found this Bearded One slowly decreased as he carefully kept his distance from us.

The man stayed along the river for many days before finally heading away towards the escarpment. It was soon after his departure that we saw the first tracks of a small herd of Impala that had come down to the river to drink. Then the following morning we heard the whistle of the Fish Eagle. These were the first signs that life was returning to the lowveld. As the days went by we saw more and more animals and heard the calls of birds, some familiar to us and some still unknown.

Two moons after we had seen the Impala spoor we heard the rumble of a strange elephant. Both Ndlovu and I replied. A short time later a small family consisting of a mother, a small calf and three young females came out of the bush. The mother stood under a thorn tree sheltering her calf between her legs and stretching her trunk out towards us. Her ears widened but she took care to keep them down so as not to signal any threat to us. Ndlovu and I detached ourselves from the herd and walked carefully towards her. When we saw her flatten her ears against the side of her head we stopped at once and stood still waiting for her to move. I ate from a small acacia to show her that we meant her no harm. Ndlovu followed my example and quietly grazed around the small acacia. After a long time the strange elephant came slowly out of the shade and walked towards us with her ears gently flapping forwards and her trunk slightly raised. Touching trunks with me and then with Ndlovu, she stood quietly while the rest of her small family gathered behind her. I rumbled gently to her and then to our herd, warning them not to approach. Instead I turned and with Ndlovu walked slowly back to the herd. The new elephant hesitated, and then followed us to the herd. Everyone remained quiet and only after some time did each member of the herd greet the new arrivals with touches of the trunk. In this way they became part of our herd. The mother's name was Fika, "to arrive", and her baby's isiFike, "new". The two oldest of the young females were Buyisa and Buya, "to restore" and "to return". The fourth member of the small group we named Jabula, "happiness", in remembrance of little Jabula whom we had lost in the land of the Amazulu.

We could feel the world around us returning to what we had known in the Nyathi Plains. The pain of our losses was eased by the gaining of the new family. The sounds of the herd were once again comforting. The smells and sounds of our new home were forming an envelope around us. Yet it seemed that our struggle to survive was not yet over. For only a few days after Fika and her group had joined us, Bearded Ones on horseback began bringing their moving houses down from the escarpment into the lowveld. The fear we had so often felt before, and believed that we had left behind us, came surging back again. This time it was not only fear but a feeling of hopelessness. We had come to the end of our world. We knew that only hardship lay in all directions. There was nowhere else to go. Perhaps it was this feeling of hopelessness that caused me to keep the herd along the river. The human intruders were moving to the south, so I turned the herd towards the escarpment, but did not move far.

As time passed, however, we saw little of the Bearded Ones. In twos and threes, some of them occasionally came up the river. But at no time did they threaten us. Instead their body language was peaceful and friendly. Soon we became used to seeing them near us. But we always slowly gave way, melting into the bush. Then more of them came, together with many Amazulus that we had seen to the south in the Nyathi Plains. Like an army of ants they ate up the bush, making tracks as wide and straight as the bands of rock on top of Mabutu Mountain. They worked for many moons, their growing paths stretching far into the bush. As they disappeared into the bush to the north, I led the herd back down the river to the south. At the first wide path the Bearded Ones had made, the herd milled about, shaking their heads in clouds of dust, rumbling and moving forwards and backing away from the path, straightening their trunks before them and their tails behind them. The red earth that the Bearded Ones and Amazulu had scraped to the side of the path rose in ridges like the track of Wenya the Crocodile. The smells were strong and strange and the piles of stones and bush along the track blocked our way. With the herd getting more and more restless behind me, I finally found a gap in the piles of thorns and, with my head held high and tail curled over my back, I rushed across the path. The openness of the path, running away into the distance to the sky on either side of me, frightened me, but I kept my fear to myself. Once I was across and looking back there seemed to be little to fear. Yet it was only with much rumbling and trumpeting that the herd eventually managed to cross the path after me.

As the river swung towards the mountains of dawn, a barrier like the rawhide riems the Amazulu had pulled across the narrow valley lay before us. Again the herd milled and rumbled at the barrier. Trunks reached out towards it. The tip of my trunk touched a thin vine of the barrier. A searing pain jerked through my trunk and I screamed in fright. This turned the whole herd away from the barrier, running in panic up the river. I never forgot the pain of that barrier, and none of us ever approached it again.

It took many moons before we got used to what the Bearded Ones had done. During this time strange objects, shaped something like beetles but as large as Mvubu the Hippo, began creeping along the paths that they had made. These objects seemed to have many very small legs that moved like those of Shongalolo the Millipede across a twig. We stood silently in the bush watching these unknown objects going up and down the paths. They gave off a pungent odor that caught in our trunks, but it was quite different from the smell of the Bearded Ones. When they moved they made a low rumbling something like that of Ngonyama the Lion admonishing a cub. We could see no sign of danger about them, and they never threatened or charged us, so quite soon we came to accept them as harmless, whatever they were. We saw that they usually stopped whenever they came near any place where we were standing in the open, and that they stayed still for a time before moving off slowly, so at first we thought that they might be scared of us; but then we noticed that they did the same with every other animal, large or small. In fact they would even stop if little Skilpad the Tortoise were crossing the path ahead of them, so whatever their reason was, it could not have been fear. After that we usually paid these strange objects very little heed.

The Bearded Ones who had made the long straight paths through the bush had also built camps in places along the river. Each camp was surrounded by bare tree-limbs planted in the ground with riems running between them like those we had seen in the south. At sunset, like dung beetles rolling their balls of dung along the paths, all the objects went into the camp. There we noticed another strange thing about them: once they had stopped inside the camp, the objects each gave birth to up to four or five Bearded Ones at a time, and what is more, these newborn Bearded Ones emerged fully grown. The Bearded Ones in their camps would often gather to watch us drink and bathe in the river below. They never went out of their camps at night, leaving the bush to us. In the mornings, we soon saw, something even stranger happening in these camps. The objects that traveled along the paths could not only each give birth to four or five Bearded Ones at a time: each one could also eat four or five of them at a time, and every morning this is what they did. And the strangest thing of all was that the Bearded Ones seemed almost eager to be eaten by them, for every morning they would go to the objects and climb inside them very willingly, while the objects sat still, not even needing to chase them. The whole business was altogether most peculiar.

Slowly we came to accept all this strange behavior and these new things. They became part of a world that was beginning to feel safe and secure. More of our kind could be heard and sometimes seen along the river which was now our home. Mvubu the Hippo had come back to the river and we could hear him grunting at night as he came out to graze on its banks. Ingwe the Leopard returned to the shelter of the dark fig trees and the warning call of Mfene the Baboon could be heard once again. Once again, too, Lamithi the Giraffe could be seen swaying through the thorn trees. Herds of wildebeest, zebra and buffalo grew and the coughing call of Ngonyama the Lion traveled once more through the evening air as we had always heard it do. At the setting of the sun, one day early in the wet season, Ndlovu and I went alone into the bush. The next morning we returned to the herd with little Nkosi wobbling at my side.

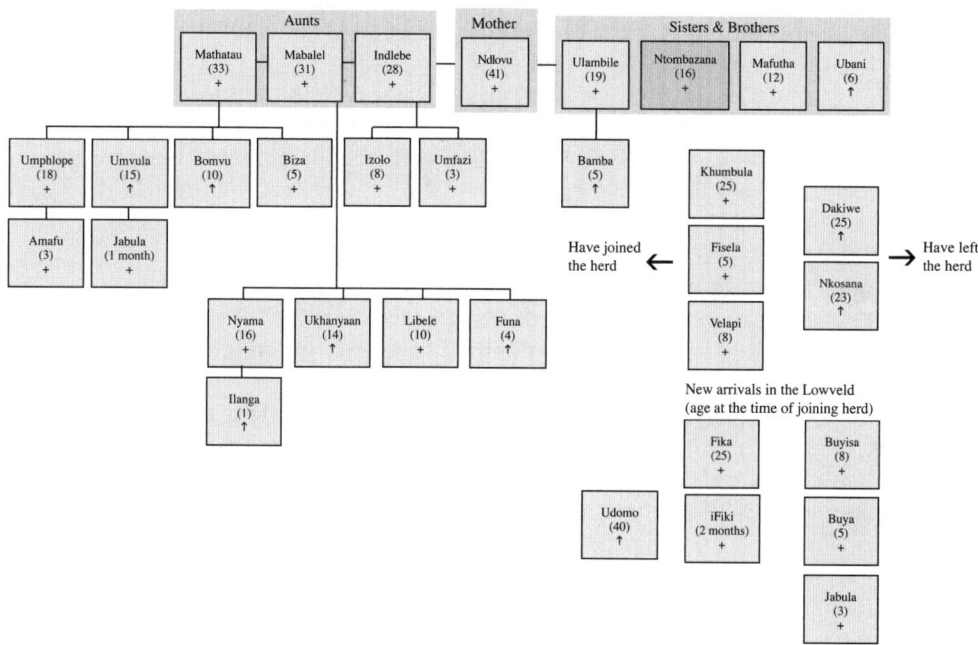

Epilogue

The ending of Ntombi's story is a new beginning. As checkered as the beginning might have been, a sanctuary does emerge and the herd will survive and even prosper.

The Kruger National Park which is the sanctuary found by Ntombi and her herd had its beginnings in a proclamation issued by the Volksraad of the Transvaal Republic and President Kruger in 1898. The Anglo-Boer War postponed the actual founding until 1902.

By that time the wildlife had been decimated over much of South Africa, first by an economy that depended upon the exploitation of wildlife and then by a bitter and long war of attrition. The home ranges of elephants on the Nyathi Plains and the Escarpment had long been lost. Even the potential sanctuary was largely devoid of animals.

Preservation was pursued as a strategy to maintain wildlife as a resource and not to conserve it. Game reserves were selected not because they provided adequate habitats but for a variety of reasons: endemic diseases, climate, poor soils, lack of minerals, they were unsuited for human occupation and exploitation.

Stevenson-Hamilton, (1), the first warden of the park, commented after entering the southern region of the present Kruger National Park in August 1902 that "one would have expected to see at least some indication of large wildlife. Yet there was not even an old spoor to indicate that anything of the kind ever existed". (p 46) And later "It was not until the third day that we came across a few tracks of Zebra, waterbuck and impala." (p. 46)

Elephants had disappeared from the escarpment (White River area) before 1870. In 1903 (p 191) seven bull elephants were seen north of the Olifants River. It is likely that these bulls had crossed the Lebombo Mountains from Mozambique. The first reserve, the

Sabi Game Reserve, in the southern part of the Kruger National Park covered an area of 2895 square miles, more than twice the size of the State of Rhode Island. By the late 1990's the Kruger National Park measured some 225 miles from north to south with an average east-west width of 45 miles, occupying an area the size of the State of Maryland. By 2002 protocols with Mozambique and Zimbabwe created the Greater Limpopo Transfrontier Park, the world's largest game reserve.

These expansions, including the incorporation of private preserves especially on the western side of the park, have restored access to old habitats and opened old migration routes. The two maps, shown overleaf, illustrate the evolution of the Kruger National Park from its inception to its current configuration.

Yet shadows still hang over the park. With a current population of 12,500 elephants, concerns about habitat destruction have been raised. Elephants are a 'keystone species' which means that they serve other species by maintaining habitats such as grasslands in the bushveld. However, when too many elephants are concentrated in a single area, habitats are destroyed. Mineral exploitation in the Kruger National Park poses an ever-present threat. People-park conflicts erupt, particularly on the boundaries where encroachment of animals and humans into each others' territories pose problems. Yet we should remember that it was public opinion that brought about the Kruger and other national parks (such as those in the United States). If parks are managed for the benefit of both animals and people, Ntombi's sanctuary will be secure.

(1) *South African Eden: The Kruger National Park* by James Stevenson-Hamilton, Struik Publishers (Pty) Ltd. Cape Town, 1993. pp 334.

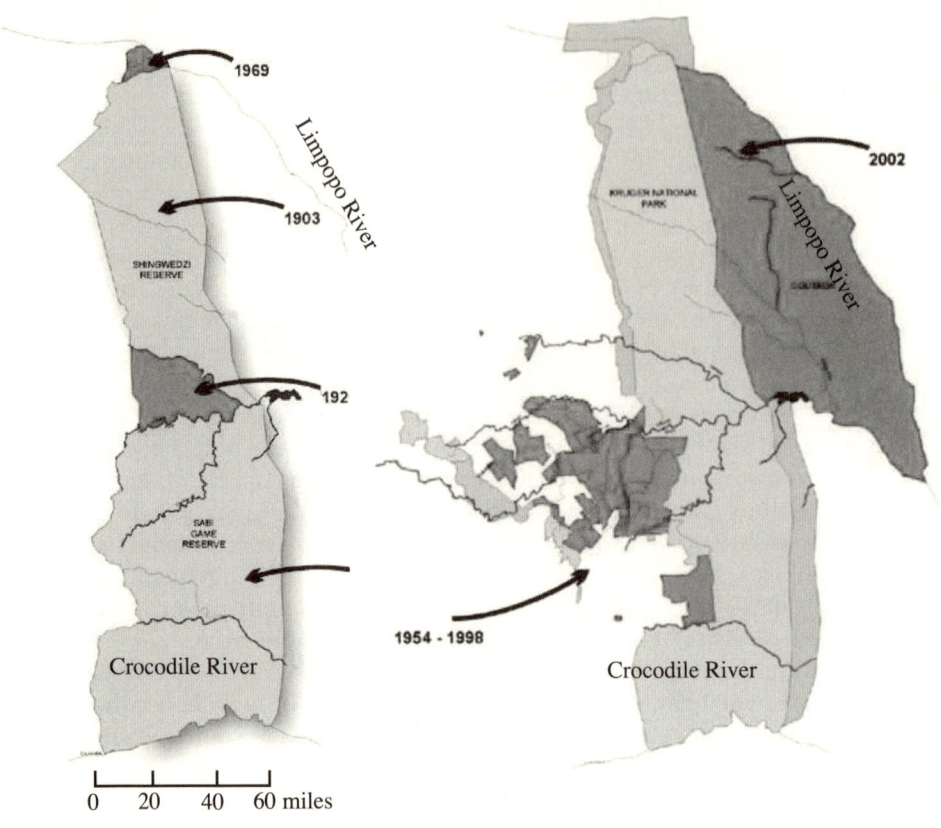

Maps from http://www.kruger2canyons.com

Author's Note

Ntombazana was originally written for my grandchildren. Strange and exotic places are rapidly disappearing from a world being homogenized by technology. Far away times and places need to be captured and kept. So I have retained a letter written to my grandchildren introducing each book for it is really addressed to children everywhere and of all ages.

A Letter to Zouella and Rodes

The stories that Ntombi tells you of her family of elephants and their adventures are set in the part of Africa where I grew up. The Nyathi (Buffalo) Plains and the Balele Mountains are real places. Almost all the other places that Ntombi goes with her herd are places I explored when I was a boy. Mostly I went with Mbusana, my Zulu friend, and Tippy, my dog. Tippy was a cross between a fox- and a bull-terrier and was a very brave dog who loved hunting. Mbusana, whose name means "goat" in Zulu, was the same age as myself. We grew up together and he taught me to speak Zulu. He called me "Jabajaba", which in Zulu means "the one who talks too much".

I was born not far from Ntombi's Hidden Valley, just around the corner towards Mutwa the Magician's kraal. Your great-grandfather Tom was born in the same house. Your great-great-grandfather Albert Garstang came to South Africa from England in 1889. He went to the new Colony of Natal and eventually to the Nyathi Plains. There he met and married your great-great-grandmother Henrietta Jemima Dicks. The Dicks family had already been in the southern and northern ends of the Nyathi Plains for a very long time. Your great-great-great-great-grandfather and -grandmother Joseph and Jane Dicks had moved to the small village of Howick back in 1850. There Joseph once saw a herd of thirty-five elephants. The country was still wild and only a few settlers were moving onto the Nyathi Plains, which by then was being used as grazing lands by the Amazulu. Your family lived to see the great elephant herds and other animals leave the Nyathi Plains, to be replaced by people after two great wars—one between the English and the Amazulu and the other between the English and the Boers. The stories in Book 1 and Book 2 take place before all this happened. In Book 3 Ntombazana and her family meet and have to face the newcomers to their land.

The kranse or cliffs of the Balele (Sleeping) Mountains rose up almost from our backyard. Aasvoëlkrans (Vulture Crag) was behind my Uncle Maurice Dicks's farm. We usually rode our bicycles to get there. It was far enough away for me to make a little box that fitted onto my bicycle's carrier for Tippy to ride in. We would go up the Ingagane River to the waterfall and then behind Aasvoëlkrans into the Hidden Valley. It was wild in the kloofs, with Mpala antelopes, Iphiti the Duiker, Imbabala the Bushbuck, Emfene the Baboon, Logwaja the Hare, Mbili the Rock-rabbit and, of course, lots of vultures. One day I even saw the golden shadow of Ingwe the Leopard in the Hidden Valley.

Mbusana, Tippy and I would leave soon after the sun came up over the Ipumalanga Mountains. We climbed up on the Balele Escarpment along a path which led us on an easy way up the kranse. We took sandwiches, some fruit, and biltong, if we were lucky enough to have some, in a backpack. We usually didn't carry water onto the escarpment because the streams were crystal-clear and perfectly drinkable. If we ventured out onto the Nyathi Plains, though, or towards Mabutu Mountain, we had to carry water with us. Sometimes we would take a small tent and camp out overnight. The first time we did this I woke up in the middle of the night and saw a huge baboon standing right in front of the tent. Earlier that afternoon, while we were pitching our tent, we had seen a whole tribe of baboons nearby. The big alpha male had sat up on a rock barking his displeasure at our presence. Now in the night I was sure that this was him coming to get us, and I was as scared as anything. Tony, my big brother, was with us on this occasion, so I woke him and told him in a very shaky voice that there was a big baboon right in front of our tent. He looked out and laughed. It was only a big rock that in the moonlight looked a bit like a baboon.

From our house you could see the great range of the Drakensberg (Dragon Mountains) far to the west. In the story I use the Zulu name for the Drakensberg: Inkonto Quathlaba, which means the Barrier of Spears. I also give the northern part of the Inkonto Mountains the name of Ntshonalanga, or Mountains of the Sunset, because that is where the sun went down. Majuba Mountain or Hill of Doves is a real mountain, as is Mabutu. Mabutu Mountain has a real cave in it which goes right through the mountain. We used to try to get through it, but it was pretty scary because you had to crawl on your belly through very low places. There were bats, scorpions and snakes in the cave. We were especially afraid of the very poisonous snakes called puff adders because they are so slow to move away (though quick to strike) and you could easily put your hand on one. It was very dark in the cave and even with flashlights you couldn't see into all the dark crevices and cracks. One day when we had gone about fifty yards into the cave we heard a terrible roaring. So we scrambled out backwards, to find out that an aeroplane with three engines—an old Ford Trimotor, I think—had just flown right over the cave. We had left two friends outside who saw the aircraft, the first one that any of us had ever seen. Mbusana and I never saw it—we just heard it.

When my family first came to the Nyathi Plains there were still small groups of San Bushmen living in the caves of the Inkonto and Balele Mountains. Their paintings were on the sandstone walls and roof at the entrance to the cave in Mabutu Mountain. The place with the most paintings was on a high roof of sandstone which made an overhang, not a cave. It looked out over the river and plains. You could see for miles from this shelter, which gave you a great view of all the animals grazing on the plains and feeding along the river. Once when Mbusana and I shot a rock-rabbit, it fell into a crevice in the rocks. We crawled into this crevice, which led us deep down into the pile of boulders. When we got deeper the narrow crevice opened up into a chamber. On the floor of this chamber we found pieces of old pots and even some nearly whole clay pots. It must have been a Bushman hiding-place long ago.

Another time we were pushing rocks over the edge of the krans, making them crash down onto other boulders and start mini-avalanches which roared down into the valley. We worked hard to get one big boulder loose and started it rolling towards the edge of the krans, but instead of going over, it stuck on some bushes. I went down to give it a final push with Tippy following me. As I was pushing the boulder over the bushes, one of my not very smart friends rolled another rock down onto us. It hit Tippy on the rump and sent him flying over the edge of the krans. The fall was terrific, maybe a hundred feet or more. I feared the worst for Tippy but I had to try to find him. I struggled down a narrow ravine that split the krans, hoping that I would find him, but knowing that when I did he might be dead or at the very least badly injured. I had climbed about a hundred

feet down when I heard a rustling in the ravine below. Then Tippy's ears and face appeared, and he came struggling up the ravine. He was limping and had a patch of fur rubbed off his rump, but otherwise nothing seemed to be hurt or broken. I could only suppose he had landed in one of the thick bushes that grew at the base of the krans. But I knew he was one tough dog. That incident helped to teach me that you should never roll or throw rocks down a mountainside.

Further down across the Nyathi River I had another uncle, Henry James, whose nickname was "Jinks." My brother Tony and I used to ride our bicycles to Uncle Jinks's farm on the Nyathi River and spend part of our summer holidays there. We crossed the Nyathi River on a railway bridge. This bridge had no walkway, and you had to step from cross-tie to cross-tie with nothing between you and the water far below. You did this carrying your bicycle, backpack and gun. I can remember being pretty scared.

Occasionally our whole family—my father, my mother Ethel, my sister Pam, Tony and my Grandmother Ball—would go to visit Uncle Jinks. All six of us squeezed into our car, which had a canvas roof, open sides with no windows, and wooden-spoked wheels. There were no roads across the Buffalo Plains, only tracks, and we often got lost when we chose the wrong one. Sometimes we would get stuck in the sand and have to dig the car out with the shovels that my father always brought along. There were no road bridges across the Nyathi River, so when we arrived opposite Uncle Jinks's farm we took a big tin washtub down from the roof of the car where my father had tied it. The washtub was big enough for Granny Ball to sit in and my father and Uncle Jinks steered her across the river in it. The rest of us had to wade or swim across, leaving the car on the Nyathi Plains side of the river.

The Badlands and Gramadoelas are also real places. They are not quite as big as in the story about Ntombi's father, but they were impossible to cross, even on foot.

The big vleis (marshes) which I call Umzimkulu and Amanzimtoti, the Big Waters and the Sweet Waters, are about where I say they are. We used to hunt duck and Spurwinged Geese in these vleis. There were Golden Otters, too, but no longer any crocodiles or hippos. By the time I grew up all the elephants and other large animals had gone from the Nyathi Plains and the Balele Highlands. But they used to live there, and the stories that Ntombi will tell you are about the time when this valley and these mountains were full of animals. Book 1, *The Dry Season*, is about the part of the year that Ntombazana and her mother Ndlovu, the matriarch of the herd, would spend on the Nyathi Plains with their family group. Book 2, *The Wet Season*, tells how Ntombi's mother would lead the herd onto the Balele

Highlands in the other part of their yearly cycle. In Book 3, *Losing Our Home Ranges*, humans start to take over the Nyathi Plains, and Ntombi becomes the matriarch of the herd and must try to lead them to safety.

The stories she tells you in these books are tales which I heard when I was growing up. For example, when I was small and did not want to go to bed or do something I was supposed to, I was told that if I did not do it, "the Tokolosh would get me". Since baboons used to raid our garbage cans in the back yard and I "knew" that the Tokolosh rode on the backs of baboons, I was pretty sure that the Tokolosh *could* get me. Ntombi will tell you more about the Tokolosh.

Vusamazulu Credo Mutwa was a real and famous sangoma or healer. He was also a great story-teller and keeper of the traditions of the Zulu nation. I learnt about tribal history and legends from his books and from the books of many others. I have watched elephants and other animals for many hours on many days during many years. Some of this has been part of my work trying to learn the language of elephants, but much of it has been because of the pure fascination that these great and wonderfully intelligent animals have always held for me. The stories that Ntombi tells you in these books are a mixture of all of these things.

When Book 2 starts Ntombazana is almost six years old. That may not sound young to us, but at this age she is growing up quickly, and she learns something new almost every day from her mother, aunts and older cousins. In the second book she tells you about the elephant's wet-season range. The Balele Highlands, on top of the escarpment behind the house in which I lived as a boy, are a very different place from the Nyathi Plains. Up there the tallest mountain—Thaba Insimbi, the Mountain of Iron—rises to fully ten thousand feet, and most of the highlands are between four and six thousand feet above sea-level. Even in mid-summer the nights are cool and the skies filled with so many stars that if you stretch out your arms on a moonless night you can see your hands clearly.

In the rainy season there are violent thunderstorms, with lightning and cracks of thunder that echo up and down the kloofs. Mbusana, Tippy and I were sometimes caught in these storms and had to be careful where we found shelter. Lightning would strike the boulders and once we saw a ball of fire, the kind of lightning called St Elmo's Fire, run down the kloof. We had to avoid exposed places, but streambeds were also dangerous because a rushing wall of water could be upon us without warning.

Once Mbusana, Tippy and I were trapped between the small streams that form the Second and Third Waterfalls as they drop over the edge of the escarpment. Our hunt had taken us a long way towards the Pass to the Unknown and we had only just begun our

return homeward when huge towering black clouds formed above Ndumeni, the Place of Thunder. By the time we reached the stream of the Second Waterfall it was a torrent of foaming brown water. There was no way to cross, and we knew that the stream going over the Third Waterfall would also be in flood. We were trapped. Without a tent or blankets and with only some dried fruit left in our kitbag, we were in trouble. Luckily we had shot two guinea fowl earlier in the day and we always carried some salt and a box of matches. Finding a place to shelter and dry off in was our main concern. After rain the nights are cold up there. Unless we could get a fire going to warm ourselves we were in for a very miserable night.

In the soft sandstone of Mabutu Mountain there are caves, but not in the hard rocks of the high escarpment. The stream plunging over the Third Waterfall lay in a deep kloof. The rock walls of this kloof were fractured into columns and blocks eons ago when the hot rock cooled. In a few places the cracks had moved far enough apart to allow one to squeeze through. Sometimes a fissure opened into a dry space big enough to shelter in. Luckily for us, there was such a place in the kloof next to the Third Waterfall. We found it just as the light of day was fading from the dark rainy sky.

As we were squeezing into the narrow passage Tippy started to growl, pushing past our legs with the hair standing up along his neck and back. It was already too dark to see what he was growling at, but we suspected that it was Nyoka the Spitting Cobra. This was dangerous, because the snake could blind Tippy or one of us if we got too close to it. Mbusana shouted at Tippy to back off and told me to get my rifle ready. Then he threw one of the dead guinea fowl into the entrance of the passage. As the bird hit the ground with a dull thud the open mouth of Nyoka, glistening in the fading light, closed in a flash onto its neck. I had neither time nor space to aim, but fired on instinct, killing Nyoka before he could draw back into his lair. We quickly cut the neck and head off the guinea fowl because we did not want our supper to be contaminated by any cobra venom.

We still felt a bit uneasy about what might be in the rock shelter. Usually Nyoka was by himself but we could not be sure. Mbusana searched until he found an old aloe with dried-out leaves hanging down around the base of its trunk. He carefully broke off the driest leaves, crumbling pieces into my hat. Then we piled the aloe leaves up in the entrance of the passage and placed small twigs on top of them. After a lot of blowing, the pile flamed up and we were able to light a branch of a dead ironwood tree. By the light of the burning branch we could see into the passageway and small chamber. It was empty and looked dry and snug. With our wet clothes clinging to our bodies, we shivered as we moved the fire into the small chamber and brought in more ironwood to get a hot blaze going.

As we plucked and cleaned the guinea fowl that had saved us from Nyoka, Tippy, who was as hungry as we were, kept a keen eye on everything we were doing. By the time we had finished roasting both guinea fowl our clothes were mostly dry. We shared the roasted guinea fowl amongst the three of us, making sure that Tippy did not get any of the splintery bones. Except for having to get up at intervals during the night to put more ironwood on the fire, we were warm and slept well. The worst part of the whole adventure was dealing with our very worried mothers when we got home the next day.

In Books 1 and 2 Ntombi is still young, and when we were at the same stage of our lives, life for Mbusana and myself was simple and full of fun. Sticks and stones were all that we needed for many of our early games. To play kennetjie, for instance, you placed a short stick about four or five inches along across a groove made in the ground and flicked it out as far as you could with a longer stick. After that there were complicated hits you made with the longer stick on the short one. Miss a hit and you were out. Other games needed only an old tennis ball. Sometimes we made a ball by wrapping rubber strips around a rock; to make a soccer ball we stuffed the bladder of an animal with rags.

As we got older we found that we needed money to buy cartridges for the bigger rifle we were using and shotgun shells for the single-barrel shotgun I had been given for my birthday. Mbusana would sell some of the birds and small game that we hunted to the Zulus who lived in the area. They were eager for game to eat because they would slaughter their goats or cattle only on special occasions. All of them were poor. I worked in the machine shop on the mine where my father was a foreman. Mbusana was my helper and I shared my earnings with him. We made the large bolts used in the hooks that attached the coal-cars called golovans to a long endless cable. This was how the coal was hauled from the mine to the

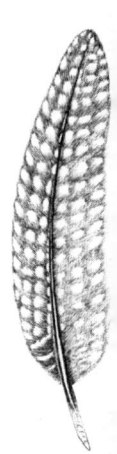

screening plant. We were paid half a crown (about 50 cents) for each finished bolt. Because the lathe we worked on was in use during the day, we had to work after hours, from four o'clock to midnight. We eventually became very good at producing the bolts, making up to 40 in one shift. This made the regular day-shift workers unhappy and probably jealous. Because we were not qualified fitters and turners they banned us from the workshop. We then got a job laying track on the slag-heap where the waste rock and poor-grade coal were dumped. This slag-heap was always burning and gave off sulfurous fumes and smoke. It was very hot and dirty on the burning black coal-dump under the blazing summer sun. To make matters worse the pay was much less than we had earned making bolts.

One day I was walking through the screening plant where the coal was crushed, washed and sorted into different sizes. There were a number of conveyor belts which carried the coal. One of these conveyors consisted of an endless loop of steel blades dragging coal down a channel. The blades were attached to chains which ran over wheels at each end of the channel. Rolling over these wheels at one end, the blades were sent down into the channel and then at the other end they were sent up again and returned over the lower blades like the treads on the track of a caterpillar tractor. Tippy was following me through the plant, and while we were going up a steep flight of steps, he slipped and fell into this steel conveyor. Each time he tried to get out, a returning blade caught his neck and nearly beheaded him. I had to run down the steps and along a narrow plank walkway to save him. When I reached him I had to wait until there was a gap between the upper and lower blades and then quickly grab him and pull him free. Amazingly, just as when he went over the krans, he wasn't hurt, but I was left shaking with fright.

In Books 1 and 2 Ntombi describes a pattern of life that once went on uninterrupted for many, many generations of elephants. Since time immemorial, her kind had lived through the same peaceful annual cycle. Year in and year out, the herd would set out for the Balele Highlands as the wet season began to turn the veld from brown to green, and year in and year out, with the onset o the dry season they would return to the Nyathi Plains. Then in Book 3, which takes us about a decade further on in her life, she tells of the coming of people, especially white settlers, in the elephant's world. With them come change and disruption, and in only a short time the elephants' way of life is changed for ever. Until now tranquility has always reigned in the elephants' world: now fear, pain and grief overtake the herd. She and her family are forced to enter into a struggle for survival. For the elephants it becomes a matter of life and death. She herself has to take on responsibilities beyond her years, and use all the skills she has learned from her mother Ndlovu.

In Book 3 Ntombi tell you the final outcome of the story of her family.

Changes of a very different kind also began to disturb and then disrupt the lives of Mbusana and myself. Although he and I still spent many days on the Balele Highlands or on the Nyathi Plains, both of us were starting to think about what we would do in the changing world ahead of us. Mbusana went to school for only a few years. He could not go to the same school that I attended. For the first time he and I realized we were living in a land where we were not treated as equals. Growing up with Mbusana, I knew that he was very smart. He could beat me almost every time we played a chess-like Zulu game called marabaraba. He often learnt and understood new things more quickly than I did. Yet his school, although new, had few books and much less of all the things that my school had. My parents knew the value of education and made sure that we finished high shcool and that, if it was at all possible, we would go on the university. But Mbusana's parents needed the help of their children to survive. So instead of finishing his schooling, Mbusana had to help plough the fields for growing mealies and millet as well as look after his father's small herd of goats and cattle.

Great changes for all of us came abruptly when the Second World War broke out in 1939. My brother Tony and most of my uncles joined the army or air force. The older men in the village, including your great-grandfather, were organized into a home guard. The German forces were winning everywhere, especially in North Africa. Even though we were far from any large city, and even further from the fighting, British soldiers and sailors came to stay with us for a rest on their way around the tip of Africa. Two of these soldiers who came from the famous Welsh Guards Regiment, went hunting with Mbusana and me, and we were amazed that they could not shoot nearly as well as either of us boys—in fact they hardly knew how to shoot at all. Because of the war we could no longer buy ammunition for hunting. Every now and again I was able to obtain a few cartridges, and sometimes Mbusana and I would climb the escarpment or go to the Hidden Valley behind Aasvoëlkrans with only two cartridges. We would walk all day for those two shots and had to be very certain that we hit our mark. We were especially careful not to wound any animal. Perhaps this helped us to be good shots.

During World War II I was the only English-speaking student at our small school of eighty boys and girls. All the other students were Afrikaners and spoke Afrikaans. Many of them did not like the British and hoped that Germany and Japan would win the war. I had lots of fights at school because of this. Old wounds from early colonial days and from the bitter Anglo-Boer War were reopened. These feelings of dislike and even hatred between some of the English- and Afrikaans-speaking South Africans were later to affect the course of my life.

Before I left for university Mbusana and I went on a last long hunt. I had only ever been on one train journey away from home, and that had been with a group and not on my own. Now I was leaving home and leaving Mbusana behind. He had little to look forward to. It was not a happy hunt. Tippy had contracted an eye disease that could not be cured. First he lost the sight in his left eye. Then his eyesight gradually failed altogether. He was still fit and badly wanted to go on the hunt with us but could not. My brother Tony, home on leave from the army, was the one who took Tippy to the vet for the last time.

I took a camera with me on that last hunt. At university I joined the photographic club and developed the pictures of our hunt in the club's darkroom. I sent Mbusana some enlargements together with a letter. He wrote back thanking me for the pictures but asked whether I could please send him the camera.

During the university winter vacation Mbusana helped me with a first-year thesis that I had to do. I had chosen to do a project on the Badlands and Gramadoelas between Mabutu Mountain and the Pumalangas. I wanted to find out why these Badlands were there. One of the tests we had to do was called a "percolation test". We had to dig a one-cubic-foot hole in the sandy soil of the badlands, then pour four gallons of water into it and record the time it took for all the water to sink away. Then we had to repeat this in a number of places. The trouble was that, as you know, there is no water in the Badlands. Nor were there any roads, and there was no way to get a vehicle anywhere near where we were working, so we had to carry the four gallons of water five miles from a spring near Mabutu Mountain. Four gallons of water weigh about 50 pounds. After the third trip Mbusana sat down at the spring and said, "Look, Jabajaba, I know you are a university student who has read many books, but why don't we dig the hole in the ground at the spring and pour the water in there?"

Deeper and uglier changes began to affect our lives soon after I went to university. The government of South Africa changed to one which drew sharp lines between English- and Afrikaans-speaking and between black and white South Africans. Differences between people were written into law. Barriers were erected which prevented Mbusana from attending good schools, finding work freely and choosing where he might live. His family was moved from the home he grew up in to what was called his "homeland", a place that neither he nor his family had ever seen before. There was no work in the Zulu "homeland" to which Mbusana's family was moved. He had to leave his family to find work in some city. Here he was lost in the crowds of young men all trying to survive. For a time I knew that he had gone to a small town to work as a gas station attendant. There I could help him for a while, but then I too had to leave the country I was born in, losing him, the Nyathi Plains and the Balele Moutains.

The barriers I faced were of a kind more subtle than those Mbusana had to deal with. Jobs and positions, especially in government, were no longer awarded on merit, but on whether one's heritage was English or Dutch. Your grandmother Elsabé Mostert and I had met during our first year at University. Elsabe's family had come to the Cape two hundred years earlier than mine. Her family spoke both English and Afrikaans with ease and did not support the policies of the new government. We made the huge decision to get married and to leave our families and our country behind us. I joined the British Colonial Service as a meteorologist and was posted to Trinidad in the West Indies. I had to complete a six-month training course in London, England, before going to the Caribbean.

We left by ship at the height of the South African summer only three weeks after we were married. Neither of us had been to sea before. We were fascinated by the blue of the tropical ocean and by clouds like fully rigged ships sailing in skies as endless as those of the highveld. The sense of adventure obscured the loss of family and country. While we did not realize it at the time, we would now carry the memories of the place of our birth in our hearts but would find our home in some place new and unknown.

After we had crossed the equator, meeting King Neptune and earning our Pollywog status, the skies and seas began to change, especially once we had left the island of Madeira. Now greys supplanted blues and the towering cumulus was replaced by banks of clouds and fog which clung to the northern horizon. We were now sailing into mid-winter. Yet pleasant surprises were ahead. On the boat-train from Southampton to London on a luminous day such as only England seems to be able to produce, we passed through fields so green that they seemed to be lit from below. How could such green fields exist in the middle of winter while the veld of summer that we had just left was a sea of brown? Surely, if we stopped to walk in these fields we would come across elves and fairies. Instead, we saw rabbits with soft ears not nearly as large as those of Logwaja the Hare, pheasant with plumage to rival that of a Purple-crested Lourie and cattle so round that they looked like Mafutha when she was six years old. Later we were to find that this green grass of England had none of the brittle dryness of the highveld grass that cracks and pricks under one's bare feet. It was as soft and smooth as a spaniel's ear.

Then came the outskirts of London, with unending rows of houses and even more rows of chimneypots. The houses looked grey and grimy and the backyards minute and cluttered. Gone were the vistas of veld and ocean. Soon after arriving in London we found out what a London fog was all about. While many a Sherlock Holmes movie had prepared us for the gloom and faint glow of street-lamps in the middle of the day, nothing had prepared us for the grime and sulphurous smell of smog.

Although this was more than seven years after the end of the Second World War, blocks of the city were still nothing but rubble. We had to get ration books for butter, meat, coal and other things that we had always taken for granted. To us these were minor inconveniences. To the worn and pallid Londoners they were a continuation of years of privation. Soon, however, we found a small flat on the outskirts of London with open fields and forest adjacent. None of the drawbacks of life in post-war Britain could dampen the excitement we felt at being in London, with Peter Pan in Kensington Gardens, Eros in Piccadilly Circus, Nelson's Column in Trafalgar Square, Big Ben, Tower Bridge, the Tower of London, Buckingham Palace, the changing of the guard, and Dickensian characters around every corner. Stories we had grown up with, from Peter Rabbit to Caliban, made England seem warm and familiar.

Six months later, at the height of the English summer, we boarded another ship bound for the Caribbean and Trinidad. Even though the training course had been an intensive one, we had seen quite a lot of England, including the white chalk cliffs of Beachy Head near Eastbourne in Sussex, where your great-grandmother Ethel Ball was born. We also sought out the town of Garstang in Lancashire and explored the legends and history of the family. Our earliest known ancestor is claimed to be Oswald Thorald Gar, a Viking chief who landed at Jarrow in the year 803 near the present city of Newcastle on the river Tyne on the east coast of England. The Ancient Book of Records at Jarrow-on-Tyne documents the arrival and establishment of Thorald Gar. Thorald Gar claimed the title of King of Northumbria but was killed by Penda of Mercia in the wars of the Heptarchy, a period of many co-existing kingdoms of Angles and Saxons in Britain. His eldest son, Edwin Thorald, regained the title and reigned until the peasant rebellion of 827. Victory in this rebellion gave Edwin Thorald claim to be the first King of England. The family made its home at Hexam Castle in Northumberland, then called Pond Aetu. Guthrad Thorald followed Edwin but both he and his eldest son died together fighting Alfred for the freedom of the north of England. Malcolm of Scotland now claimed Northumbria as his Fief and for a time the kingdom was lost to the family. In 1039 Seward Thorald regained Northumbria and reigned until the time of William the Conqueror in 1066.

His eldest son, Edwin Thorald the second, joined forces with William of England and went on the first Crusade to the Holy Land. From this time onwards right up to the time of Henry VI the head of the family worked with the reigning kings of England. They crossed to France with Henry IV and lived alternately in France and England through the reigns of Henry IV, V and VI. During the reign of Henry VI the family moved south, giving all its possessions (except the Castle of Hexam) to the Percys in exchange for their possessions in Lancashire. The ruins of the Castle of Hexam stand to this day. Moving to the land of Oswaldeston, Stang and Longton, they chose Stang as their home. They then adopted the name of Gar-of-Stang which became Garstang. The house in Lancashire was finally built in 1103 and still stands.

Our Coat of Arms with its motto "Amor et Pietas" ("Love and Duty") was granted in 1190 by Richard the Lionheart. The shield bears the Cross of the Crusades, the Lion of Richard, the Dagger of France. The Pen of the Magna Carta and the Fleur-de-Lis granted by the Black Prince were added later. The record of the Coat of Arms is now lost. It could be reconstructed from a complex heraldic description that we have.

The record of our family seems to be clear up until 1737, when the line is broken. Missing from the register at Longton Hall, Longton in the County of Lancashire is the birth, marriage and death of Betty, Countess of Idden. If this missing page in the register could be found, we might prove to hold the oldest name in England.

In Granny Elsabe's life and mine, coconut palms, orchids, Scarlet Ibis, Agouti and the beautiful beaches of the north coast of Trinidad now took the place of the flat-topped acacias of the Nyathi Plains and the kranse of the Balele and Pumulanga Mountains. The sounds of steel drums replaced the whistles of the fish eagle and reedbuck. The calls of the morning doves could not match the mournful call of the emerald-spotted wood dove. Black vultures soared in skies as blue but not as high as those in which the Lammergeyer sails. Instead of Ingwe the

Leopard, dogs barked, and no booming calls of Mfene the Baboon greeted the rising sun. Wet seasons followed upon dry, and the cold and damp of winter in England quickly receded in our memory.

After four years in Trinidad our lives took another turn. First we returned to South Africa, where Stephen was born, and then we left again for work and study in the United States of America. A whole new life began for Granny, Stephen and me. Michele, your mother, was born in Tallahassee, Florida, to complete our family. Research projects took us to Barbados, the far eastern Atlantic, the coast of West Africa, Germany, England, Thailand, New Zealand, Pacific islands, Brazil, and back to southern Africa. Michele and Jamie, and then Stephen and Kathy, were married. Zouella, you were born in Richmond; then both families came back to live in and near Charlottesville. Rodes, you were born soon after Michele and Jamie came to Seven Gables. Now your Grandmother and I had, and have, not only a home but a place of birth as well: far from the valleys, plains and mountains where we began our lives, but ours too, just as they are yours.

Jabajaba

Appendix
Zulu and Afrikaans Names and Words

Zulu names and words are mostly pronounced the way they are written, with each syllable being enunciated. For example, Im-ba-ba-la, the Bushbuck.

"N", "M", and "Im", as in Ntombi, Mbusanam and Mpala or Impala, are soft sounds, and are hummed, while the next letter is sounded: m-m-m-Pala or n-n-n-Tombi.

Sometimes there are hard sounds like "gwa" and "cha" as in Logwaja, pronounced Lo-gwa-cha, the Hare.

The most difficult sounds to say are the clicks, which made by sucking the tongue off the roof of the mouth. Clicks are signalled by "X" or "Xh" as in Xoxo (the Frog) or Xhosa people. To pronounce Xoxo, you make two clicks with your tongue, each followed by a short "aw". Zulu, like other southern African languages – especially San, the language of the Bushmen – is spoken both exhaling (as English words are spoken) and inhaling to make the so-called glottal clicks. There are only a few words in the book that are as hard to say as Xoxo.

The prefix "Ama" means "the (plural)": thus Amazulu means "the Zulus". "Kwa" means "of the": thus Kwazulu means "of the Zulu". "I", as in Idube the Zebra, means "the", as does "u" in uBhejane (the Rhinoceros), though the "u" is often left out. The first syllable in Bhejane is pronounced "betch" and the second "wan", so Bhejane is pronounced "betch-wan".

Langa is the sun.
Puma is to come out or up.
Shona is to sink.
Pumulanga is sunrise.

Shonalanga is sunset.
Nkosi is God or the Great One, or Great Chief.
Nkosinkulu is the Greatest One.
Abantu means "the people".
Sabona is a greeting meaning "I see you".
Sapele is a polite question: "Are you well?"
Bayete is a royal salute.
Indaba is a council meeting.

Here are some Afrikaans words. (When you say them, the letter "r" is always rolled, not smooth. Practise pretending to be a motor-bike's engine being revved—"r-r-r-r-r-tn, r-r-r-r-r-r-r-tn"—to make this sound.)

An aasvoël (literally "carrion bird"; the first part is pronounced "ah-ss" and the second rhymes with "who'll") is a vulture.

The kwêvoël (literally "Kweh-bird", named after its call) is the Grey Lourie or Go-'Way Bird.

The kiewiet (pronounced "kee-veet") is the Crowned Lapwing or Crowned Plover.

The hamerkop (literally "hammerhead"; pronounced "harm-er-kawp") is an unusual waterbird with a long, thick beak and a crest that projects backwards from its head.

A bobbejaan (pronounced "baw-ber-yarn") is a baboon.

A klipspringer (literally "rock-jumper") is a small antelope with specially adapted hooves that enable it to move safely even on smooth, steeply-sloping rock surfaces.

A duiker (literally "diver"; pronounced almost like "day-kuh") is a small antelope that can hide easily even among fairly low shrubs.

Wildebeest (literally "wild cattle"; pronounced "vill-duh-beer-st") are known in English as gnu.

A dassie (rhyming with "fussy") is a rock-rabbit or hyrax.

A meerkat (say "me-er-cut" quickly) is a suricate mongoose.

An aardvark (literally "earth-pig"; pronounced "aart-fark") is an ant-eater.

A skilpad is a tortoise. (The first syllable rhymes with "will"; the second sounds like "putt".)

A miskruier (literally "dung-carrier"; pronounced "miss-cray-er") is a dung-beetle.

A krans or kranz (rhyming with "chance") is a mountain-crag or high rugged cliff.

A donga (pronounced "daw-ng-gar") is a deep, dry gulch or gulley.

A vlei (pronounced "flay") is a marsh or lake.

Veld (pronounced "felt") is open prairie or grassland.

A kloof is a canyon, gorge or ravine.

An assegaai is a spear (in Zulu: inkonto).

A knobkierie is a stick with a knob on one end. (The "k" is sounded and the "b" is soft: "k-nawp-kirri".)

Gramadoelas are badlands. (The "g" is pronounced like the sound at the end of the Scottish word "loch", and the whole word sounds like "grah-mah-doo-lah-ss", but spoken quickly.)

A riem (rhyming with "him") is a long, thin strip of leather.

Haakdoring (pronounced "hark-dour-eng") means "hook-thorn".